T0191252

I AM SOMEBODY

I AM SOMEBODY

Why Jesse Jackson Matters

David Masciotra

BLOOMSBURY ACADEMIC
LONDON • NEW YORK • OXFORD • NEW DELHI • SYDNEY

BLOOMSBURY ACADEMIC
Bloomsbury Publishing Plc
50 Bedford Square, London, WC1B 3DP, UK
1385 Broadway, New York, NY 10018, USA
29 Earlsfort Terrace, Dublin 2, Ireland

BLOOMSBURY, BLOOMSBURY ACADEMIC and the Diana logo are trademarks
of Bloomsbury Publishing Plc

First published in Great Britain 2020
Paperback edition published 2023

Copyright © David Masciotra 2020, 2023

David Masciotra has asserted his right under the Copyright, Designs and Patents Act,
1988, to be identified as Author of this work.

For legal purposes the Acknowledgments on p. xv constitute an extension
of this copyright page.

Cover design by Adriana Brioso
Cover image: Rev. Jesse Jackson, 1983. (© The Denver Post/Getty Images)

All rights reserved. No part of this publication may be reproduced or transmitted
in any form or by any means, electronic or mechanical, including photocopying,
recording, or any information storage or retrieval system, without prior permission
in writing from the publishers.

Bloomsbury Publishing Plc does not have any control over, or responsibility for, any
third-party websites referred to or in this book. All internet addresses given in this
book were correct at the time of going to press. The author and publisher regret
any inconvenience caused if addresses have changed or sites have ceased to exist,
but can accept no responsibility for any such changes.

A catalogue record for this book is available from the British Library.

ISBN: PB: 978-1-3504-0054-2
ePDF: 978-1-8386-0427-1
eBook: 978-1-8386-0426-4

Typeset by Deanta Global Publishing Services, Chennai, India
Printed and bound in Great Britain

To find out more about our authors and books visit www.bloomsbury.com and
sign up for our newsletters.

This book is dedicated to Sarah, for keeping hope alive.

If history is to be creative, to anticipate a possible future without denying the past, it should, I believe, emphasize new possibilities by disclosing those hidden episodes of the past when, even if in brief flashes, people showed their ability to resist, to join together, occasionally to win. I am supposing, or perhaps only hoping, that our future may be found in the past's fugitive movements of compassion rather than in its solid centuries of warfare.

—Howard Zinn, *A People's History of the United States*

I may be poor, but I am somebody! I may be on welfare, but I am somebody! I may be in jail, but I am somebody! I may be uneducated, but I am somebody! I am black! Beautiful! Proud! I must be respected! I must be protected! I am somebody!

—Jesse Jackson, *Leading an audience call and response in 1969*

CONTENTS

THE ROOT OF JESSE

By Michael Eric Dyson

Jesse Louis Jackson was born poor and black in the South seventy-five years after slavery ended. Even though the shackles were removed, oppression remained. American apartheid seemed to get the last laugh by extending the warranty of oppression and etching "colored" on his birth certificate. Jim Crow filled the sky of black destiny. The wings of segregation shadowed the lives of colored children in its destructive flight. His mother Helen Burns was barely in her teens when she delivered him into poverty and personal peril. At sixteen, she was more than half the age of Noah Robinson, the married man next door who had a son with her that he would seldom see except through the mirror of his child's desperate nostalgia—and then not till fame had kissed him into a precocious legend. The brutal mark of his "bastard's" origin was branded on his generous forehead like an invisible "B." The circumstances of his birth sometimes blurred his eyes with grief and at other times moistened them with lament. His foremost biographer Marshall Frady noted his "propensity for tears" at an early age, showing just how wrong are those who say he only sobs with cameras in view.

Jackson came of age when it was literally against the law for black folk to drink water, or ride buses, or share a meal, or stay in hotels, or vote, or go to school with white folk. It was nearly illegal to imagine that you could do something about it. If you dared to dream that you could rise above your station, there were policemen standing by to remind you of your place by clubbing you upside your head in a show of racial sadism. He came of age when black women were routinely raped and black men were castrated and lynched at the drop of a rope. He came of age when black servicemen returning home from war in their uniforms were murdered by vengeful bigots at bus stops where they waited to join the families they left behind. Dodging the bombs and bullets of exotic enemies, they met death at the hands of domestic terrorists who hid behind religious cloth and crosses.

When it came time for him to get his lesson, as the old folk described formal education in their charming vernacular, he called on a rich cast of characters who bathed him in love: coaches, who instilled discipline on the gridiron and around the hoop; teachers, who fed his huge intellectual appetite; neighbors, who saluted his eerie self-confidence even as a boy; college presidents, who spotted his academic promise and egged him on; and ordinary men and women, who lent him encouragement in the often proud and affirming black world that segregation had no idea that it had helped to create. We often said to oppressors who forced us to live together back then what Joseph in the Hebrew Bible said to his brothers who sold him into slavery but only made him greater: "You meant evil against me, but God meant it for good."

While Negroes divided ourselves by shade of skin and pocketbook, racism imposed a lovely and efficient unity on black life—a practical solidarity. Whether we were doctors or ditch diggers, lawyers or landscape architects, automobile mechanics or accountants, carpenters or chemists, nurses or nannies, farmers or pharmacists, secretaries or social workers, or judges or prisoners, we were all colored and just didn't count that much in the white world. Our grand sororities and fraternities didn't impress them. Our big churches didn't make them testify to our spiritual genius. Our thriving colleges and universities didn't make them see how much sense we had. True, the way we hit a hanging curveball or a high "C" eventually made the white world take notice, but the ordinary Negro rarely crossed the average white person's mind except when he served him a cold drink or passed him by on the street with his hat in his hand to show proper deference. No matter our pedigree or profession, we were often just another nigger. And when white folk took the time to worry about Negroes, it was either our sexual menace or our uppity attitudes that called for adjustment or retaliation.

This is the black-and-white world that shaped Jesse Jackson. This is the world that called forth his stirring oratory, his vital leadership, his gift of prophecy. He had already cut his teeth on local protests in Greenville, South Carolina, where he was born, and, later, in Greensboro, North Carolina, where he went to school, before he burst onto the national scene during the events that led to the famous protest in 1965 at Selma, Alabama. His eagerness to serve and his ambition to lead caught the eye of Ralph Abernathy, the veteran activist and best friend of the movement's greatest leader and mouthpiece, Martin Luther King, Jr. Jackson soon earned his way as an apprentice prophet of sorts, throwing in with the band of men and women who helped to change the world before there was an internet or social media. They didn't have Facebook to market their revolution; instead, they faced being booked into jails and relied largely on black-and-white television to beam their unjust imprisonment to the world. They couldn't use Twitter to tweet their message of social redemption, but they could set the nation atwitter with their bold and daring efforts to tweak social change. Before he became a commanding general in the war to remake America, Jesse Jackson was a street soldier who did grunt work to turn the nation even further toward true democracy and real freedom.

When King met his bloody end in Memphis, Tennessee, Jesse Jackson was there with him at the Loraine Motel that evening. Some folk have held this chance occurrence, or this divinely appointed rendezvous with destiny, against him, as if he had something to do with King's demise, as if he sent that bullet hurtling across air to collapse time and space to a crushing few seconds where, as the rapper The Game brilliantly says, "the future took a head shot." But The Game amplifies the suspicion of Jackson when he asks in his rap devoted to King: "I wonder why Jesse Jackson didn't catch him before his body dropped/ Would he give me the answer? Probably not." The Game's piercing questions echo the sentiments of those who believe that Jackson was overtaken by an ambition so fatal that he would as soon see King die than live and prosper. But that's a mix of bad history and terrible sociology. King was already symbolically dead before he got sent into the ground with an exploding report inside his skull. He was wildly unpopular, he didn't routinely draw big crowds, his former allies fell off, and he would have hardly earned a national holiday had he not been blasted into martyrdom when he got caught in a bigoted assassin's crosshairs.

Yes, Jackson had a big ego to match his big Afro. You'd think rappers—and for that matter, preachers and politicians too—would be the last folk to complain about anybody's big ego. You can't be great unless you have what Quaker spiritual writer D. Elton Trueblood called "the habitual vision of greatness." And not only do you have to see it but you've also got to want it bad enough to sacrifice your way there. The late great Kobe Bryant saw greatness in Michael Jordan and wanted some championships of his own. Al Sharpton saw greatness in Jesse Jackson and wanted some civil rights victories of his own. Nicki Minaj saw greatness in the Queen B Lil' Kim and wanted some honey of her own. Yes, Jesse Jackson wanted to be great; yes, Jesse Jackson wanted to lead. But he got what he got the old-fashioned way: he worked hard for it, as hip-hop stars Method Man and Notorious B.I.G. admonished us to do. Nobody works harder than Jesse Jackson.

Before his historic gait was slowed and stiffened by the onset of Parkinson's disease, he got up earlier than most and went to bed later too. Even now as the disease progresses, he defies its deadening lethargy with every fiber of his considerable being. For more than fifty years he's been speaking, agitating, writing, thinking, marching, protesting, strategizing, building, traveling, organizing, arguing, resisting, and fighting for us. I've been with him in London when he worked from sun up till sun down, meeting with Mandela in a leader's home, lunching with a billionaire media titan, preaching in churches full of common folk, kibitzing with songstresses Anita Baker, Natalie Cole and Patti Labelle, and then talking, talking, talking, like Sinatra sang, into the wee small hours of the morning. I've been with him in Texas when he worked with union laborers to get a fair wage and a decent standard of living. I've marched with him in Illinois as he argued against zero tolerance to policies that jilted the future of young black males.

Jesse Jackson has led us with style and substance, with flair and formidable intelligence. While King's rhetoric reflected a jazzman's pace and improvisational instincts, Jackson upped the oratorical ante by sprinkling street speech in his lyrical dance; he laced dazzling displays of urban authenticity and verbal bravura into his melodic rhetoric. He was dropping couplets and rhymes a full decade before the Sugar Hill Gang and Kurtis Blow. "Down with dope/up with hope." He was spinning mantras before Tina Turner or Oprah or Deepak Chopra: "Keep Hope Alive." In 1966, he was already saying it, and I heard him say it forty-five years later, on a bright Sunday in 2011, in renowned pastor Freddy Haynes' magnificent Friendship West Baptist church in Dallas: "I am—Somebody. I may be poor, but I am—Somebody! I may be on welfare, but I am—Somebody! I may be uneducated, but I am—Somebody! I must be, I'm God's child. I must be respected and protected. I am black and I am beautiful! I am—Somebody!" It makes perfect sense; indeed, it seems inevitable, even necessary, that David Masciotra would choose this title for his masterly mediation on the meaning and importance of one of the greatest public moralists in the nation's triumphant and tragic history.

Jesse Jackson closed the distance between the sacred and the secular and taught us that we could embrace Moses in the Bible— and Black Moses Isaac Hayes and his Hot Buttered Soul with his bald pate shining black sensuality to the world. Jesse Jackson looked good while doing good: he donned dashikis, sported sideburns, blew out his 'fro, draped his neck in medallions—his version of a Jesus piece—and jumped into leisure threads or Brooks Brothers suits to make his point. He was a Country Preacher—and a country's preacher. He has been a public moralist who has preached redemption to the masses and elites alike. He visited the short—and short-tempered—singer Little Willie John in prison long before another Weezy or T.I. got locked up. He shot hoops with Marvin Gaye, hung out in the studio with Stevie Wonder, preached on Aretha Franklin's second gospel album—her Daddy, the legendary preacher C. L. Franklin had, after all, helped to ordain him— performed the wedding of *Ebony* magazine's heir apparent Linda Johnson Rice, and preached the funerals of everybody from Ron Brown to Sammy Davis, Jr. "Let Mr. Bojangles rest," he pleaded over Davis' body. "He has earned it."

Jesse Jackson has been our leader and prophet at one of the most difficult times in our people's journey. After King forecast his demise the night before he was slain, Jesse Jackson had to play Joshua to his Moses. "I just want to do God's will," King thundered in Mason Temple. "And He's allowed me to go up to the mountain. And I've looked over. And I've seen the Promised Land. I may not get there with you. But I want you to know tonight that we as a people will get to the Promised Land."

Jesse Jackson has not been, like King wasn't, the only leader of our people. So many brave souls and sharp minds have helped to fashion our fate with their words and actions. But he was the most visible and vital black leader since King's death. But unlike King, who was aided immeasurably by his martyrdom, Jackson has had to stick around and see his fortunes rise and dip even more sharply than King's. But King only lived to be thirty-nine and only had twelve years to serve. Jackson has been in public service for nearly half a century and will be seventy-nine this year, more than twice King's number. Though we wish the martyr's death on no one—and no one can detract from the ultimate price paid by King, and by Malcolm, and by Medgar, and hundreds more who gave their lives—there is a historical advantage to early death that often escapes the survivors. Jesse Jackson has endured the loss of reputation, and the battle with self-destructive forces, in public, that King only briefly engaged. Jesse Jackson has lived from the time when black folk could barely make the news to where they become fodder for the tabloid industry. He has seen his greatest flaws magnified in a celebrity-obsessed culture hungry for details about the lives and hypocrisies of icons and flashes in the pan alike. But through it all, he has stayed the course. He has fought the good fight from the 1960s till this third decade of the new millennium.

He celebrated the beauty of blackness and shouted that it was "nation time" for black folk in the early 1970s. He led us through the wilderness of white backlash in the mid-1970s. He helped navigate us through the assaults on affirmative action in the late 1970s and on through the 1980s till today. He helped to combat cultural listlessness during the simultaneous rise of black narcissism and the epidemic of crack in the late 1980s and early 1990s. He helped defend the black poor at all times. He called on parents to turn off the television and teach their children to read and to take them to school. He fought the policies of racially insensitive presidents and urged racially sensitive presidents to do more for the vulnerable and dispossessed. He rescued prisoners on foreign soil, met with heads of state around the world, retrieved hostages, and encouraged political bullies to behave better. He did brilliant battle with right-wing ideologues, bested conservative intellectuals in conversation, and marshaled a dizzying array of facts in hundreds of speeches, sermons, and lectures every year he has been in, and outside, of the spotlight. And by the way, he twice ran for president of the United States, and paved the way for Barack Obama's successful pilgrimage to political power twenty years after Jackson's last run.

And now, after the Age of Obama, a lot of folk have written Jesse Jackson off. A lot of folk wonder if he's still necessary, if he still matters as Masciotra states. A lot of folk say he should shuffle off stage and shut up. A lot of folk just wish he would go away. Well, there's definitely always a need for new blood and fresh ideas and other leaders. But there will always be a unique place for Jesse Jackson. Without Jesse Jackson our black prophetic ministry wouldn't be as vital as it is today. With Negro preachers addicted to the pornography of prosperity, he has constantly begged us to pay attention to the folk who are locked out of this nation's vast riches. It's not that he doesn't want black folk to get a bigger piece of the economic pie; after all, he has hosted a Wall Street initiative to bridge the gap between major centers of capital and destitute and needy communities. His push for black businesses has created the economic infrastructure of today's black wealth. His targeted boycotts of certain industries opened the door for black folk to get more franchises and licenses. But he has never caved in to the vicious play of materialism. Instead of pushing a Lexus, he cried to let us do right by the poor. He has never forgotten from whence he came.

That's why rappers and other young folk who take delight in dissing him ought to recognize that he's more like them than most other leaders. Mama was a teen mother? Check. Grandmother was thirteen when she birthed your mother? Check. Grew up poor without really knowing who your Daddy was? Check. People clowning you because you were "illegitimate?" Check. Big ego while spitting venom at folk who want to destroy your crew? Check. Enough self-confidence to start a small nation and to inspire your folk to believe in your genius? Check. Mad because folk are sleeping on the hard work you did to lay the path of success for the cats who come behind you? Check. Folk "pray and pray on your downfall?" Check. Folk love you when you're on top and try to play you to the left, to the far left, when you're down? Check. Baby-Daddy drama? Check.

But without Jesse Jackson we wouldn't have the black leadership that we enjoy today. Without Jesse Jackson there would be no Al Sharpton, who has brilliantly morphed into a world-class advocate for black folk and the poor. And without Jesse Jackson we wouldn't have the black political clout that we enjoy today. There would be no fiery Maxine Waters or a soulful Barbara Lee. And there wouldn't be a Barack Obama.

Sure, Jesse has clashed with Barack; Jackson has differed greatly with Obama. The prophet has called the president to task. But that's his job. Yes, to be sure, to say that you want to sever the future president's private parts is not the way to gain the love and loyalty of young black folk. But it was the public parts of Obama's condescending speech to black folk that Jackson thought the president-to-be should have kept private that motivated him. In any case, Jackson apologized for his remarks, and though the president said he forgave him, Jesse Jackson lived in political exile from the man for whom he blazed a path. It is indeed curious that alleged allies like Joe Lieberman pulled for the other team and yet weren't stonewalled like Jackson. White conservatives who prayed for Obama's downfall received more play than a black leader whose greatest fault is that he loved black folk so much he was willing to go nuts for us!

We shouldn't cast aside our prophets because they say unpopular things. We shouldn't discard our rhetorical geniuses because their speech is still freighted with unadulterated love for black folk. We shouldn't diss our leaders because they get long in the tooth but still manage to flash their fangs on our behalf. We shouldn't forget that we wouldn't enjoy the extravagant prosperity we enjoy today without his critical voice. We shouldn't forget that Jesse Jackson has prayed for us, preached for us, pleaded for us, prophesied for us, been proud for us, and has prodded us to do better for more of our folk for more years than most can even remember. He has been faithful to his calling even when it didn't gain him access to the White House. He has been faithful to his calling even when it didn't earn him brownie points with the powers that be. He has been faithful to his calling even when he has been crushed by media and panned by pundits. He has been faithful to his calling even when he was caricatured and dismissed. He has been faithful to his calling even when those he has loved have been unfaithful to him.

And he has pressed toward the mark of greatness—which is defined by Jesus as willingness to serve. He has served us with his head and heart, and with his mouth and feet. He has been courageous when we have been scared; he has given ready answer to the enemies of our people when our minds have faltered. Has he been flawed? Yes, like Moses was flawed, like David was flawed, like every prophet who ever opened his or her mouth to utter what thus sayeth the Lord has been flawed. But he has been faithful despite his flaws, valiant despite his shortcomings, useful despite his imperfections.

Those of us who know simply love Jesse. We love the way he rhymes his speech and makes us remember his ideas almost against our will. We love him for working himself every year into an appointment with the hospital for several days just to get a break from the inhuman pace he kept. We love him for the long hours and miles he logged to tell Pharaoh to let our people go. We love Jesse for being a self-assured, supremely confident black man who thought enough of us to believe that nothing should limit us except our talent and vision. We love Jesse for teaching us to Keep Hope Alive. We love Jesse for making us believe we are somebody. We love Jesse because, despite what anyone says, he loves us so much that he was willing to live for us until he dies. David Masciotra's *I Am Somebody: Why Jesse Jackson Matters* is a brilliant glimpse into the monumental life of a modern-day prophet. It is an eloquent and timely reminder of the mettle and morality of a towering public sage who has shared with us his wisdom and inspiration for more than half a century. Read this book and get a portrait of a gifted and courageous visionary who dared to seek and shape the truth of our political and social lives and lived to tell about it.

ACKNOWLEDGMENTS

I would like to thank the following people for their generosity of time and their candor: Reverend Al Sharpton, Delmarie Cobb, Karen Cecile Wallace, Frank Watkins, Butch Wing, Anthony Ramirez, Christopher Stone, Eulonda Skyles, and Judy Tanzer. Most of all I would like to thank Reverend Jesse Jackson for his stories, his insights, and his unshakable spirit. The hospitality, honesty, and joy with which he shared the details of his political life provide the foundation for this book. I will always treasure our conversations.

I owe a permanent debt of gratitude, along with my love and respect, to Alanna Ford, without whom this book would not exist. Her support, enthusiasm, and friendship have proven among the most essential and sustainable resources of my life and career.

I would like to extend my deepest thanks to Michael Eric Dyson for his characteristically profound and moving foreword, and for supporting my work more broadly. I would also like to thank Nayiri Kendir for her tireless devotion to this book, and its publishing process.

Thank you to my editor, Tomasz Hoskins, for his interest, patience, and assistance. A writer's cliché is that our editors save us from ourselves. I've never felt that way until now.

ABOUT THE AUTHOR

In addition to *I Am Somebody: Why Jesse Jackson Matters*, David Masciotra is the author of four books, including *Mellencamp: American Troubadour* (2015). He is a regular contributor to *Salon* and *No Depression*, and has also written for the *Atlantic*, *Los Angeles Review of Books*, and the *Washington Post*. He is a political essayist, music critic, journalist, and poet. He lives in Indiana, with his wife, and teaches writing and literature courses at Indiana University Northwest.

INTRODUCTION

EYES ON THE PRIZE

The only presence thicker than the humidity in the Selma Convention Center was joy. An audience of a few hundred had assembled—fanning themselves and slugging lukewarm water to keep their bodies cool as they anticipated a forum of "living legends"—the elder statesmen and women who crossed the Edmund Pettus Bridge in 1965. On that day, Bloody Sunday, an unarmed army confronted the violence of state-sponsored racism; enduring beatings, death threats, and harassment—all for the right to vote in a country that parades itself as the leader of the free world. The effort to universalize the franchise extended far beyond its immediate, practical purpose. It was an effort to transform a counterfeit democracy into a system that could make a credible claim on legitimacy and authenticity. Jesse Jackson, while eulogizing Rosa Parks in 2005, explained that "Jeffersonian democracy" has no "export value," because it includes "racial and gender subjugation." "When American leaders talk about exporting democracy," Jackson thundered, "they mean Parks-King democracy."[1] Jackson was one of the "living legends" scheduled to address the crowd in Selma for a fiftieth-anniversary commemoration of the Bloody Sunday march. He crossed the bridge in 1965 and, in doing so, crossed a threshold, stepping into the territory he would spend the rest of his life. Before leaving Alabama, he met a young, brilliant, charismatic, and already-accomplished leader of the Black Freedom Movement and talked his way into a job on his staff. Jackson would leave graduate school in Chicago to work for his new boss, Dr. Martin Luther King, Jr.

In the convention center, fifty years after that fateful meeting, Jesse Jackson's assistant sat among the restless and sweaty crowd. Wearing a stylish beret (room without air conditioning in the Deep South spring be damned) and a big smile, she beamed when I asked, "How is Reverend Jackson doing?" "Oh, he's great. He's with all his friends." Down the block from the convention center, before his arrival, Jackson had hugged the granddaughter of Hosea Williams, one of the organizers of the Bloody Sunday march in Selma, and assured her, "Your granddaddy was somebody special, baby."

One of Jackson's other longtime friends had arrived, a gold medal from Selma's mayor around her neck to distinguish her as a veteran of the original march, Dorothy Tillman. A fiery and controversial former alderman of Chicago, who once pulled a gun out of her purse during a city council meeting, she and a white man named Keith, who was also wearing a medal, took it upon themselves to entertain and enlighten the impatient crowd. Tillman told her story of marching as a teenager in Selma, while Keith described suffering an assault so severe that he spent weeks in the hospital. His crime, in the words of the assailants who bashed him with nightsticks, was being a "nigger lover." Throughout his story Tillman nodded, and gave an occasional "that's right," before explaining that whites in alliance with civil rights were often subject to even harsher treatment than blacks, because segregationist forces viewed them as "traitors." Concluding her history lesson, Tillman commanded a music group awaiting the arrival of the legends to perform. The hip-hop gospel group from a nearby black university began to beat on their drums and sing funky renditions of civil rights anthems—"Woke up This Morning," "Freedom Highway," "Eyes on the Prize." The crowd sang along with enough avidity to transform the humble setting of a small convention center, with tearing paint on the walls and leaky faucets in the bathrooms, into a roadside tent revival with a congregation singing hymns for the salvation of the American democratic experiment. Taylor Branch, the great historian who wrote a three-volume series on Martin Luther King, was in the crowd. "There's a tremendous tide of freedom that came out of the civil rights movement," Branch has written, and these commemorative events felt like an ecstatic baptism.[2] The country's first black president was in Selma too, here to not only honor those who made his political ascendency possible but also galvanize support for criminal justice reform and the expansion of health-care services for poor Americans. Like a boulder at the top of a mountain, the progress of those who stretched and strained their muscles to push and lift was visible. A black president, black mayors, black congressmen and -women, black business leaders, black intellectuals, black entertainers, and black cabinet officials all descended on Selma like a royal fleet.

The celebratory fervor might have clouded the stench of blood and barbarism that also fills the air of Selma. Few in 2015 would have guessed that merely a year later the United States would elect as Obama's successor the most hateful president of the modern era and, in the process, witness a newly emboldened white supremacist movement on social media and in the streets. The excitement of the evening might have also acted as an emotional blindfold, rendering the surrounding state of Selma invisible as crowds of thousands filled the streets of the small, Southern town with more energy and activity than it has ever seen.

When I crossed the Edmund Pettus Bridge, and felt my feet against its sacred ground during the fiftieth-anniversary commemoration, I was moved by my surroundings—people of various ages and races united in tribute to those whose faith and strength injected life into America's claim of egalitarian representation and governance. I was stirred by the immediacy of history, imagining both the beauty and brutality of what transpired on that same slab of concrete. A group of 600 civil rights activists, including current congressman John Lewis and Jesse Jackson, reached the bridge after marching 54 miles from Montgomery to demand the right to vote. For such a simple act of democratic engagement, and for such a reasonable demand, Alabama state troopers, local policeman, and newly "deputized" white civilians attacked the protesters with billy clubs. I was also shocked and saddened by the neglect of Selma's history. At the foot of the bridge, and next to a sign welcoming visitors, sits a small park of dirt and gravel. Empty soda bottles and fast-food wrappers litter the ground where plaques paying tribute to John Lewis and Hosea Williams show visible decay. It is the size of a children's playground in a tiny village of the Midwest, and there is hardly anything there to indicate its meaning in American, and world, history. The edge of the park connects with a vacant strip mall, giving visitors a coincidental connection between the decrepitude of the park and the disrepair of the American economy. Across the street is an abandoned used car lot.

With its broken surroundings, its dirty trappings, and its placement among the wreckage of bankruptcy, it is ugly; there is no other word for it. More painful than the aesthetic wound is the grotesquery of the betrayal it represents. If America cannot pay proper respect to its bravest citizens, the citizens who cried and bled to give their country credibility, then it would appear to lack any edifying sense of itself.

On the bus ride into Selma, I looked out the window and thought about the words to Lynyrd Skynyrd's rock 'n' roll classic: "Sweet home Alabama / Where the skies are so blue." Much of the state is so undeveloped, and so naturally beautiful, that the sight of the sky, stretching into space, stole the breath out of my lungs. Down below the beauty, however, is the crime of modern poverty in a nation of material abundance. Ramshackle trailers, barely able to stand, almost crumble into barren fields of dirt and burned grass. With no running water, no indoor plumbing, no central heating or air, many people here struggle to survive.

Walking through downtown Selma is like crossing the threshold of a time warp. It is not only a ghost town but also a ghost town of 1960s America. There is no real commerce, and from what I could tell, little hope for employment or opportunity for its residents. Hundreds of thousands of people had descended upon the tiny town for the fiftieth-anniversary proceedings, but food was available only through street vendors, the majority from cities like Atlanta, Birmingham, and New Orleans. Selma has no restaurants or diners of its own to serve its tourists.

It is situated in the center of Dallas County—the poorest in Alabama, and one of the poorest in America. More than 40 percent of Dallas County families and 67 percent of children live below the poverty line. Its violent crime rate is five times the state average. "America's Third World" is how two scholars rightly labeled it.[3]

Throughout the fiftieth-anniversary commemoration, there was hardly a mention of the current state of Selma. Rather, the occasion was used, often exploited and manipulated, to present American exceptionalism with a human face. "When race is involved," Taylor Branch said years before he sat in the Selma Convention Center with his wife, diligently taking notes, "there is a pronounced and proven tendency in the United States for the majority of the culture to willfully misremember the history and turn it down."[4]

Most of the speakers, all worthy of admiration and gratitude, focused on the past, providing commentary and insight on their long-ago journeys. Jesse Jackson, almost alone, in a gray suit with his tie undone at the collar, rejected nostalgia.

"Selma is a rearview mirror," Jackson told the audience, "It takes no courage to walk through a rearview mirror in one's imagination." Jackson, and no one else speaking at the event—not even elected officials in Alabama nor then president Obama—called for the federal government to preserve the house of Amelia Boynton Robinson with landmark status. Robinson played a crucial role in the civil rights movement, allowing Dr. King and other civil rights leaders to stay in her home in Selma, where they rested in preparation for the march, and also drafted the first copy of the Voting Rights Act. Her home now has boarded windows and sinks into the soil—indistinguishable from the other blown-out buildings on the same block.

The erosion and dilapidation of the Robinson home, which doubled as Selma's headquarters for civil rights tactical planning, is a sad symbol for American vandalism of its own history. "It is easy for us to talk about what Selma has done for us," Jackson concluded. "It is now time to talk about what we can do for Selma."

Jackson's explanation of what we can do now is consistent with the moral positions he has advocated since the 1960s. "We must end the war on poor people and resurrect the war on poverty," Jackson said, before describing the urgency and necessity of universal health care, affordable education, and poverty relief programs under fire from austerity. The most painful irony of the celebration was that brave men and women like Jackson, Tillman, and her companion Keith suffered insult and injury to secure the right to vote, and that same right had recently slipped away as a result of a controversial Supreme Court decision—*Shelby County v. Holder*—which many state governments have used to resurrect voter suppression schemes. Jackson, nearly alone in the commemorative weekend, spotlighted the specter of Shelby, which haunts the victory of Selma.

"Shelby gutted Selma," Jackson explained, referring to the case as a touchstone moment of American decline. Shelby County sits 100 miles north of Selma, and the bloody bridge, if voting rights are to remain operational, must now extend between the two points of contention. In a regressive decision, the Roberts court nullified sections 4 and 5 of the Voting Rights Act, declaring that because former Confederate states no longer show signs of voter discrimination, they were no longer subject to federal oversight, rule, and regulation. Justice Ruth Bader Ginsburg, in her dissenting opinion, likened the decision to confiscating a man's umbrella during a rainstorm on the grounds that he isn't wet.[5] Jackson, always armed with a metaphor, offered a lesson of historical contextualization and comprehension.

"When the Civil War ended," Jackson instructed the audience, "There was a brief period of freedom for blacks in the South, because the troops were there. The troops protected the rights of blacks. We could vote, run for office, walk down the street without fear. After Reconstruction when they removed the troops, tyranny came back, slavery came back." Resting his hand on his chin and taking a pregnant pause as if to emphasize that the point is on its way, Jackson settled into his crescendo: "Section 4 and 5 were the troops. We've removed the troops again."

The removal of governmental protections of voting rights constitutes a threat to the liberty and agency of already-depleted sources of energy in the country. Any attempt to suppress the vote of largely poor, mostly minority demographics throughout Southern states is akin to draining the fuel tank of an automobile without a battery, or as Jackson put it, "With Shelby we now have the car without the key." A Harvard Law school study shows that the cost of obtaining a Voter ID card, which Republicans claim will cure the nonexistent plague of voter fraud, is $175, when including the costs associated with documentation and transportation.[6] Long lines are also preventative and punitive. Destitute voters are least likely to have the money for the identification, and they are also least likely to have the time to wait in line at a government office, filling out forms and answering questions throughout the afternoon. Clairvoyance is not a requirement to determine the end result. In Texas, Tennessee, North Carolina, and Florida, participation continues to decline as identification mandates continue to calcify. Many states are brazenly discriminatory in the voting laws they have passed with their newfound freedom. In Texas, a gun ownership ID card will gain a voter access to the polls, but a student ID will not.[7] North Carolina has steadily removed voting precincts from college campuses and black neighborhoods.[8] "After the Civil War, we left our rights in the hands of former slavemasters," Jackson continued. "Now we are leaving our voting rights in the hands of former segregationists."

The Confederate Flag may no longer fly from government buildings in South Carolina, but the neo-confederate assault on the promise of multiracial and multicultural democracy continues to register a body count as it migrates from former slave states into the American Heartland. Donald Trump won the state of Wisconsin by under 23,000 votes, and yet alleged voter suppression techniques obstructed hundreds of thousands of blacks and college students from making it to the polls.[9] The same is true in Michigan, North Carolina, and Florida. Stacy Abrams, the first black nominee for governor in Georgia, lost an airtight race in 2018 to Brian Kemp, who as secretary of state was the monitor of voter registration. To outsiders it seemed he was the referee in his own boxing match. In resemblance of a banana republic that would draw denunciation from the American government in any other country, Kemp personally prevented 53,000 black Georgians from voting by refusing to process their registration applications.[10] If Selma in 1965 sought to authenticate a counterfeit democracy, Shelby has begun to transform it back into fool's gold.

Jesse Jackson, one of America's great orators, did not receive the uproarious response other speakers provoked in Selma. Even among a liberal audience, few welcomed the man who chips away at the gold-colored paint to reveal a cheap and dirty center. The ascendency of black wealth and power in the United States becomes increasingly visible on television, but far removed from the zoom lens of expensive cameras exist countless Americans, disproportionate percentages of them black, who exist on the periphery of privation and powerlessness. Alienated from any viable source of capital, geographically desolate, and unable to participate with efficacy in the political process, they are strangers in their native land.

Jesse Jackson himself, with the heightened drama of the times in which he grew up, moved from the shadow side of America—a stranger to privilege, born to a single mother, poor in the Jim Crow South—to the ornate and ostentatious legislative chambers and boardrooms where the rich and influential manipulate the mechanisms of power. Through his own determination, self-will, and intelligence, Jackson elevated himself out of the jail cell, where he sat for attempting to check a book out of a local library or order coffee at a diner, to a place of prominence where former presidents and current governors return his phone calls. Even though he maintains borderline celebrity status, his public image has sustained severe blows in the past two decades. Conservatives view him as a nuisance at best, an anti-American saboteur at worst, while far too many progressives, regurgitating right-wing propaganda, castigate Jackson as a publicity seeker more focused on his own aggrandizement than the improvement of public conditions. The majority of Americans, who surveys reveal often struggle to identify major government officials and Supreme Court Justices, look at Jackson's role in helping to shape America into a more equitable and hospitable society as they would a soft fog in the air as they drive down an illuminated street. Perhaps, they are aware of its presence, but they do not consider it worthy of much thought or appreciation.

At a precise and urgent moment in American history, exactly when movements of regression should inspire an intimate inspection of a radical and consistent leader on issues essential to racial and economic justice, *I Am Somebody: Why Jesse Jackson Matters* aims to rehabilitate Jackson's presence in the historical pantheon, and offer his accomplishments and expertise, along with his defeats and failures, as tutelage for Americans of conscience currently suffering confusion over the future of their country. Jackson's life is not only an instructive rearview mirror but also a roadmap.

Jesse Jackson, at Selma in 2015, was emblematic of America's past, but also a challenge to America's future. This duality captures the essence of Jackson's current identity in the American story. Jackson, one could argue, is a "blues hero," to invoke the wisdom of Albert Murray. A hero in the blues needs a challenge against which to define himself. Aware of the existence of the challenge, he does not deceive himself into believing that he can eliminate his pain, nor does he cower at the inevitability of injury. To protest the existence of dragons, Murray argued, is naïve. True heroism rests in the maturity, bravery, and tenacity of fighting dragons.[11] With dragons spitting fire across America, it is essential for the restoration of the democratic promise that Americans study and consider its dragon slayers. *I Am Somebody: Why Jesse Jackson Matters* does exactly that.

When having coffee with Jackson in Selma, he told me that as Dr. King was preparing his staff for a march under threat of violence, he detected anxiety troubling his young aide. "'I can tell that you are nervous and frightened,' Dr. King told me," Jackson recalled before continuing, "They are going to call you 'nigger,' and they are going to throw rocks at you, and threaten to kill you. But you just keep going. Stare straight ahead. Don't give them your attention. Keep your eyes on the prize."

For fifty years, from Selma of 1965 to Selma of 2015 and beyond, Jackson has kept his eyes on the prize. *I Am Somebody: Why Jesse Jackson Matters* measures and appraises Jackson's commitment, and addresses the disparaging attacks which emanate largely from the right. Far from a publicity-driven egotist, or a corrupt "shakedown artist" seeking only to enrich himself, Jackson remains one of the most committed forces for racial and economic justice in America, employing his notoriety not for purposes of celebrity, but to humanize and moderate a too-often exploitative system of American life.

I Am Somebody: Why Jesse Jackson Matters provides intimate narration of Jackson's work to end Jim Crow with Martin Luther King, his victories for economic integration in a discriminatory economy in the 1970s, his historical campaigns for president in the 1980s, without which hundreds of black officials, including Barack Obama, would not have won election, and his tireless advocacy for organized labor, social welfare policies, and criminal justice reform. A true pleasure and privilege of my life is a personal relationship with Jackson. As a journalist, I have interviewed him countless times, observed his work from a front-row seat, and developed a truth-telling rapport with his staff. As a white man in his thirties, I know that I make an unlikely storyteller of the Jackson saga, but my own connection to his work serves, I hope, only to emphasize the reach of his influence.

Exhausted, hungry, hot, I sat in the back of a coach bus full of volunteers for Jesse Jackson's civil rights organization, the Rainbow/PUSH Coalition. The streets of Selma had rededicated themselves to their typical profile—desolate and barren. Long past the expiration point for the commemorative events, the only evidence of human activity still visible was empty water bottles rolling to the curb, tossed-away fliers on cracked sidewalks, and the occasional car passing by our window, likely en route to a town with the minimal vitality of an open diner or working gas station. "Why aren't we moving?" a woman shouted from the back, creating an echo of similar inquiries. Having grown restless and eager to return home, the volunteers were understandably confused, and beginning to anger over the stationary status of our bus. "We were supposed to leave a half-hour ago," another insisted. Despite the volunteer protests, the bus driver did not turn the key, and replied only with vague assurances of "getting on the road soon." Another fifteen to twenty minutes passed. The streets of Selma, at that point, decorated only by our bus. I rested my forehead, reddened from sunburn, against the window.

From around the bend, a surreal image cut through the humid haze of the empty streets. On the back of a John Deere trailer, like a wounded quarterback, Jesse Jackson was sprawled out in his three-piece suit, ankles swollen from walking, standing at podiums, and marching for three days straight. His diligent and dedicated traveling assistant, a young minister from Chicago, was at the wheel. At a snail's pace, the trailer reached the bus door, and after Jackson's assistant put it in park, he helped Jackson to his feet. Struggling up the stairs inside the bus, the PUSH volunteers greeted him with an ecstatic ovation. Leaning his large 6'4" frame into a seat at the front, Jackson took the bus PA system in hand, and thanked everyone for representing Rainbow/PUSH in Selma. Then, he offered a more personal message.

"We have someone who is sick with us today." Measuring and deliberately planting each step, Jackson made his way to the side of Lisa, a middle-aged woman who was wearing a scarf to cover her bald head. She made the trip even with cancer. Drops of sweat falling down his grimacing face, Jackson nearly collapsed when he lowered himself to one knee. He took Lisa's hand, while requesting that everyone bow their heads in prayer.

> Dear God—Fifty years ago, right here in Selma, we endured great pain to arrive at a moment of healing. We suffered so that we might experience restoration and redemption. Please make this the spot and the moment when you begin to heal our friend Lisa. Then, just as you heal Lisa, please begin to heal our land.

Jackson, breathing and laboring heavily, barely made it to his feet with the help of his aide and Lisa's crying husband. There wasn't one eye on the bus without tears. Jackson shook everyone's hand and encouraged them to vote in an upcoming Chicago mayoral primary race. He then left the bus, lumbered a few steps toward the tractor bed, and sat down. As the vehicle pulled out of view, he raised a hand in the air, slowly closing it into a fist.

Chapter 1

REMOVE NOT YOUR ANCIENT LANDMARKS

"The sore is still raw," Jesse Jackson said with a tear in his eye as he began to describe the murder of America's greatest moral and political leader, Martin Luther King Jr.—a gruesome and history-halting event that took place more than forty years before our conversation in Jackson's private office at the Rainbow/PUSH headquarters in Chicago, Illinois. The civil rights organization operates out of an architecturally grand synagogue on the South Side of Chicago, with the nickname, "Dr. King's Workshop."

"What was so different about that sermon," Jackson remarked in reference to King's final public speech, which he gave begrudgingly at the Bishop Charles Mason Temple in Memphis, Tennessee, "is I saw grown men crying. There was a pathos to his message, to his presentation." Jackson's eyes enlarged as if he was looking upon the tragic drama of King's prophecy for the first time, "It was a transitional speech—'I'm fearing no man,' 'My eyes have seen the glory of the coming of the Lord,' 'I may not get there with you.'" The leader, just as in the gospel, was more aware of the proximity to Golgotha than his disciples. "We all knew of the threat of death," Jackson said, "It was always with us. But he was more intimately aware. He felt the pressure. He felt the burden of leadership. He felt it on his back."

The cry for justice in America is always a whisper in a storm. It can, on some sweet occasions, find amplification, but it often is blown into oblivion.

"The next day was relaxed in the hotel room," Jackson began to recall. "And I remember coming across the courtyard in the afternoon as we were preparing to leave for dinner. He said to me, 'Jesse, we're going to Rev. Kyles home for dinner, and you don't even have on a tie.' I said, 'Doc, the prerequisite for eating is an appetite not a tie.' He laughed, and said, 'You're crazy.'" King's eyes met those of Ben Branch, a musician and civil rights activist, whose rendition of "Precious Lord" on the saxophone had deeply moved King just weeks earlier. "I want you to play my favorite song tonight," King offered as request. "I will Doc," Branch assured him, articulating the last words King would ever hear.

"That's when it hit," Jackson said, bringing his hands together in a thunderous clap. "It knocked him against the door."

"I then took the longest ten steps of my life," Jackson said softly and slowly, as if his words must move at the same pace of his feet on that fateful day in the home of the blues, "I called Coretta Scott King, and I couldn't quite say what I saw. I told her that he was shot in the shoulder."

As Jackson spoke to King's wife, she was already a widow. The bullet fired from the rifle of James Earl Ray, an undistinguished white supremacist, killed King on impact. His blood began to empty onto the balcony. Jackson moved up the stairs, embraced King's lifeless body, and in a spiritual exercise and execution of the Christian belief and Baptist refrain, "There's power in the blood," allowed his vital fluid to soak his sweater. He would leave that mark on his body during his television appearances throughout the next twenty-four hours.

> Precious Lord, take my hand
> Lead me on, let me stand
> I'm tired, I'm weak, I'm lone
> Through the storm, through the night
> Lead me on to the light
> Take my hand precious Lord, lead me home

"The pathology, the sickness, the neuroses of Memphis, of this society is what really pulled the trigger," Jackson told a television reporter less than a day after King's heart beat for the last time, "The white people do not know it, but their best friend is dead."[1]

White America rarely, if ever, truly detects friendship, and what promises improvement for the universal American experience. Racism, in addition to all the words a mourning Jackson used to describe it on April 5, 1968, is what Toni Morrison calls, "a fantasy."[2] So lost in the spell of its own hypnosis, white America cannot recognize the obvious veracity of what Jackson explained to me as the "residual benefits of the civil rights movement." "Before the Voting Rights Act," Jackson said, "white women could not serve on juries. College students could not vote on campus. There was no bilingual voting." With characteristic rhetorical verve, Jackson also delineates the social, political, and financial rewards of tearing down the "cotton curtain"—"You could not have the Tennessee Titans behind the cotton curtain, the Carolina Panthers, the Atlanta Braves. The players would not have been able to ride on the same bus together. You couldn't have a BMW plant in South Carolina behind the cotton curtain. Furthermore, you couldn't have had presidents Carter, Clinton, or Bush. The shame of segregation and lynching would have prevented their politics from going national."

In the lobby of Rainbow/PUSH, there is a lifelike mock-up of Jackson and King standing together on the balcony of the Lorraine Motel. The description underneath the image anoints King as the "architect of American democracy." The much-ballyhooed brain trust of the Founding Fathers could not envision a system of self-governance without slavery and with an unlimited franchise. King could. Few Americans realize that the Soviet Union's most popular and effective propaganda tactic to divert attention away from American criticism of its routine human rights violations was the slogan, typically attached to visual depiction, "And you are hanging blacks."[3] The FBI, most elected officials, and the majority of white

Americans saw King as subversive, when in reality he was America's most powerful defender, just as Jackson, suffering through similar slander, remains an advocate for the genuine article America, what Walt Whitman called, "Centre for equal daughters, equal sons . . . Perennial with the Earth, with freedom, law, and love."[4]

The tragic sweep of America's failure to support King's transition from civil rights advocate to economic justice crusader emerged in full proportion a month after his assassination. It was the late leader's dream to converge on the National Mall of Washington DC with a poor people's march. He hoped it would triumph just as the 1963 march on Washington where he gave the most famous of all his speeches—"I have a dream"—and gained a momentous victory for black freedom under American apartheid. To prepare for the demonstration, thousands of impoverished and dispossessed citizens of the world's richest nation constructed a shantytown in the capital, calling it "Resurrection City." It was Occupy Wall Street, but only in earlier and grander form. Residents of Resurrection City elected Jesse Jackson as their mayor. The grief emanating out of King's untimely death coalesced with the relative lack of success of the Poor People's Campaign, and as Resurrection City was preparing for collapse, its constituents looked to their mayor to "give them something," to use Jackson's simple phrase.

"We were all depressed," Jackson said. "I had no money to give them. I could not get them back home. We did not change any laws. I looked in their tired faces, and said, 'You still have worth. You may be hungry, but you are somebody.' Then, I asked them to say it, 'Say, I am somebody.'"

Jackson alchemized as inspiration an old poem by Rev. William Holmes Borders, Sr. to, in the absence of anything material, provide the least of his brethren with those qualitative gifts that can never disappear without consent—hope, faith, and self-respect.

The Jesse Jackson story is encapsulated in the words of his most famous refrain. It is a mission to assert his own identity, integrity, and agency—his own *somebodiness*—in the service of forcing America to honor the *somebodiness* of everyone living within its multiracial, multicultural, multireligious milieu. King's death had left Jackson, and all of the aides and activists "disoriented," to use his own word, and in a biblical rhythm, an assortment of apostles would have to spread the gospel, meaning "good news for the poor," without their founder, leader, and director. The subsequent journey would include milestones and missteps, triumph and tragedy, mountainous heights and cavernous lows. At King's funeral, Jackson assured his fallen friend and teacher that he would "never stop fighting." From the man in the coffin, he had already received his necessary training and education.

Architecture leads to construction, and every construction project begins with a stake in the ground mapping the point of origin for development. Racism and white supremacy formed the stake in the ground from which Jackson could begin his dedication to authentic activation of American democracy. He came of age not only black, suffering under the oppression, limitation, and terror of Jim Crow, but also poor. To intimately experience both state-sponsored racial abuse and state-enabled and -ignored deprivation, is to gain expertise in the gaps of contradiction separating what America trumpets as its persona and practice, and how it actually behaves, from the local to the federal level of governance, and from the loan office at the neighborhood bank to the gilded and gated entryways of Wall Street.

Far removed from America's central junction box of political or corporate power, Jackson once requested his driver to take us down a bumpy road in Greenville, South Carolina. Giving further instruction for the driver to pull to the curb, he pointed out the house where he was born and raised. "A small house, we didn't have much, but there was a lot of love," he said. In his 1988 speech at the Democratic National Convention, he offered poetic reflection on his humble roots—"Wallpaper as decoration? No, as windbreaker." Jackson assured me that this was not merely oratorical panache, but an accurate description of the desperate tactics a family takes to vainly fight the cold in a house constructed with thin walls when the furnace is faulty, and the savings account is empty. Because he was born to a teenage mother, out of wedlock, he also endured taunts and harassment from his peers. "I am somebody," is not merely a refrain Jackson asks audiences to repeat for their own edification, but a mantra containing hard-earned truth he had to battle and toil to internalize.

"Our money was counterfeit," Jackson said. "We could not shop in the grocery store, could not stop in a hotel." He described his stepfather—his mother would later marry—having to sit behind Nazi POWs at an Army base during the Second World War, because they were white, and he was black. The white advantage of Jim Crow, briefly, extended even to the foot soldiers of the Third Reich. "The first time I was arrested was for trying to check a book out of the library," Jackson offered as testimony of his own baptismal fire into civil rights activism and leadership. On break from North Carolina A&T, a historically black university where he studied sociology, he looked for a necessary text in the black library, and unable to find it, the librarian assured him that her friend, a librarian in the white library, would assist him. Naïve and grateful, Jackson rushed over to the other side of town. The librarian told him that she would hold the book for him, but that he could not check it out at that moment. "Why?" I asked, "I'm here, and I need it for a project this weekend." A police officer who happened to be in the library did not give the librarian time to answer the question. Forcefully grabbing Jackson by both arms, he manhandled him out of the door, and threw him down on the pavement. "I sat down on a bench and cried," Jackson said.

He and a group of seven friends, eventually earning the moniker of the Greenville Eight, decided to practice civil disobedience in an attempt to challenge the stratification of library resources and the discrimination of public accommodations. "Our pastor told us to remain calm and respectful no matter what anyone calls us or how anyone treats us," Jackson recalled before laughing, "When the police showed up at the library and threatened to arrest us, we ran back to the church. I said, 'Pastor, they were going to arrest us!' He said that's what is supposed to happen. So, the next day we went back and did it again."

To prevent further activism, and to guard against any possible pressure for integration, the Greenville City Council temporarily closed not only the black branch of the library but also the main branch. The closure of both libraries acted as a symbol for how the politics and policies of white supremacy, in a rich irony, inflict damage upon white institutions, and the poor and working-class white citizens who rely on their largesse. Studies often indicate that support for social welfare programs, even among white constituents who would benefit from them, plummets when there are also black beneficiaries. "A house divided against itself will not stand," Abraham Lincoln famously warned when fearing that a civil war would result in the death of America.

"The Civil War never ended," Jackson declared in a conversation not long ago. Up until July of 2015, the Confederate Flag—a banner celebrating slavery and segregation, and a calling card of the Ku Klux Klan—flew from public buildings in Jackson's home state of South Carolina. As contemptible as it was to officially sanction a symbol of hatred, as long as the Confederate Flag flew from government buildings, the state of South Carolina did offer truth in advertising. Jesse Jackson grew up not so much in the United States of America, but under occupation of the Confederacy. He not only endured the legal torment and torture of an apartheid regime but also lived under threat of terror, as all illegitimate governments rely on violence, both its direct use and the whisper of its underlying possibility, to maintain its power and order. It is not merely the matter of a police officer accosting a teenager attempting to check a book out of the library, but the terrorism of lynching. "4,400 blacks were lynched in the United States," Jackson said. "The KKK was not an outlier. They enlisted support of the white gentry, the police— often lynchings were advertised in the newspaper." Jackson remembers the frisson of fear he felt as a child when news spread around black quarters of Greenville that a "missing" African American man who was teaching illiterate blacks to read, and attempting to mobilize others in an effort to challenge racial oppression, was not lost or missing at all. He had been lynched.

Speaking on the streets of Charleston after the funeral service for black churchgoers who were massacred in a hate crime in 2015, Jackson said,

> We're on Calhoun Street, named after a slaveholder, and it runs right into Meeting Street, where they sold our people. This place is dripping with a kind of indecency, a kind of barbarism. I mean, slavery, 246 years, was real. And the extension of slavery was even worse, in many ways, because at least slavemasters tried to protect the health of their slaves enough for them to work and reproduce. But after slavery, when slavocracy lost to democracy and kept the political and military power, 4,400 blacks were lynched, 163 lynched in this state without one indictment, often carried out by judges and police.[5]

No one was ever arrested, much less charged or convicted, for the murder of the Greenville activist of Jackson's childhood.

Jesse Jackson became a force for democratic transformation in American society, partly because he never actually experienced authentic democracy as a citizen, voter, or resident of South Carolina. "Under slavocracy, the slave owner kept the slaves alive because they were worth something to him. Lynching was the dark side of democracy," Jackson said during our discussion. "If there were 10 slaves, but only one slave owner, the slaves had more votes, and were therefore politically dangerous." It is for this reason of practical interest that lynching reached its peak not during slavery, but subsequent to the Emancipation Proclamation. Historian Douglas Blackmon documents and depicts in his book, *Slavery By Another Name*, how even after slavery ended, black life became criminal—loitering laws, for example, made it illegal for more than one black man to congregate on a corner— and black convicts became prison laborers. Meanwhile, various schemes and tricks of suppression prevented black Americans from voting, thereby rendering them subjects to political occupation, rather than participants within democracy.[6] "It is good that the flag has come down, but the flag agenda must come down with it," Jackson declared in response to South Carolina removing the Confederate emblem from its buildings. The "flag agenda" amounts to anything that preserves separation to protect the economic advantage of the ruling class, or as Jackson put it, "In 1870, we were supposedly free with the right to vote, but the infrastructure was still in place to destroy us." It was within that infrastructure that Jackson spent his formative years, and against its muscular engineering that he pushed for liberation.

Jackson might now live with the full protections of American citizenship, but the policies of his home state, and many others including those not originally within the Confederacy, prove that not only is the Civil War ongoing, as Jackson asserts, but it is also without a clear winner. Barack Obama became the first black president of the United States only to greet the most overtly white supremacist president of the modern era, Donald Trump, as his successor. The policies that play out in the push at the table are those that Jackson identifies as belonging to the "Confederate flag agenda."

Voter suppression schemes, such as those made possible by the *Shelby v. Holder* case that effectively stripped the Voting Rights Act of its substance, are part of the flag agenda. When black officials win election in Southern states, they still find themselves living under the flag agenda, and riding on, what Jackson calls, "the back of the legislative bus"—"Stacking and packing of districts in which gerrymandering puts blacks in the districts with the fewest resources renders them powerless."

The flag agenda not only protects the political asymmetry of white supremacy but also organizes all of its strength to prevent any progress against poverty, especially when privation, at least according to public perception, has a black face. "The flag agenda is turning down money for Medicaid when 350,000 people in your state have no health insurance," Jackson said referring to South Carolina's rejection of $4.1 billion in funds allotted to make President Obama's Medicaid expansion possible in that state.

If all this seems rather "subtle," to use a favorite qualifier of liberals who meekly criticize the Confederate agenda, one might want to consider that "slavery by another name" still persists. According to Jackson, "twenty five percent of the population in South Carolina is African American, and 75 percent of the prison population is African American. Twenty percent of those do prison labor for 30 to 80 cents an hour."

As much as citizens of conscience can applaud the removal of the Confederate Flag from public property, perhaps the banner, along with streets named after slaveholders and monuments to treasonous generals, should remain in clear sight as a signal of where the loyalty of, at least, half the country rests—not with democracy, but with slavocracy, not with Martin Luther King and Jesse Jackson, but with Robert E. Lee and George Wallace.

The heart of hope continues to beat. After Jackson's driver turned the key in the ignition and lowered his foot on the gas pedal, he steered our way into the parking lot of Grandma's Kitchen, a legendary soul food restaurant. During dessert, two young blonde women, with voices out of a Tennessee Williams play, excitedly greeted Jackson, pleading for pictures and autographs. As he happily complied, they explained that they work for a voting rights organization in the state, summoning all their intellect and energy to combat the suppression schemes in fashion and operation since *Shelby v. Holder*. The two women smiled brightly for the camera, and then asked if he would consider speaking to their group. After they exchanged information, and as we could hear the click clack of the ladies' high heels echo as they approached the door, Jackson looked at me, smiled, and said, "That's the new south."

If a new south comes into fruition, it will have largely begun to germinate in the 1960s when Jackson, and many like him, decided that they would no longer tolerate the tyranny and terror of the old south.

"We performed moral jujitsu on evil," Jesse Jackson told me, while forcefully mimicking a martial arts maneuver in his chair, bright and early on Thanksgiving morning in 2014. He was reporting on an exchange he had with a few college students during a recent commemorative event honoring the Greenville Eight. The proceedings included the airing of footage of Jackson, and seven of his friends, sitting at a diner counter, politely asking for coffee. They had money in their hands and were willing to pay, but the "White Only" sign in the front window meant that they were breaking the law. The manager of the restaurant was screaming at Jackson and the other young men, calling them "niggers," threatening physical harm, and appearing deranged, especially in juxtaposition with the respectful stoicism of the Greenville Eight. "How did you remain so calm?" a student asked Jackson. Like most of us would, she was likely placing herself in that situation, unable to imagine not retaliating to such vicious invective and hostility. Jackson explained to her that not only was nonviolence a political necessity—whites had the law and all the guns on their side—but it was also culturally persuasive. The diner manager looks demented, because the Greenville Eight looks polite, upstanding, and superior in their comportment and ethics. By not dropping to his level of barbarism, the Greenville Eight used the weight of his own mad dog hatred against him. Like a professional grappler in the ring, they allowed him to fall with the momentum he created. They "performed moral jujitsu on evil."

Despite Jackson's characteristic amplification of persuasive language harmonizing political savvy and theological poetry, what biographer Marshall Frady aptly called, "gospel populism," civil rights leadership and foot soldier support were not exposing the hideous and disfigured face of racism to America with the idealistic hope of changing hearts and minds. They were summoning all of their strength and sophistication and risking life and limb to transform laws and alter public policy. The pathos of King's "I Have a Dream" speech is what most people remember, but the entire first half—the half before he reaches the soaring heights of poetic rhetoric at its finest—is a presentation of a legalistic and political case for the reformation of American law, regulation, and ordinance.

I once asked Jackson for his reaction to Catholic Worker Movement leader Dorothy Day's declaration that America needs a "revolution of the heart." Jackson surprised me by shaking his head, and saying, "That's wrong." While he certainly shares the sentiment, he accuses the late Day of naivete. "We live in our faith, but we live under the law," Jackson said before explaining that, contrary to the assumption of most political observers, hearts often change last, not first, during times of tumult and periods of rebellion.

"If you were a racist in Alabama and you rode the bus to work every day," Jackson said pointing his finger at me,

> As long as the law makes blacks ride on the back of the bus, and allows you to ride on the front of the bus, your racism is protected—never challenged. But when the law changed, you might have to sit next to a black woman on the bus. You might not like it, but you no longer have a choice. Maybe it happens again, and again after that, and again and again. Then, maybe you start to notice that you're still getting to work on time. The bus doesn't move any slower because you have to sit next to a black person. And maybe she's nice. Maybe one day you drop your papers, and she helps you pick them up. Maybe, and only then will you start to think, 'maybe I had it wrong.' The rhythm is that the law changes, which forces behavior to change, and beliefs change when behavior changes.

Jackson's sharp analysis cuts through the moral sanctimony that has come to dominate too much of leftist politics in the age of social media. Many insightful and important contemporary movements, dealing with racial, economic, and gender injustices, such as Occupy Wall Street, Black Lives Matter, and MeToo, resemble snow falling from the sky on a day too warm for accumulation. The wisdom of Jackson, gathered over years of civil rights triumphs and defeats, beginning with the Southern Christian Leadership Conference, would benefit young activists, because it insists on measurable and legislative changes in governance and policy, rather than the emotional satisfaction of creating big media moments with political theater. Jackson's motto is: "A revolution of the heart doesn't mean much without accompanying changes in the law." To illustrate the veracity of Jackson's analysis, polls regularly indicate that the majority of Americans support more rigid gun control regulation, and universal, publicly funded health care, and yet, because of the calcification of conservative politics and corporate influence, gun laws remain dangerously lenient and decent health-care coverage still eludes millions of Americans.[7] Too many young activists appear to substitute prideful grandstanding through social media–shaming campaigns for strategic planning to rearrange the prevailing legal apparatus. Policing language and behavior through digitized peer pressure, Jackson warns, is unlikely to produce any long-lasting effects, and will ultimately fail to have significant impact on the overwhelming majority of average Americans who do not use Twitter.[8]

Jackson began his lifelong commitment to civil rights as a college student not with the daffy hope of ending racism, but with the more attainable and realistic goal of ending racist policies. "When walls go up so does hatred, ignorance, and fear," Jackson told me. "The walls also block the sun so one side gets most of the light, plants blossom, gardens grow, but the other side is left in darkness. When the walls come down, hatred, fear, and ignorance go down with them, and we are able to grow together." "We've managed to survive apart," Jackson said to punctuate his point, "we must learn to live together." Education is impossible under a regime of laws enforcing illiteracy.

Subsequent to graduating college with a bachelor's degree in sociology, Jackson was ready to continue his own formal education, choosing theology over law, and moving to Chicago to study in the Masters of Divinity program at the prestigious institution where Barack Obama would later teach, the University of Chicago. In 1965, three courses shy of degree completion, Jackson heard about the upcoming march on Selma for voting rights and protections in the South. Jackson told a group of white and black classmates that they were to leave immediately to make an all-night drive to Alabama. It might seem abstract to current students of history, but America in the 1960s threatened anyone preparing for the road trip Jackson organized with imprisonment, or even death. Andrew Goodman, Michael Schwerner, and James Chaney, one black and two Jewish civil rights activists, respectively, were murdered by the Ku Klux Klan in Mississippi just one year earlier, while on a drive to help black Southerners register to vote. One of the coconspirators in the killing was Lawrence A. Rainey, a county sheriff. Neither the danger nor the unfinished academic business of the semester could deter Jackson. One of his classmates recalls that it all came together without hardly any of them stopping to think. "That was just Jesse's style," he explained.[9] The persuasive power of Jackson's charisma and command of an agenda was already proving that he possessed the mysterious substance of leadership.

Exercising and evincing the cliché, "fortune favors the bold," Jackson also made an impression on his hero, Dr. Martin Luther King, Jr. When he managed to locate and meet with the civil rights leader in Selma, he did not ask or even apply for a job, but announced that he would benefit King's organization, SCLC, and after only a few minutes of conversation, demanded a position. He became the youngest aide on King's staff, and promptly left graduate school. The Chicago Theological Seminary, however, would award him his master's degree in 2000, counting his years of civil rights leadership, human rights advocacy, and roving ministry as far more valuable than the nine credits he had left to earn when he joined King after Bloody Sunday in Selma.

Jackson might have left the Chicago Theological Seminary, but he certainly did not abandon Chicago. For the next fifty years of Jackson's life, he would operate out of the city of big shoulders, using its combination of blue-collar character and multicultural struggle to steer a flagship containing critical elements of Americana and cosmopolitanism. Al Sharpton credits Jackson with "fashioning a generation" into civil rights advocacy and political activism by appealing to teenagers who, in the 1960s, diverged from King in everything ranging from militancy to fashion. "Jesse made it appealing to me, as well as other kids, who were more nationalist," Sharpton said, "To get involved in the traditional civil rights movement. I'm 13 years younger than Jesse. He was 12 years younger than King. So, his style and approach was almost a generation ahead of his time." As an aide for King, Jackson helped to convince his boss to stretch the muscular reach of the movement into Union cities, and while the initial campaign in Chicago had mixed results, it could boast of a profound cultural achievement. By bringing King to Chicago, Jackson and SCLC began to urbanize and Northernize the movement and, in doing so, appeal to adolescents like Sharpton, who, while growing up in the inner city of New York, found it difficult to identify with middle-aged ministers in Georgia and Alabama. By helping to persuade King to launch a Chicago campaign, Jackson also demonstrated the political cunning and courage necessary to expose the dangers of the American myth, still in motion today, that racism, in policy and practice, was a predominantly Southern glitch in the software of American life.

"The Northern bigotry," Sharpton explained,

> was button downed. Jesse understood that in the South, you were white or black. But in Northern cities, you had blacks from Africa, blacks from the American South, blacks from the Caribbean. In the city, you also had to know how to navigate neighborhoods—Irish neighborhoods, Jewish neighborhoods—which were friendly, which were hostile. He was born in the South, but based in Chicago. So, he understood the complicated terrain.[10]

Chicago, more than most major American cities, has a black identity. It is the political hometown of Barack Obama, the country's first black president. Michael Jordan was an ambassador to the world throughout the 1990s, dazzling audiences with his unprecedented excellence and acrobatics on the basketball court. And more than any city, with the possible exception of Memphis, Tennessee, Chicago is identifiable with the blues. It is also one of the most segregated cities in America, and not merely in residential patterns, but also the distribution of resources, the quality of schools, the representation of municipal governance, and the brutality and blight of poverty. A cursory look out the window of a moving automobile is all that is necessary to observe the lethal malevolency of Chicago's racial and economic stratification. The majority black South Side, where Jackson's Rainbow/PUSH office is located, suffers under the oppressive weight of deprivation, visible with dilapidated housing, bankrupt and dysfunctional public schools, street gang turf wars erupting in drive-by shootings and carjackings, shuttered store fronts, and a marketplace where it is easier to find a crack rock than an organic food product. The largely white North Side, by comparison, resembles an Edenic paradise, blooming with business, beautiful brownstone homes, and some of the nation's most elite public schools. The canyon separating black and white life in Chicago has a long history of redlining, police harassment, discriminatory regulations and ordinances, and even strategic highway construction so as to build a physical barrier between white and black neighborhoods. Its destructive legacy persists, as historian Paul Street, who spent several years as a researcher for the Chicago Urban League, notes in his book on racial inequality in the Windy City, explaining that his study "provided invaluable lessons on the powerfully persistent grip of white supremacist race apartheid and anti-black discrimination in American life in the post-civil rights era."[11]

The absence of fair housing laws in the 1960s consigned blacks, regardless of educational or financial attainment, to slum living conditions. Consequences of Chicago's cruel policies manifested politically and culturally, rendering racial integration all but impossible, but also individually and ancestrally with blacks wearing the chains of "slavery by another name," and paralyzed by the pervasive politics of white supremacy. They could not exercise their right of free movement or assembly, they typically could not improve their living conditions no matter how inventive or diligent, they often could not matriculate into high-earning positions due to hiring and entry discrimination in businesses and trade unions, and they could not buy property of significant value, effectively eliminating the possibility of passing on any fruits of labor to progeny.[12]

It might seem otherwise to anyone closely attuned to political media or attached to an academic institution, but ignorance of America's racial history abounds. Most school systems, especially those in predominantly white districts, reduce the black struggle under white power to slavery and segregation, giving the false impression that King's "I Have a Dream" speech cast a magical spell over America, righting every wrong and creating a democratic and egalitarian utopia.[13] The extension of King's work into Chicago was one of the first of several major efforts to display precisely how vast and virulent white advantage dictated the terms of American life.

Shortly after his arrival in Chicago in July of 1966, King attracted attention with the media-savvy maneuver of living in a slum tenement with a black family for several days. The broadcast and print press dutifully reported on his visit, enabling him to, with characteristic eloquence, describe the disgraceful living conditions for the inhabitants of Chicago's limited housing for blacks. King determined it was best to capitalize on the media coverage of his live-in with a march through the South Side neighborhoods with largely white and ethnic working-class demographics. The demand for fair housing laws was not met with polite objection. As King, Jackson, and the SCLC staff led a march down Chicago streets, a white mob formed, screaming slurs and epithets, but also throwing bricks and other solid objects. A stone hit King on the forehead, causing him to bleed, but the injury did not deter him from the course of the march. A particularly deranged and menacing racist, who was never identified, fired a gunshot in the air. Video footage of the event shows King flinching at the sound of a bullet exploding out of the barrel, but not breaking pace.[14]

Michael Pfleger, a priest on the South Side who has earned a reputation in Chicago as one of the Midwest's most committed fighters on issues of racism, gun violence, and poverty, attended King's march as a teenage supporter. He recalls pedaling his bicycle home and thinking that King was either the "most beautiful and courageous man" he had ever seen or a "total lunatic."[15] There was no moderate explanation for how someone could act with such stoic courage in the face of extreme danger. Much of Pfleger's current work aims to make American Catholicism more progressive, appropriate considering that Jackson has said that he and King "never saw hatred, not even in the Deep South, as severe as what we encountered in Chicago with the ethnic, Catholic whites." He elaborated that in Alabama, for example, the fear was always that the Ku Klux Klan or the police themselves, as in Selma, would turn violent on the protesters. In Chicago, it was almost as if the entire white majority was overcome by wicked mania, acting out their psychosis without shame or restraint. Ordinary men, from school teachers to auto mechanics, were charging the marchers, attempting to intimidate and assault them. The violence was so shocking, even to King and company, that a follow-up march planned for the nearby suburb of Cicero was canceled. Chicago's draconian mayor, Richard Daley, agreed to a set of demands including open housing, exerting pressure on banks to provide loans to qualified black applicants, and the creation of a real estate board to monitor fairness in sales, tenant treatment, and other residential related measures. The document, however, was without teeth or claws. Because Daley did not submit to any rules of enforcement, he was quickly able to rescind or neglect most of his promises. Much like the Montgomery Bus Boycott of 1955 helped to nationalize the civil rights movement, the Chicago campaign, despite its local failure, galvanized a nationwide push for reform, resulting in the 1968 Fair Housing Act, signed into law by President Lyndon Johnson, shortly after the assassination of King.

Too many liberals and leftists, especially when lost in the radioactive fallout of Donald Trump's 2016 electoral victory, stepped directly into the pitfall of false dichotomy. Mark Lilla amplified the aggrieved voice of many liberals when he wrote that the left must mute their advocacy on issues of race, gender, and sexual orientation in order to broadcast an agenda of economic interest that will unite all poor and middle-class voters, regardless of demographic characteristics. Attempting to claim the mantle of martyrdom and leadership, Bernie Sanders contradicted himself when he implored Democrats to declare a cease-fire on identity politics so that they might better appeal to the "white working class." One of his 2020 rivals, Kamala Harris, protested that ridicule of "identity politics" amounts to little more than preemptive shaming of those who seek to spotlight racial and sexual injustice. Christopher Parker, a political scientist at the University of Washington, not only agrees with Harris but also breaks with Lilla by arguing that Democrats can win only if they maximize turnout from minority voters, providing a clear incentive to wrestle the megaphone away from Sanders to do just what the Vermont senator condemns—speak loudly and clearly about race.[16]

The organization and advocacy of Jackson, beginning with the Chicago Freedom Movement, undresses both groups for their deficit of imagination. The history of America makes it impossible to talk about class without talking about race, and vice versa. Slavery was an economic and racial injustice, just as many years after the passage of Thirteenth Amendment, whites will often conceal the beast of bigotry with a mask of economic consternation. The south suburbs of Chicago experienced one of the most rapid and rapacious takeoffs of white flight on record in the United States.[17] Few white homeowners were so brazen to cry "there goes the neighborhood" at the sight of a black family moving into a new house. Instead, they would articulate seemingly benign worries about property values. The justification for segregation in the 1960s was largely the same, but anyone throwing bricks at pacifist ministers is probably not contemplating real estate listings.

The example of Jackson is important for anyone seeking to develop insight into why white America is largely hostile to democratic reform. He identifies "four stages of the struggle." The first was "246 years of legal slavery," and the "segregation season" of the Reconstruction period following the Civil War until the Civil Rights Act of 1965 was the second. To secure the right to vote and universalize the franchise in a multicultural democracy constituted the third stage in the struggle. "The fourth stage, which we are still fighting," Jackson explains, "is access to capital and economic rights." He often repeats during speeches, "free but not equal," going on to say, "When we won our freedom, we became free to fight for equality. What we have found is that many of our freedom allies are not our equality allies."

Many people forget, and it is rarely even taught in history courses at the university level, that Martin Luther King's last political activity was not a march against segregation or racial discrimination, but leading a rally on behalf of Memphis sanitation workers striking for decent wages and safe working conditions. When King made it to Memphis, the threats on his life had grown so prevalent and unpredictable that many of his aides advised him against making the trip, including Jackson, who got into a heated argument with King when he tried to convince him that he should focus more on the efforts of economic integration that Jackson was already leading since the Chicago campaign. King insisted that he made a promise to the Memphis garbage collectors, and it was "the right thing to do." The courage of King provides him with a towering grandeur in the eyes of history, but it is important to remember that anyone standing close to King, especially in public and on the open street, also flirted with the trajectory of rifle fire. With gravitas rarely visible in affluent society, these men accepted vulnerability to violent death not only for their own benefit but also for the extension of life, liberty, and justice to neighbors and strangers, generations born and not yet conceived.

"I get frightened now when I think how close I came to not getting into the movement," Jackson confessed. "I was brought up in a materialistic, individualistic society, and might never have escaped."[18] Charles Taylor, philosopher and author of *The Ethic of Authenticity*, argues that generating an independent identity is an empty accomplishment if it does not include the service of something larger than one's own profit and prestige.[19] Jackson certainly could have flourished in a variety of lucrative fields. Upon graduating high school, he rejected a contract with a minor league baseball team. An undeniable economic sophistication, along with his ability to negotiate deals with powerbrokers in business and government, indicates that a successful career in law or finance was within his grasp. Bernard Lafayette, one of the organizers of the march on Selma, said that Jackson instead "modeled himself entirely after King."[20] The replication of King's soaring oratory and the duplication of his synthesis of spiritual combat with political engagement from outside the system of governance do not fully capture how King's influence on Jackson was "total," to use Jackson's own adjectival description. The final steps of King's life would sketch a dream that Jackson would spend the next fifty years attempting to bring to bear in the world of the lucid.

"The last major meeting we had was less than a month before Dr. King's assassination," Jackson told me in reference to a March 14, 1968, summit.

> Dr. King had convened a strategic summit with the purpose of organizing the poor. We were at the meeting, of course, representing black America. There were white labor leaders from Appalachia, organizers of Latino migrant workers, Native American activists and tribal leadership, and Jewish anti-poverty workers and thinkers from New York. We were trying to determine how we could harness our collective strength to fight poverty and achieve economic justice.

It was a genuine rainbow coalition.

The meeting was the culmination of a steady realization from King that even a magical erasure of racism would not eradicate the virus of the soul infecting America. Behind the concealment of democratic rhetoric, a technocratic-corporate state was marshaling its brilliant machinery for the immiseration of life. The bombs and Agent Orange transforming Vietnam into a poisonous crater, the children dying in backwoods outposts and on city streets for lack of medicine, and the massive fist of Jim Crow colliding with the face of black America were not alien to each other; rather, they were all emanating out of the same source of death. Harry Belafonte remembers King telling him, "I worry that I am integrating our people into a burning house."[21] Having witnessed the end of the segregation season, and having secured the right to vote, King and his aides were then aiming to extinguish the flames. They were going to commit to a mission as ambitious as the moral restoration and democratic regeneration of America. The murder of King left an empty chair of command.

Despite appearances to the contrary, as white supremacists gain steam in political culture and income inequality continues to become more extreme, the movement is not without its triumphs. "The first time I was arrested was for trying to check a book out of a public library," Jackson once told me when I asked how he maintains the hope and will to continue fighting when bad news is on the doorstep every day,

> My father had to sit behind Nazi POWs on base. Now, we've gone from picking cotton to picking presidents and governors and mayors. We went from the balcony of the Lorraine Motel to the balcony of the White House. Sometimes

when you're trying to climb your way out of a hole, you become so fixated on how far you have left to go, that you forget to look behind you, and see how far you've come.

The Black Freedom Movement, as Jackson explained in his eulogy for Rosa Parks, is the keystone to American democracy. It is the most effective civilizing and humanizing force in American life, as it not only legitimates the Bill of Rights by extending its protections to all citizens, regardless of skin color or ancestral background, but also permeates into other precincts of American life, generously offering its victories and benefits to all constituencies of citizenship. On the South Carolina trip when Jackson showed me his boyhood home, he also spoke in a large, black church about the necessity of Medicaid expansion and, in turn, the need to apply political pressure on then governor Nikki Haley, who would later accept a cabinet position in the Trump administration, to accept funds from the federal government to enlarge the state-administered health-care program for the poor. Jackson made part of his pitch the data indicating more whites would benefit from Medicaid than blacks. It was simple arithmetic. The majority of poor people in South Carolina, and therefore the majority of state residents without health insurance, were white. Jackson saw Medicaid as an opportunity for coalescence. Whites and blacks who care about themselves, their children, and their sick or disabled neighbors could transcend racial difference, and organize around the common cause of good health.

A young woman in a "Black Lives Matter" T shirt stormed the microphone during the audience question and answer portion, challenging Jackson to explain "why we should worry about white people." "They don't worry about us," she said, "so, why should we care if what we do helps them?"

I felt several sets of eyes turn toward me, the only white person in the audience. Jackson quickly attracted all attention, however, when he told a story about visiting Russia when it was still the flagship country of the Soviet Union, and still America's enemy in the Cold War, during the 1980s: "More Russians wanted to talk to me about music than politics," Jackson said.

> They knew I never played music, but they asked me if I knew Michael Jackson, or if I knew Diana Ross, or Prince, or Stevie Wonder. Now imagine if we always just stayed in our own neighborhoods—if say, the Motown artists, only played their music for each other in their own section of Detroit. We can start on our side of town, but then cross over to the other side of town, and the entire city gets better. We've always made America better.

To understand how America became better, but also how it can regress and become worse, it is essential to remember the wisdom of Prov. 22:28, a scripture Jackson is fond of quoting: "Remove not your ancient landmarks, which thy fathers have set."

Chapter 2

THE APOSTLE OF ECONOMICS

The "fantasy" of white supremacy, to recall Toni Morrison's description, finds competition in manipulative power only from the myth of meritocracy. Even after endless revelations involving insider trader schemes, savings and loan scandals, and the "gaming of the system" from big banks, major corporations, and billionaires who manage to pay little, if any, taxes, the majority of Americans continue to believe that hard work is a guarantee of success.[1] Even liberal politicians betray and encourage a certain naivete when they draw applause by arguing on behalf of struggling Americans who "play by the rules." The rules, one could posit in a country where the top 1 percent of income earners control more wealth than the bottom 90 percent, is precisely the problem. Martin Luther King, while being held captive in the Birmingham Jail, attempted to appeal to his white guard's humanity and predicament, when he explained that, because they both belonged to the exploited working class, they had much more in common—and shared much greater interests—than their different pigmentation of skin would otherwise suggest. Race might bring one to a critical crossroad, but one will soon find that the road on which they travel runs right into class.

Once when preparing to conduct a live interview with Jesse Jackson in front of an intimate audience, Jackson's son, Yusef, suggested that at an opportune moment I ask his father a "question about sports." "There are few things dad loves more than sports," Yusef said about the former college football quarterback. If memory serves me right, I asked him to give a prediction about the Chicago Bears regular season record, but Jackson's football analysis was hardly the most memorable use of athletic language during the evening. When addressing the myth of meritocracy, and the simple goal of the Black Freedom Movement, Jackson said, "Why is it that blacks and whites can come together and play on the football field without any conflict? Why is it that athletes from all over the world can compete in the Olympics without the tension we have in our politics?" Jackson asked before answering his own set of questions, "Whenever the playing field is even, rules are public, goals are clear, referees are fair, and score is transparent, we can all make it together. We can win or lose without challenging the result." The popularity of professional sports is predicated upon a universal expectation of fairness, consistency, and transparency. Jackson said that "no one would watch or take seriously the NFL, if there was one team with all white players, another team with all black players, and touchdowns were worth 10 points for the white team, and only 5 points for the black team—the black team had to move the ball 12 yards for a first down, but the whites were required to go only 8 yards."

Jackson's hypothetical prompted laugher of comprehension from the audience. The absurd football competition he imagines is precisely how the American economy has functioned, to varying degrees, from the Declaration of Independence to the present. This is not to say that diligence and effort do not offer any rewards, but that the rewards are easier to access, and greater in value, for some than they are for others. Imploring people to work hard, or explaining the benefits of raising children within a marital union, might make for sound advice, but, contrary to the narrow thinking of the far right, it does not amount to a political program. When I asked Jackson about conservative pundits who dismiss systemic causes of the racial gap in economic fortune with invocations of "personal responsibility," he offered a simple demolition of the argument: "They're just stating the obvious. Of course, children will typically do better in a home with two loving parents instead of one, but then what?"

Libertarians and conservatives lack an answer to "then what?" but that is the exact question Jackson started fighting to answer after the death of King, concentrating on not only bigotry but also the "infrastructure in place to destroy us"—much of which was economic and would prove much more wind and rain resistant than the house of Jim Crow.

Operation Breadbasket began to operate in 1962. Limited to the city of Atlanta, Georgia, its aim was to enhance the economic opportunities of black Americans, who, in spite of talent, intelligence, and the will to work, were endlessly pacing narrow, asbestos-infected halls outside of closed doors. Few white businessowners would employ blacks, and even fewer banks would lend to aspiring black entrepreneurs and homebuyers. Meanwhile, trade unions largely refused to admit black laborers just as local and state governments rarely, if ever, awarded contracts to the black companies that did exist. King's concern about integration into a structure set to tumble down in flames was deeply spiritual, but on the immediate, practical level, there was also anxiety that newly won freedoms earned blacks only the freedom to live in poverty. Operation Breadbasket began in Atlanta as a corrective means to harness the same power of activism that defeated public transit segregation in Montgomery, Alabama, in the application of pressure on financial institutions, and the mechanics of commerce, in order to create a more equitable economy for black citizens. Thirty ministers in several Southern cities began to direct Breadbasket chapters, but despite their commitment and sound intentions, they floundered and struggled, leading only small boycotts and boasting marginal achievements.

It was not until 1966 when Breadbasket became operational in Chicago, its second northern city after Philadelphia, that it became a local economic success and, as a result, a national cultural influence. The muscularity of the economic mission did not begin to grow in strength and flexibility until it found an effective leader and spokesman—a young, innovative, and increasingly militant aide to Dr. King whose tactics extended beyond the niceties and modesty of middle-aged,

Southern preachers—a man who, for his efforts, would earn the nickname "Apostle of Economics" from *Ebony* magazine: the Reverend Jesse L. Jackson.[2]

With his ties already developing in Chicago from his study at the Chicago Theological Seminary, and his service as associate pastor at Fellowship Baptist Church on the South Side, Jackson had an ability to navigate the local terrain of a Union city that made Confederate policies more technological, more institutional, more smooth, and less violent, than the Jim Crow South. Already married and a father of three children in 1966, Jackson and his family were no strangers to the monetary degradation of their constituents and stakeholders. It was not until several years later when Jackson began to attract the patronage of sponsors that he could move his family into a decent home, have a car to drive, or even good shoes to wear. One of Jackson's early sponsors, the CEO of Jou Louis Milk—a dairy company founded by the champion boxer—recalls seeing Jackson slip on the sidewalk due to tears in his old sandals. The business executive reacted by purchasing him a new wardrobe—one that signaled a dual identity for Jackson, who, in the first years of Breadbasket, was dividing his time between Chicago and southern campaigns with Dr. King. When he was in the entourage of the latter, he wore conservative suits and sweaters, but in Chicago he began to adopt a more radical look and comportment—African clothing, bell bottoms, heeled boots, and jewelry. It was not until after King's death that he would grow out his afro and sideburns, just as it was not until after King's death that he would formally commit to directing Operation Breadbasket, full time.[3]

Jackson might have cultivated the fashion of Black Power, but unlike the Panthers, his tactics of political and economic agitation were not far from the mainstream. Many of his critics view him as subversive, but Jackson has always sought to reform, not repudiate, the working institutions of American democracy and society. When I accompanied him on a speech at a community college, one student asked him for his advice on getting "outside the system." Jackson offered no such advice, seeing the young man's question as idealistic in intention, but delusional in practice. "You're in the system whether you like it or not," he said. "When you're born, you have a birth certificate, and when you die, there will be a death certificate. You're going to have to pay taxes, you're going to drive on roads built by the system, and right now you are studying in a school that is part of the system. So, the question isn't how to get out of the system, but how to make the system work better for you."

Black separatist organizations, as Louis Farrakhan, leader of the Nation of Islam, most famously articulated in his address at the Million Man March in 1995, have always entertained the fantasy of thriving with no connection to white institutions. The Jackson method, while perhaps not as romantic to some, is much more realistic, and as a consequence, more effective. Just as King invoked the Declaration of Independence and US Constitution in his case for political integration, Jackson attempts to use the incentives already in place within white capitalist structures to "make the system work better."

The first campaign Jackson directed for Breadbasket engineered exactly that improvement, albeit on a small scale. Enlisting the support of nearly every black church in Chicago, Jackson organized a boycott and many public protests against the major food chains in black neighborhoods—all of which rarely employed blacks, almost never carried products from black businesses, and never had blacks in management positions. When a chain, or even a single store, would agree to implement changes, Jackson would publicly announce it, and hold a Saturday morning event—a "Forum"—to announce the terms of the deal and give an update on compliance. The Saturday morning forum, although wider and broader in scope, still takes place on a weekly basis under the auspices of Jackson's own organization, the Rainbow/PUSH Coalition. Within six months of the first campaign against grocery stores, all major food chains in Chicago signed pacts with Breadbasket, and all black businesses saw significant increases in sales to those chains, with one food producer boasting of a 600 percent spike. A&P began to stock the products of twenty-five black manufacturers.[4]

Jackson's style of negotiation was certainly unconventional. A theological and pastoral practice of deal making, it would allow Jackson to seize the moral high ground in a fashion so direct it was borderline comical. He and his staff, which typically included black and white ministers, would enter a corporate boardroom, and before even broaching a topic of pecuniary interest, would request to open with prayer. Jackson would have the board members join hands in a circle with his staff, and then ask God to "help these men see the light." If the meeting went well, Jackson would then close with prayer, thanking God for the "moral redemption of these men's souls." One white businessman called Jackson and his staff the "moral mafia," but it was not merely an ethical appeal Jackson relied upon to make progress against the infrastructure of economic segregation. With the media-savvy and rhetorical brio for which he would later become famous, Jackson would marshal almost every black church and organization, attract widespread journalistic coverage, and convince many sympathetic whites to support his campaigns, making the daily routines of commerce hell for those who would dare defy him. Jackson also led a committed staff of young and skillful strategists. Frank Watkins, a white graduate of the theology program at Anderson University of Indiana, took his first job as Jackson's point man in the suburbs, which Watkins playfully translates as "getting the support of white people."[5] By 1971, the fifth year of Jackson's leadership of Breadbasket, *Life* reported that the effort was responsible for directly helping 4,000 blacks in Chicago gain suitable employment, and was also instrumental in the acquisition of an additional 10,000 jobs related to their victories in support of black products, entrepreneurship, and contracts.[6] One particularly salient example of how Jackson nationalized the economic campaign after Breadbasket and PUSH's initial success is the $460 million agreement he negotiated with Burger King in 1983, convincing the fast-food company to commit those funds to an effort that increased black-owned franchises by 15 percent within five years, and recruited 20,000 minorities for managerial positions nationwide.

"I never felt powerless," Jackson told me when I asked how he summoned the strength to make demands on men with far greater wealth and influence. "If you locate the power source through incentives," he explained, "you can locate your own power. Businessmen care about profit, profit is tied to consumers, and I had the consumers on my side." Jackson also told me that, in addition to beginning meetings with prayers that would implicate the executives, another unconventional tactic of negotiation—one that he would later practice when meeting with foreign dictators and tyrants—was to begin with the "disarming" question, "What can I do for you?" The inquiry would surprise those expecting Jackson to initiate conversation with castigation. "Some of them would raise a business matter," Jackson recalled, "While others were more personal. I'll never forget that one CEO became emotional; asked me to pray for his daughter. She had been in an accident."

The *New York Times* recently ran an old photo of Jackson in 1969, leading a rally of 4,000 aspiring construction workers to protest the exclusion of blacks from the trades. Wearing a suede vest with fringes in the chest, and a hardhat, Jackson has his large arms in the air as he appears to make a loud appeal over a crowd of police officers. "The same people who called us lazy locked us out of the trade unions," Jackson told the newspaper and stretched the connective tissue between structure and culture; policy and psychology. He then said, "We're still fighting these barriers to equality and justice."[7]

Jesse Jackson's birthday is October 8th, and every year on that day, Jackson follows the instruction of Martin Luther King, who believed that birthdays are not for self-aggrandizing celebration, but service. One should express and exercise gratitude for life with, in the words of Jackson, "compassion and cultivation of a thirst for justice." On King's final birthday in January of 1968, he spent the morning planning the Poor People's Campaign, spoke to several student groups in the afternoon, and then strategized with the anti-war movement in the evening. In 2014, I spent the day with Jackson, watching as he acted on the inspiration of King's example. He spent the anniversary of his birth not in an ornately decorated banquet hall or in the warm embrace of a luxurious party, but inside the thin and cracked walls of Chicago's underfunded public schools.

Before he left his office, and while his staff and supporters ate a spread of eggs, bacon, sausage, and grits, he told me, "We must have the courage to reimagine our struggle. Even as we gain traction and make progress, we must maintain the ability to see the ways our struggle changes and stays the same."

The struggle endures throughout different stages of the average American life—a country where the majority of citizens have less than $500 in savings,[8] and blacks and Latinos, on average, face even greater financial precarity. For those who navigate the night side of the "land of opportunity," the struggle begins somewhere like Chicago's Farragut Academy High School. The student body is predominantly poor and Latino, and Rainbow/PUSH made a visit to host a morning assembly not only so that Jackson could offer a characteristic combination of motivational speech and political encouragement but also to make a special announcement. Rainbow/PUSH established a relationship with Farragut after learning that the football team did not have adequate funding to equip and protect its players with enough helmets and pads. Many players were sharing helmets, which increases the risk of concussion, and many were unable to practice due to lack of padding. Rainbow/PUSH secured funding for the football team, and in the words of Farragut's assistant football coach, "Made the players safer."

Debates and disturbing discoveries about the dangers of football under any conditions aside, one doesn't need the imagination of Charles Dickens to realize that high schools on the wealthy, North Side of Chicago—or in the rich suburbs—don't have a problem getting their football players the best, newest, and safest equipment. The same is true for excellently trained teachers, current textbooks, classroom technology, and functional infrastructure. The playing field, in innumerable ways, is uneven for the children of Farragut. At birth, the child who lives in a neighborhood with high property taxes, and rich schools, is far ahead of a child in a neighborhood where bullets fly and families fall apart.

Jackson ended his speech at Farragut by asking all the students to stand and join him in the recitation of the "I am somebody" refrain he made famous in the 1960s. The students reacted with a roar, shouting with the strength of a full-force gale—one girl, standing behind me, fighting back tears—"If my mind can conceive it, and my heart can believe it, I know I can achieve it. I am somebody . . . ." It was a moving affirmation of the students' basic humanity, and it was an attempt to empower them to speak in the active voice and project themselves as actors, rather than meekly accept roles as the acted upon.

During the same week of 2014, there was a small Ebola scare in the United States. One man, Thomas Duncan, who was black and had just visited West Africa, died from the infection. At the request of his family, Jackson had spent the day before his birthday in Dallas, Texas. At the time, Duncan had not yet died from Ebola. Jackson met with the Duncan family and Mike Rawlings, then mayor of Dallas, to discuss the cruelty of the for-profit health-care system. Texas Presbyterian Hospital initially sent Duncan home—even though he had a 103 degree fever and had informed hospital staff he had just returned from Liberia—because he did not have health insurance. "He was poor. So, in many ways the treatment of him was typical," Jackson said. "We often talk about the immorality of the health care system, but this highlights its irresponsibility."

The denial of Duncan's humanity—the measurement of his life according to a bottom line, insurance card criteria—put his friends, family, and neighbors at risk for Ebola infection. It is chilling to contemplate how many uninsured patients suffering from other contagious diseases are sent back into their homes and offices, without receiving a test or diagnosis, because a hospital deems their treatment unprofitable. Hospitals and schools are public institutions of collective investment and return. If America does not invest the capital, energy, and effort to make them great, it should not feign surprise and disgust when men with Ebola wander outside hospital doors back into the street, and children do not, in the words of Jackson, "choose futures over funerals."

Keeping eyes on the prize while climbing up the ladder means confronting the ugly reality that with each rung there is another layer of discrimination and obstruction.

"The media see the police shoot a black teenager, and think, 'oh, that's a black story,'" Jackson said, "But they don't think anything to do with high tech and finance can be a black story. They don't think it is a diversity issue."

As much as the horrific killings of unarmed black Americans deserve extensive media coverage, they do, as Jackson implies, fit the stereotypical script of the black story. Minority-owned investment firms and Silicon Valley are nowhere near any mainstream media script. That is why Rainbow/PUSH became shareholders in the major high-tech companies—Google, Facebook, Twitter, Pandora—and demanded that they release their hiring numbers.

Do the boards and management offices of companies communicating with the world, and acquiring the information of billions of people, reflect the diversity of their customers and clients?

The high-tech industry attempted to evade this question; some companies even resorted to taking legal action to secure the privacy of their employment data. If not for the investigation by Rainbow/PUSH, no one could confirm what many have long suspected: the technology industry is overwhelmingly white and male. Blacks and Hispanics account for 28 percent of American Twitter users, but only 5 percent of Twitter employees. Pandora is located in Oakland, a city of exciting racial and ethnic variety, but 71 percent of its employees are white. Over a third of its users are black and Hispanic, but its offices are so white that a visitor would need sunglasses to make it through the door.[9] "This is like the music industry," Jackson said, "Where blacks and Hispanics are over-indexed in the product and in purchasing, but not in employment and business."

It is not just the technical division of these companies that is monolithic, but the management, legal, and communication departments. "The only person with a technology background on Zuckerberg's board is Zuckerberg," Jackson noted, referring to Facebook founder, Mark Zuckerberg. "There is not a shortage of talent. There is a shortage of opportunity," he added. John Thompson, an African American, is chairman of Microsoft, and David Drummond, a black lawyer, incorporated Google. The talent, and often the education and expertise, is there, but the opportunities are behind locked doors, and the same is true in debt capital markets. Rainbow/PUSH has uncovered that most Fortune 500 Companies—from McDonalds to Boeing—have few to no relationships with minority-owned broker dealers.

An easy assumption to accept is that once people—of any race or background—acquire educational pedigree and sufficient capital, they've made it through the velvet rope and now have VIP access to the American dream. While owners of broker dealers are not comparable to the students at Farragut, they are still kept in the basement of the high-finance mansion. A network of cronies combats the diversification of their world, limiting opportunities for broad inclusion of the American polity and stifling potential for minds with the talent of Thompson and Drummond. "They aren't George Wallace," Jackson said describing the owners and administrators of tech companies and major corporations, "but they operate according to cultural blindness." Karen Cecile Wallace, an attorney who worked for PUSH in the 1990s, describes a similar situation in the legal field, calling it one of the "least diverse" in the country. Her principal task, under the direction of Jackson, was to advocate for black lawyers in a variety of fields, building relationships with companies and organizations to bolster the opportunities and prominence of black attorneys who might provide superior representation to minority consumers, workers, and stakeholders than an exclusively white and patrician legal office.

As Rainbow/PUSH moves from Wall Street to Silicon Valley, they expose the sociology of inequality. "People do business with those they know, trust, and like," Jackson said before echoing the insight of Joseph Stiglitz that "economic inequality creates social distance." He punctuated his point with a local example that generalizes, especially as gentrification and racial displacement become larger crises in nearly every major city: "If there is a new shopping mall in development on the South Side of Chicago, who is going to buy up the surrounding properties to prepare for the jump in real estate value? Not the people of the community, but those who know the developers."

The machinery of inequality within American corporate capitalism operates so that it becomes visible, albeit with different shades of subtlety, at various levels of society—from the poor, underfunded public schools where children pass through metal detectors, and the district cannot afford to purchase new protective equipment for students playing its most dangerous sport, to the opulent suites of technology firms doubling as cliques of culturally obtuse tycoons. Jackson first confronted the legal apparatus and associative social pattern of extreme inequality in the 1960s as director and spokesperson for Operation Breadbasket. Battling neighborhood grocery store chains might seem simpler and easier than grappling with multinational corporations, but Jackson would quickly learn that it was all part of learning that the free market promise of bountiful waters is little more than a mirage.

In the late 1960s and early 1970s—in Chicago and from coast to coast—there were laws, ordinances, and corporate policies, both spoken and those that fall under "gentlemen's agreements," coalescing to maintain white authority.[10] Jesse Jackson's rejection of Dorothy Day's position on the salvific potential of a "revolution of the heart," and his insistence on using actual rules and regulations to measure racism, invites a new definition of "white supremacy." One early Sunday morning when I was with Jackson during his radio broadcast, he made an amusing admission during a commercial break: "An inside joke with black people is whenever someone white commits an egregious act of stupidity or ineptness, we would often say, 'There they go being superior again.'" Jackson's assistant Alanna looked at me, laughed, and said, "It's true." If his policies were not so destructive, and his rhetoric not so incendiary, one might have the temptation to have a laugh on white America for the election of Donald Trump. There they go being superior again. "White supremacy is that which maintains white authority," Jackson has said. It is hard to imagine that anywhere near a majority of white Americans believe that they actually belong to a master race, genetically endowed with superior intelligence, talent, and skill, but the more insidious form of white supremacy, using the Jackson analysis, is the system of laws and official practices that allow whites, all other things being equal, to enjoy superior access to career opportunities, finance, and education than their black counterparts.

Operation Breadbasket, like the campaign for public accommodations and suffrage, focused on reformation of American law, policy, and institutional procedure, but any battle requires the enlistment and energy of rank-and-file soldiers. The civil rights movement began to gain power not only because of the brilliance and charisma of its leadership but also because of its swelling ground level support from "everyday people," to cite the Sly Stone lyric. The discriminatory and predatory effects of Jim Crow were obvious, and, as a result, the recruitment strategy was just as clear. With Operation Breadbasket, Jackson and his staff had to work to persuade a critical mass of people to make a difference in the Chicago economy, and beyond. "The only thing worse than oppression," Jackson has said, "is to adjust to it." In 1968, Jackson would have to exercise his own creativity to convince people, without power, wealth, or influence, to become, in the words of King, "creatively maladjusted."

Jackson's first invention was "Black Christmas," featuring a parade of black officials, athletes, writers, entertainers, and beauty queens. Presiding over the parade was not Santa Claus, but the "Black Soul Saint"—a character combining traditional African fashion and the accessories of 1960s militancy. He came from the South Pole, rather than the North, and instead of bearing gifts, he promised "love, justice, peace, and power." The imagination of Jackson shows that he was capable of creating memorable images, or in internet parlance, "memes," long before such messaging activity became an obsession for millions of people on social media. Jackson conducted a similar event surrounding "Black Easter," and its symbol was a black lamb, suggesting that the story of Jesus Christ as exile was similar to the mistreatment of blacks in America. Unlike many social memes, which appear to function as the ends in themselves, providing amusement and gratification, but doing little to alter actual politics and institutional relations, Jackson's assertion of new imagery served a pragmatic purpose. It was to first inculcate pride in his followers and observers so that they might gather the strength and willpower to join his campaign for economic inclusion and opportunity. "If we are proud to be black," Jackson said at a Black Easter event, "we can spend our money where we are." It is hardly any secret that Christmas is the most significant shopping season for retail, and to a lesser extent Easter, so Jackson would use these events not only to attract media attention, and recruit new supporters, but also to kickstart boycotts of businesses that would not comply, or even negotiate, with Breadbasket's reasonable demands for better treatment of black applicants, consumers, and workers.[11]

The success of the black holiday celebrations inspired Jackson to organize what would soon become his most famous commercial activity, the Black Expo. Beginning in 1969, Jackson began hosting an exhibition of black business, artistry, music, and service providers. It was also something of an activist convention where the various organizations, large and small, working in the Midwest on issues of civil rights and economic justice would unite to strategize, share successful tactics, and, when possible, join forces.

The effectiveness of Operation Breadbasket shocked even the most hardened critics of Jackson's fiery style, which often clashed with older leaders of the civil rights movement. In addition to securing thousands of jobs and slots in trade unions for black workers, Breadbasket also negotiated over $100 million of benefits for black entrepreneurs, firms, and neighborhoods by winning product placement in grocery chains, government contracts for black businesses, and fair loans to startups. Meanwhile, the Expos became a national apex of black culture with performers like Curtis Mayfield, Donny Hathaway, Aretha Franklin, and Stevie Wonder often headlining. Jackson even summoned Breadbasket's leverage to win better recording contracts for many of these musicians. He would also apply pressure to Chicago radio stations to increase staff pay for low-level workers, and feature more black on-air personalities if they were going to continue to play music by black artists.[12]

In December of 1971, tensions between Jackson and the Southern Christian Leadership Conference became irreconcilable. Ralph Abernathy, and other leaders of King's old organization, believed that Breadbasket was siphoning off too many funds, but Jackson countered that his campaign "not merely for rights, but for power," should define the future of black advocacy and activism in the United States. Unable to reach a compromise, Jackson launched his own organization, PUSH—People United to Save Humanity. A few years later, Jackson would wisely change the name to the less melodramatic, People United to Serve Humanity. PUSH took advantage of the Breadbasket momentum by continuing the struggle for economic inclusion—organizing boycotts, walkouts, picket lines, and PUSH Expos, events exactly like the Black Expos. Even with the triumph of Breadbasket, and later, PUSH, Jackson's efforts attracted criticism, and not merely from the usual suspects of right-wing demagoguery and slander.

The American left attacked Jackson for sublimating his obvious charisma and persuasive power into an organization that, even if its results were laudable in the short term, was not working toward the mitigation of capitalistic excess at the policy level, much less aiming to achieve victory for democratic socialism in the United States. Unlike King in the year of his death, Jackson was not devoting significant time or energy to discussion of health-care disparities, educational divergence, and differences in standards of living that were consequences of public policy, not private bigotry. King was reticent about Breadbasket, because he believed that its victories would amount to an injection of the "tranquilizing drug of gradualism," to use a phrase from the "I Have a Dream" speech, into the body politic. The only substantive and permanent solution to black poverty—like that to white poverty, Latino poverty, Native poverty, and Asian poverty—was a massive overhaul of the American economic system, beginning with the increase of the minimum wage to a living wage, full employment, an expansion of the social welfare state, and more just distribution of resources through progressive taxation. King was never shy about loudly declaring himself a Democratic Socialist, while Jackson has never self-applied the term. It was not until the 1980s that Jackson would demonstrate great vehemence in his demand for socialistic policies, but even then, in steadfast refusal of appeals from supporter Michael Harrington, would reject the ideological label.

Shortly after the foundation of PUSH, Jackson spoke to a gathering of 3,000 black nationalists, attempting to temper the ridicule of his economic agenda. "We are part of the white capitalist system even if we do not give it our moral endorsement," he said.[13] The American right has often depicted Jackson as a revolutionary subversive who, if possible, would take a flamethrower to every institution of society, but regardless of fantastical desire, Jackson has always displayed a tendency toward ritualism. Sociologist Robert K. Merton defines a "ritualist" as someone who goes through the motions of life even if he does not adhere to the values of the systems that demand those motions. In a political context, the term might apply to someone who works within a structure to manipulate it to improve the outcomes, rather than seek to destroy the structure itself.[14] The resulting dichotomy is that if Jackson was not a ritualist, he would have never succeeded to the extent that he did, achieving more than nearly any national leader to push America into a more equitable, just, and fair state. His savvy for working the various levers and mechanisms of democracy to the ends of justice is responsible for his major victories of the 1960s, 1970s, and 1980s. One cannot help but wonder, however, given Jackson's extraordinary ability to persuade and influence, how he might have fared as a revolutionary working entirely outside the system.

Jackson's simultaneous navigation of the political system and the world of radical dissent has enabled him to act as a credible broker in times of tumult. After the Chicago Police Department killed charismatic Black Panther leader, Fred Hampton, in a 1969 raid—a raid that the testimony of participating FBI agents confirm was conducted with the sole purpose of assassinating Hampton at the behest of the federal government—Bobby Rush, the cofounder of the Illinois Black Panther Party, went into hiding. Fearing that he was next on the hit list, he intended to remain underground—the risk of which was that law enforcement might escalate its unlawful war against the Panthers, and other civil rights organizations in Chicago. "I remember one morning—about two o'clock in the morning—Bobby Rush called me," Jesse Jackson told an interviewer in a documentary on Chicago's violent racial history, "He said, 'I can't talk long. I'm a fugitive. But I would like to turn myself in on stage with you, because if the public sees the police arrest me, I'm protected. They can't kill me." The following Saturday at the weekly Forum event, Rush surrendered to the highest-ranking black officer in the Chicago Police Department with Jesse Jackson at his side. Rush would later become a member of the Chicago City Council, and subsequently a congressman in the House of Representatives. In the latter role, he has distinguished himself as a stalwart for justice, consistently advocating for legislation that is anti-war, pro-civil rights, and expansive of health-care access for the poor. The trajectory of Rush, from fugitive to lawmaker, illustrates the veracity of Jackson's claim that "out of great turbulence came strength of leadership."[15]

It is easy to argue that the three most consequential black leaders of modern American politics are Martin Luther King, Jesse Jackson, and Barack Obama. Each history-making figure presents a different model for engagement and agitation of the establishment with King and Obama at opposite ends of the spectrum. Obama himself was wise enough to recognize his distance from King when a reporter asked him in 2008 if he believed that the civil rights leader would endorse his candidacy for president. The charismatic candidate who would eventually become president speculated that King would not endorse any candidate, but instead lead a movement in the streets to make sure whoever wins serves the interests of the people.[16] Obama began outside of the system as a community organizer—dedicating himself to precisely the kind of work Jackson made his focus in the 1970s—but soon experienced a political conversion, believing that true change can only transpire due to a cataclysmic force on the inside. He then played the part of the predictable script for acquiring elite status—attending law school at an Ivy League university, seeking political office, and crawling toward incremental change within the comfortable confines of the American duopoly. King never expressed any ambition to run for political position, and met with governors, senators, and presidents only as an advocate—a moral tribune giving prophetic witness to a desperate legal and spiritual ache for justice. Jackson has occupied landmark territory between King and Obama. He twice ran for president, but even when collaborating with the Democratic Party, has maintained the role of the heyoka at the ceremonial dance. The heyoka is a Native American dancer who moves in the opposite direction—against the crowd—when dancing around the fire. Jackson is a participant, willing to adopt the rites and fashions of power, but unlike Obama, resistant to political conformity. Jackson's "reverse warrior" status—another Native tribal term—is the primary reason why criticisms of his life and legacy have such dramatic variance. Power brokers view him as subversive, and they are partially correct, whereas revolutionaries view him as conservative, and they are also partially correct.

"It was not only his style that related to us," Al Sharpton said while explaining how Jackson's youth and ability to negotiate two political worlds on the left acted as a strength, "It was his ability to break down corporations for our economic reciprocity. We ought to be getting contracts. We ought to be on boards of directors. We ought to be part of the mix at the highest levels. He had a slogan, 'cut us in or we'll cut you out.' That was edgy to us as teenagers and in our twenties [sic]. It was different, in an inspiring way, from the Southern appeals to people's goodwill. It was nonviolent, but it was confrontational action."

Theories of political efficacy might conflict, but it is impossible to argue with results. Operation Breadbasket, and its later incarnation of Operation PUSH, is, in the words of one historian, "the least well known of the most important civil rights organizations of the twentieth century."[17] The victories of Operation Breadbasket and the early triumphs of Operation PUSH transformed Chicago into an epicenter of black business, finance, and profit. The first black-owned banks opened in Chicago, along with several black PR firms and publications. Jackson's immediate post-King efforts might have predominantly focused on economic gains and black pride, but they were not absent a politically motivated fighting spirit. In fact, on several key issues, Jackson demonstrated his acuity and aggression for demanding and forcing political reform.

Beginning in 1969, Jackson thundered through Illinois, highlighting subcenters of urban decay on the South Side of Chicago, but also making appearances in the rural southern sections of the state and mid-sized cities, like Rockford and Springfield, to address hunger in the first world. Jackson had personally met with families subsisting on less than $200 a month. Bizarre and defective state policies not only failed to address starving citizens in a global superpower but also exacerbated their wounds and woes. Illinois was receiving hundreds of millions of federal dollars in "subsidies," and directing most of it toward farmers who did not have enough crops to maintain the cost of their land. Only a tiny fraction of those dollars—typically around 5 percent—went to impoverished families. Jackson often indicted the political bias and cultural distortion that would praise aid for white, middle-class farmers as "subsidy," but bash benefits for the poor—often black or brown—as "handouts" or "entitlements."

The provocation for Jackson's leadership on hunger and food insecurity was not the mere existence of thousands of people, even in the neighborhoods surrounding his offices, suffering from deprivation and malnourishment, but then speaker of the Illinois House of Representatives Ralph Smith's announcement of a bill to reduce state funds for social welfare services. Jackson met with sixty followers—an impressive alliance of attorneys, social workers, economists, and labor activists—to draft oppositional legislation. Their proposal demanded that Illinois declare hunger a natural disaster, increase the welfare subsidy to minimum wage levels, and create emergency job training centers for those who are able-bodied, but failing to meet their basic, physiological needs. Jackson also exercised an acuity on use of language—a trait that linguist, George Lakoff, argues is rare on the American left—by including in the bill a change in terminology from "welfare" to "subsidy." He recognized that governments, on the state and the federal level, are quick to subsidize businesses in need of bail out or protection. Why not, Jackson asked with his reorientation of the standard vocabulary, apply that principle to poor people?

With what is now his vintage oratorical style, Jackson combined data and logical argument with impassioned jeremiad in a rare address to the Illinois State Legislature. "The biggest problem for you to face is the need to change your attitudes," Jackson said, "You look upon help given the farmers as a 'subsidy' and yet you call aid to the poor and disadvantaged 'relief.' The people need subsidy not stigmatization." The next day, he led a rally of four thousand people on the steps of the Illinois Capitol. Jackie Robinson made a surprise appearance, calling on the country to "have the courage of Jesse." Buckling under the weight Jackson artfully dropped on his shoulders, Speaker Smith withdrew his bill to slash social programs, and allowed Representative Harold Washington, who would later become Chicago's first black mayor, to introduce a bill similar to the one Jackson and allies had written. Colleagues of Smith remarked that it was the first time they ever saw him surrender on legislation he personally wrote or sponsored.

Meanwhile, the odious mayor of Chicago, Richard M. Daley, propagated the lie, hilarious in its absurdity, that "there is no hunger in Chicago." Little did Daley realize that Jackson had already convinced WTTW—Chicago's public television station—to run several segments on the issue that would feature Jackson providing a Dickensian tour of the squalor that made life hell for many residents of one of the world's wealthiest cities.

Writing in the *Chicago Defender*, the city's oldest black newspaper, Jackson broadly linked hunger with the "health-care crisis," citing statistics of high infant mortality rates in poor neighborhoods and condemning the disparity in medical services separating the upper and lower classes. With the politicization of Jackson's mission to assist the black poor of Chicago, moving from the corporate suite to the capitol building, he began to gain his own intimate awareness of the totality of injustice in America. Like King, he began to realize that demolition of one oppressive barrier only exposes the construction of another steely obstruction.[18]

"It costs less to take care of people at the front end with schools and health care than it does to react at the back end with jails and welfare," Jackson offered in rhyming analysis during a conversation I had with him in his office. The derivation of the word "radical" is the Latin term for root, meaning that a radical analysis or solution seeks to identify and treat the root of the problem, its underlying cause and point of origin. Gore Vidal observed that it is precisely for this reason of etymology, and its political implication, that the label "radical" has undergone consistent demonization, so much so that mainstream media commentators often refer to Islamic terrorists as "radical Muslims."[19] Nearly every debate over a contentious issue in American politics, but especially crime and illegal immigration, undresses America's intellectual and political class as unwilling or unable to excavate. They either cannot or will not look at the root of the problem.

As Jackson moves through the ascending maze of capitalist interest—from ghettos to gilded offices—his work aspires to civilize each sector without losing sight of the root: America's systemic abuse, neglect, and exploitation of the poor, manifesting itself in the daily brutality of health-care inaccessibility, savage educational inequalities, and, as a result of a multidecade drift to the right in national politics, a consistent shredding of the social safety net. Days after the announcement that Darren Wilson, a white police officer who shot Michael Brown under suspicious circumstances in Ferguson, Missouri, would face no charges, Jackson organized and hosted a "die-in" at the intersection outside of the headquarters of Rainbow/PUSH in Chicago. After a brief speech about police accountability and racial justice, Jackson lowered his large, then 72-year-old, body slowly onto the pavement of the cracked and dirty street. He was wearing a black suit and fedora and propped himself against the backs of two young men seated side by side to provide the elderly leader with lumbar support. A PUSH staff member handed Jackson a megaphone. "We will stay here for twenty minutes," Jackson announced as news crews of local television stations captured the demonstration. Each second passed with the silence of the grave, save for cameras clicking and the ambient soundtrack of nearby traffic, as dozens of young men and women, not much older than Brown whose resting state was not an act of political theater, but all too real, laid on the pavement, eyes closed and limbs outstretched as if they were waiting for a chalk outline. As soon as twenty minutes elapsed, two of Jackson's staff members helped to lift him off the ground. With a slight hobble, Jackson labored past me. The expression on his face was one of the most profoundly sad I have ever seen. He looked as if someone punctured his heart with an icicle.

"There are Ferguson's everywhere, and there are Michael Brown's everywhere," he said just a few minutes later in his office, visibly exhausted. He then proceeded to describe an undercurrent of violence in the American experience—not only white police officers shooting unarmed black men, typically without consequence, but also the explosion of gang violence in Chicago. Too many young blacks, many of them not even old enough to vote, have resigned to a nihilistic dedication to vanquishing each other—risking life and limb on a daily basis for drug profits, the expansion of gangland turf, and bragging rights. One of the most provocative comments Jackson ever made, and his only statement the American right ever quotes approvingly, was when he briefly lived in Washington DC in the early 1990s, and in reaction to a spate of shootings on his block, including one when his wife was outside their home, he said that it "breaks his heart" that if he is "walking down the street at night, and hears footsteps" he feels safer if those trailing him "are not black." I asked Jackson about that confession, and he reminded me that it came within a certain context—a response to a particular criminal outbreak from black gang members in his own neighborhood, and that there were many times in the 1960s, 1970s, and 1980s, that he would find relief when turning to find anyone nonwhite. The multiplication of tragedy that is young men showing complete disregard for their own lives, and the lives of those in their own communities, is a predictable result of what Jackson called "46 years of systemic neglect." Coining a memorable phrase, Jackson said, "We have replaced a domestic Marshall Plan with martial law."

Fresh off the pavement in an imitation of a corpse, Jackson delineated the "death culture" in American politics: "High unemployment and low graduation rates result in guns and drugs in and jobs out, hospitals and public schools closing, poor health care for poor people." Jackson continued with reference to a congressional study of the race riots in the 1960s that, extraordinarily at the time and given the racial and class demography of Congress, argued that the cause of unrest in Detroit, Los Angeles, and other American cities was the structural exploitation and neglect of poor neighborhoods, especially those that were black: "40 years after the Kerner Commission Report, we still have not seen a significant national plan to rebuild urban America. If we were serious about addressing violence in our cities, each state every year would issue by federal mandate a detailed report on its progress in closing the gaps between black and white, rich and poor."[20]

The riot in Ferguson following the announcement regarding the police officer who shot Michael Brown, like the subsequent furor in Baltimore after Freddie Gray, a black man who died of a broken neck in police custody, provoked many predictable calls for "peace and quiet" from mediocre pundits and politicians. Jesse Jackson objects not only to the philosophical implication of the phrase but also to the coupling of the two terms altogether: "They should never go together. Quiet is the absence of noise. Peace is the presence of justice. If you don't want noise, you must have justice."

Any system can become fairer and more efficient. The education of Jesse Jackson was such that by attempting to make the system operate according to its own promises—"equal opportunity," "one man, one vote"—he learned that softening the edges might spare many people from cuts and bruises in the interim period, but the only tenable long-term solution was to reform, even reshape, the entire system. King was reticent about the efficacy of Breadbasket with good reason. The desperate need for policy to prevent eruptions of violence in towns like Ferguson became abundantly clear when Operation PUSH began to shove its way inside predominantly black public schools.

Few failures of modern America are more devastating than the extreme divergence in quality of public education. Poor and working-class children suffer through decrepitude and dysfunction, as underpaid and overstressed teachers struggle to prepare them for adulthood with little resources, often in neighborhoods of aesthetic blight, commercial deprivation, and traumatic crime. Meanwhile, upper-class children take for granted the luxuries of a wealthy nation—the best textbooks, the most advanced technology, full funding for extracurricular activities in sports and the arts, and the highest-paid and -educated teachers in the country. In order to address American inequality at the "front end," Jackson and many of the nation's most revered black educators founded PUSH Excel, short for "Push for Excellence," in 1975.

Not long before the foundation of PUSH Excel, Jackson joined an advocacy campaign to rename a high school on the South Side of Chicago after Martin Luther King, Jr. When the campaign succeeded, Jackson spoke at the official naming ceremony. Later he would learn that graduation rates at the school were quite low, and he would often spot teenagers sneaking out of the school building; cutting class to play dice or wander the streets. "This is not what Dr. King fought and died for," Jackson told a close associate.[21] He believed it was important to inspire black youth to take their own educational opportunities seriously—even if they paled in comparison to those belonging to citizens with pale skin. Jackson devised a plan for academic achievement, encouraging students to sign pledges agreeing to devote a certain amount of time each night to homework, never miss class without good reason, and strive toward college acceptance. He would rely on his charisma and powerful oratory to sell the program and persuade students to sign the pledge. After receiving grants from the Ford Foundation, an American philanthropic organization, and the Carter administration—the only time PUSH would receive federal government support—Jackson began barnstorming Chicago and suburban schools, giving thunderous admonitions of the importance of education, and the need for blacks to overcome white racism and political adversity with personal diligence and excellence. Most of the students at any given auditorium event would sign the pledge, often awed by Jackson's personality and performance, but the results of PUSH Excel's 1970s work were dubious. The pledge, according to many teachers, would reinforce the commitments of the studious, but after a short boost to morale would soon be forgotten by the academically neglectful. PUSH Excel, in the beginning, also backfired politically, as it appeared to affirm the right-wing reduction of the racial gap in educational achievement to personal problems in "black culture." One PUSH aide quit for reasons of political protest, claiming that Jackson was, with or without intention, allowing himself to become "an ally of right wing white America." Roger Wilkins, a civil rights leader and historian, likened Jackson's Excel effort to "blaming the victim."[22]

With rich irony, it is exactly condemnation of a prominent black leader for "blaming the victim" that led to one of the most embarrassing gaffes of Jackson's entire career—embarrassing because of the language, but not the message. During the 2008 presidential campaign, Barack Obama, perhaps worried that white America might view his potential presidency with racial paranoia, spoke at a black church about personal responsibility in black families. The future first black president excoriated poor blacks for feeding their children "fried chicken for breakfast," failing to take education seriously, and allowing absentee fatherhood to trouble countless households. It was a recitation of the right-wing attack on black Americans, and, to the present, still provides fodder for conservative rebuttal to leftist ideas for policy intervention in the inner city. Jesse Jackson offered a similar indictment of "black culture" in the 1970s, but by 2008 he was a reformed man with a more sophisticated sense of politics, policy, and their connection with personal responsibility. On Fox News, and unaware that his microphone was picking up his chatter, he turned to a fellow guest and friend, and said, "You hear Barack was talking down to black people? I'd like to cut his nuts off."

The crudity and violence of Jackson's casual comment, oddly out of character for an orator of poetic grandeur, shocked the politically correct, language obsessed, and increasingly delicate American press. It gave the right wing heavy artillery to escalate its attack on Jackson, depicting him as bitter and envious of Obama's unprecedented campaign success. Worse yet, it alienated Jackson from many American liberals, almost all of whom were lost in starry-eyed fervor for a messianic figure. Obama, many Democrats believed, would offer redemption for an America suffering from social ills foreign to the developed world. One of those virulent conditions is widespread privation, and the absence of a coherent and compassionate social policy of poverty relief. Among the most impenetrable cultural barriers preventing access to socialistic policies in the United States is the pervasive belief that most poor people are to blame for their own troubles. The perceived pathologies of the poor attract a level of devotion on the right that borders on religious, but even the Democratic Party in recent years has embraced the destructive ideology. It was President Bill Clinton—not one of his two Republican predecessors—who "ended Welfare as we know it," to recite his own phrase, by introducing work requirements for single mothers seeking social assistance in their struggle to raise their children in a stable home.[23] As president, Obama would make progress in poverty relief, but when addressing the black congregation, with the realization that national media cameras were capturing his sermon, he cynically directed a message over his audience to the white viewers at home, reinforcing their stereotypical and false assumptions regarding indigent black citizens. It was to this unhelpful framing of the issue that Jackson so vehemently objected, and mainstream media commentators, acting as if the deadly image of Jackson's statement was literal and not figurative, asked Jackson questions like the following from a CBS news anchor: "Are you sorry that you said it?"

Jackson answered in the affirmative, reiterating that he was a "passionate Obama supporter," but then added a crucial nuance:

> When you go to a black church and make your focus responsibility, there's a limitation. Responsibility is a universal issue. Whether you go to a black church, a white church, or a labor union hall, we must all share responsibility, but that limited message must address the structural crisis in urban America, where you have the highest infant mortality rate, the shortest life expectancy, the most children in school with teachers who have less than three years experiences, the amazing murder rate because of the free flow of guns. So, beyond personal responsibility, there is heavy government lifting that must be done.

In an exhibition of the mainstream media's standard fixation on the superficial and salacious, the interviewer followed up with questions regarding whether Jackson had personally apologized to Obama.[24]

The years subsequent to Jackson's gaffe have only validated the political criticism at its heart. Just as Jackson himself learned in the 1970s, lectures from charismatic speakers are insufficient in the battle against urban decay, familial destitution, and racial gaps in academic achievement. In the interim period separating Jackson's own motivational tour of underfunded schools and his fulsome advocacy of public policy reform on issues of education, social assistance, and wealth distribution, he continually gained measurement of the massive octopus of injustice, wrapping its tentacles around American society.

"We were naïve after the civil rights victories in the 1960s," Jackson admitted in one of our conversations, "We thought that because we became free, we would soon become equal. It turns out we were given the car without the key." The key, Jackson proceeded to explain, is the legal apparatus that ensures blacks will face greater difficulties voting than whites, more scrutiny and prosecution from law enforcement, and more economic discrimination and hardship. In the 1960s, Jackson gazed upon a landscape without "white only" signs on the front doors, but the segregationist mentality haunting corporate procedure and political practice. The success of Breadbasket illuminated Jackson's effectiveness as an organizer, negotiator, and leader, but simultaneously spotlighted the ineffectiveness, or unwillingness, of America to rectify its persistent legacies of racist law and policy.

Jackson's success in economic integration had the immediate benefit of directly aiding thousands of black workers and business owners, and long-range instructional benefit to America. Securing thousands of jobs for blacks, winning many qualified laborers admission into trade unions, and negotiating millions of dollars worth of product placement deals for entrepreneurs, despite the enormous number of individual beneficiaries, barely made a visible debt in the two-tiered economy of white capitalism. Breadbasket and PUSH effectively undraped the myth of American meritocracy, exposing the extent of its racial degradation and nepotistic corruption.

The assassination of King left all his acolytes feeling dazed and confused. In his earliest efforts, Jackson would fight for economic fairness and opportunity, and then turn toward the education system, but it was the hunger campaign that would define the rest of his career, and most forecast his mission to deploy the means of external agitation on the political system for causes of justice with as much proximity to that same system as possible. Jackson, in the 1970s and 1980s, operated according to a gradual ascension of interest and agenda. Eventually, he realized that a full-frontal, national assault on American injustice was the only adequate response to the suffering in his society.

"There are some words no corporate CEO wants to hear," Paul Holmes, a public relations specialist who often consults multinational corporations, wrote in 2002, "'The Reverend Jesse Jackson is calling for a boycott of your company' is one of them [*sic*]." Throughout the 1990s, the automaker Toyota had demonstrated a drunken gait, foolishly stumbling into two racial controversies. In the first, the company aired a television ad for the Corolla, its economy car, with the slogan, "Unlike your last boyfriend, it goes to work in the morning." Not so subtly playing on old stereotypes of lazy, irresponsible black men, the boyfriend in the commercial was African American. Not long after the withdrawal of the television spot, Toyota made the center of a print advertisement a young black man with gold and jeweled teeth. Jesse Jackson was one of the prominent black leaders who criticized Toyota for "racial insensitivity," but proceeded to investigate Toyota's hiring data and corporate board information for its American operations. Eventually, Rainbow/PUSH discovered that their record on diversity and outreach was one of the worst in the nation.

Jackson threatened a national boycott and began organizing picket protests outside Toyota corporate offices and large dealerships across the country. Experiencing conniptions of panic similar to those Holmes would predict, Toyota executives pleaded to meet with Jackson, and, in the process, promised a full-fledged reformation of its hiring practices, corporate policies on diversity, and consideration of its multicultural consumers. Jackson agreed to call back his battalion under the condition that Toyota make a public pledge at the upcoming Rainbow/PUSH Convention and allow PUSH access to its future data in order to ensure accountability. The agreement was a continuation of Jackson's multidecade commitment to diversifying the automobile industry, most notably his 1980 founding of the National Association of Minority Automobile Dealers.

Toyota announced $7.8 billion in funding for a ten-year diversity program, including a 37 percent increase in spending with minority advertising agencies, $700 million per year on procurement of auto parts and supplies from minority-owned companies, and a $7 million commitment to the creation of a program that would target graduates of historically black colleges and universities for management positions at large dealerships.[25] Jackson effectively turned an adversary into an ally.

PUSH Excel remains operational in the present, offering tens of thousands of scholarship dollars to low-income students on a yearly basis, free use of a "tech center" in the basement of its Chicago offices for neighborhood students, and an annual HBCU tour, free of charge for teenagers. Many of these charitable efforts receive partial funding from Toyota. I have watched children at work in the tech center and have observed as teenagers take photos with Jesse Jackson before filing into a coach bus for a spring break college tour. I have also seen the excitement on young men and women's faces, and the tears in the eyes of their parents, when they learn they have won a scholarship from a legendary civil rights organization. It is difficult to argue with direct aid, especially when it benefits people who the corporate–academic nexus often ignores, neglects, and even exploits. One must also wonder how Toyota and other corporations benefit from assisting Jackson's philanthropy. Does it allow them to present a hospitable façade for an entity that often undermines human progress?

Charlie Wilson, the secretary of defense for Dwight Eisenhower, famously quipped, "What's good for the country is good for General Motors, and vice versa."[26] Environmental pollution resulting in increased asthmatic rates among children, senior citizens, and pregnant women, the effects climate change, and urban planning that prioritizes traffic rather than people indicate otherwise. Jackson has also coordinated with General Motors, thereby eviscerating the rationale of Wilson's capitalistic cheerleading. If General Motors, Toyota, or any other major corporation's interests universally coalesced with the common good, the advocacy of Jesse Jackson would have no purpose or relevance. Jackson, perhaps more than any other leader outside of government, has humanized the corporate beast, helping to dull its fangs and clip its claws. Would a mission of even greater efficacy require the execution of the beast, especially considering that its claws grow back, its teeth regain their sharp edges, and history has proven it untamable?

This is an essential inquiry, especially considering that in the 1980s, Jackson's Wall Street Project, a PUSH program to diversify the white country club clique of investment firms and banks, received support from Donald Trump. "He gave us space for the Wall Street Project in one of his buildings," Jackson told me when I asked about the reality television star turned demagogic president. "He always seemed like a decent guy," Jackson continued, "We went to fights together, and he seemed like a liberal Republican." The con artistry of Trump is masterful, making his identity as mysterious as an unidentified flying object over a desert sky. For most of his life, no one—from bank executives loaning him money to ghostwriters and Jesse Jackson—seemed to know the real Donald Trump. There are even those who now speculate over Trump's sincerity as presidential candidate with rumors circulating in perpetuity that he hoped to lose and was genuinely shocked when the electoral numbers began to shift in his favor. Even if there are few certainties about Trump, it is quite a challenge to imagine he had genuine concern for racial fairness on Wall Street. It is likelier he was applying a new coat of paint on his broken-down vehicle. Jackson, in hindsight, recognizes that Trump's agenda was most likely the brandishing of their relationship in order to look like an ally of racial inclusion and justice, because simultaneous with his support for the Wall

Street Project was his appeal to the Atlantic City municipal government for assistance with casino construction plans in their city. At the time, Atlantic City's first black mayor, James Leroy Usry, presided over city hall, along with several black city council members.

There is also a push–pull process of interest at work in Jackson's current work in Silicon Valley. "The goal is not simply to be transparent, but to change the face of technology so that its leadership, workforce and business partnerships mirror the world in which we live," Jackson wrote in a letter to high-tech industry executives that he shared with me.[27] As with many discussions and debates, Jackson was an early influencer to co-opt a technological term. He consistently creates conversation surrounding a widely neglected issue, and then receives little praise for his initiation. After his campaign for diversity in Silicon Valley, the congressional Black Caucus flew to California to escalate the pressure, and, subsequently, then president Obama gave an address in which he stated, "The next Steve Jobs might be named Stephanie or Esteban."[28]

While it is true that the diversity data out of Silicon Valley exposes an oblivious avoidance of black and Latino talent, Steve Jobs, for all of his brilliance and technical wizardry, is not necessarily a leader that a healthy society should encourage its children to emulate. He employed sweat shop labor to manufacture his products. The conditions in Chinese factories became so torturous that employees began experiencing existential meltdowns in the middle of their shifts, leading them to commit suicide by leaping out the nearest window. Apple solved the problem not by treating their workers like human beings, but with the installation of nets over the windows.[29] Jobs was also notorious for cruel behavior toward his executives, often issuing public humiliation at company meetings as punishment for failure or insubordination. Beyond the moral failures of one late billionaire, there is the ongoing threat to democracy to consider. Twitter, Facebook, and other social media platforms have proven themselves frighteningly inept at policing their digital pages for hate speech, sedition, and dangerous conspiracy theories. Improving the demographic profile of their respective boards might result in more vigilance against white supremacy and other potentially lethal ideologies, as it is hard to imagine black attorneys and Native American consultants reacting to racist provocation of violence with the same blasé attitude that so often characterizes Mark Zuckerberg. A pursuit more radical and necessary than remaking the c-suites of technological giants is to consider whether they should exist at all. Everyone, from liberal senator Elizabeth Warren to libertarian law professor Glenn Reynolds, makes cogent arguments in favor of breaking up Amazon, Google, Facebook and other high-tech behemoths through application of anti-trust laws. Some institutions require renovation, while others are fit for demolition.[30]

When I pressed Jackson on the matter of monopoly, he did not hesitate to concede the point. "Many of these companies and banks do need breaking up—'too big to fail' is destined to fail." He then added the caveat, "With others, though, the problem is racial and gender exclusion, discrimination, and exploitation. We can work on those problems even before and during the move toward breaking up is underway."

The masses of voters, consumers, and workers who often feel subject to the avaricious rule of those institutions will, regardless of whether or not he was adequately aggressive, profoundly miss Jesse Jackson when he can no longer serve as the equivalent of their roving bodyguard. In his role, he demonstrates willingness to walk into the rooms of the powerful, stare down their shifty eyes, and make demands. One of the great lies of modern politics, emanating out of a misunderstanding of Adam Smith's "invisible hand" theory, is that the free market will always acquire nobility through its sophisticated self-correcting mechanisms of rational self-interest and adherence to consumer demand.[31] Through his politics of moral confrontation and methodical combat, Jackson not only has challenged the racism in the corporate economy but has also often won. The full sweep of his victories are measurable in thousands of jobs for workers, the salaries and benefits for those within labor unions, millions of dollars for black entrepreneurs, and also in the less tangible, but equally important, clarity that is accessible from the Jackson vantage point: The omniscient and omnipotent free market, left to its own devices, was helpless against the bigotry of its high priests.

Jackson's ascension of interest and agenda would take him from grocery stores on the South Side of Chicago to the boardrooms of the nation's wealthiest companies. After intimately and ideologically learning of the possibilities and limits on direct engagement with business, he would reach even higher, hoping to pull on a rock edge and lift himself atop the apex of American power.

Chapter 3

DAVID AND GOLIATH

"We came down to Columbia, Missouri, and all of these white farmers had sacks on their heads. That was a frightening scene," Jesse Jackson remembered when speaking to me about his first run for president of the United States in 1984. "We thought we had been pulled into something." The Jackson campaign was already on the receiving end of more death and bomb threats than any primary run in modern American history. A crowd of white men wearing ghoulish masks, waiting for a civil rights leader in a field, could only evoke ghastly images from the racial enmity of American history: crosses illuminating the night with the flicker and heat of hellfire, the "strange fruit" of bodies swinging from trees, and the hunting rifle–equipped executioner of a mob in a Jim Crow town where the police function as an unofficial arm of the Ku Klux Klan.

"They were afraid to let the Bureau of Farmers see their faces. They were hiding their faces not because they were planning to attack us, but because they were our supporters," Jackson explained. The year 1984 was the height of the family farm crisis in the United States when big agriculture began to dominate the market, often with government help and subsidy, effectively forcing generations of agrarian families into bankruptcy, and with it, demolishing a sustainable, rich way of life for families whose pride, identity, and legacy were as rooted in their land as the soybeans and corn they had trouble selling at a fair rate. Each state has a Farm Bureau that provides insurance and, nominally, representation for struggling farmers. Most independent farm families agree, however, that the Bureau's loyalty rests with its source of revenue. To cite the direct summary of one Missouri hog farmer, "Farm Bureau has always supported big ag., not small farmers."[1] Throughout the 1980s, there were many stories of the Farm Bureau mysteriously jacking up insurance rates for farmers who just so happened to participate in political demonstrations against the escalating power and influence of major agricultural companies.[2]

"It made me think of poor, inner city blacks who didn't register to vote, because they didn't want the government to have their name. Hiding from the oppressor was one of many things they had in common," Jackson continued, "The poor, white, rural farmer facing foreclosure, called himself 'conservative.' The poor, black displaced worker, feeling rejected, called himself 'liberal.' They were in the same situation, but they never met." The transformation of fear into revelation in Columbia, Missouri, for Jesse Jackson, and his campaign staff, animated the creation of a political tactic and its rhetorical expression that captures the essence of the American left's mission for reformation of American society. "We then began to say," Jackson recalled, "If we can leave the racial battleground to find economic common ground, we can begin to reach for moral higher ground."

The memorable moment, and the language that it inspired, poured the mortar of what would become the foundation for one of the most significant, and continually relevant, presidential campaigns in modern American politics. Jackson delineated an entire agenda, one with which some Democrats are finally catching pace, that became crucial to his barnstorming tour of Democratic revitalization under the guise of traditional campaigning: "From racial battleground—fighting each other because there are walls between us—we get the walls down, we move from racial battleground to economic common ground—both of you need a living wage, both of you need a health care plan, both of you need a good place to live, both of you need to educate your children."

"And at the end of that farmer's rally," Frank Watkins, a longtime associate and aid to Jackson told me, "There was a rainbow in the sky." The cooperation of Mother Earth in providing poetic punctuation to an already-epiphanous event only underscored the necessity of the rainbow coalition—a multiracial, multireligious alliance of America's poor and working class that Martin Luther King, just months before his grisly death, would imagine as his ultimate triumph.

"One white guy came up to me in Alabama," Jackson offered as not only memory but also political instruction,

> And said, "Reverend Jackson, I'm supporting you, but I need you to know that I was with you in Selma." I said, "I'm glad." He said, "No, what I mean is that I was with you, but I was on the other side." He was in the white mob trying to attack us, but something had happened in those 19 years. He had seen the light.

Another man who had opened his eyes to the luminosity of racial integration and cooperation informed Jackson that in the 1980s he could not bring himself to vote for a black man, but in 2008 he volunteered for the Obama campaign. The first black president himself remembers watching Jackson debate the white veterans and media darlings of the Democratic Party in 1984, consistently besting them with his policy acuity and oratorical ability. "He told me," Jackson said in reference to a conversation he had with Obama about that moment, "When I saw you on that stage, I thought, 'this thing could happen.'" The "thing" was the election of a black man—someone whose ancestors would not even have been able to vote—to the most powerful position in the US government.

The Jesse Jackson campaigns for president in 1984 and 1988 are the touchstones of how participatory democracy can activate genuine representation in traditional politics. For most of American history, politics has functioned as a contest between dueling elites who have paid a large fee to enter the game. Gore Vidal, one of the great chroniclers of American Empire, often remarked that there is only one party in American politics: "The property party with two wings." More than any other national campaign in the modern era, Jackson's surprisingly successful run for the presidency caught the egalitarian ethos like lightning in a bottle, and stretched the political imagination by showcasing what a charismatic leader from outside the property party can manage to accomplish with little money, no institutional support, and widespread derision from the mainstream media.

"A crusade is more powerful than a campaign," Jackson offers as assessment of his own attempts at gaining office. The means of measurement differ between a crusade and campaign. The only reasonable evaluation of a successful campaign is victory. Politics is a cutthroat competition with no reward for a second-place finish. A crusade reveals its onward advancement with influence, inspiration, and life after immediate political death. "When you're swimming against the current," Jesse Jackson told me, "You aren't trying to win the race. You're trying to change the flow of the river."

The 2016 race for the American presidency will stupefy and horrify American journalists and historians for decades. The two unavoidable ideas to emerge out of that odd year are the resurgence of brazen white supremacy in mainstream political organization, and after decades of austerity resulting in the liquidation of middle-class wealth, and the slow, water drip torture of the poor, pervasive hatred and rebellion against anything associated with "the establishment." The former is undoubtedly a force of evil in international affairs, while the latter is more contradictory, containing good elements, such as the growing rejection of the long-standing consensus of fundamentalist faith in private markets, and more noxious aspects, like detestation of expertise, and the administration of purity tests, rendering any and all officials with governmental experience as suspicious of corruption. Hillary Clinton, due to the complications of anti-elite sentiment in US politics, was subject to both fair and unfair criticism throughout her campaign. The discomfort many Democrats had with their own nominee displayed a schism within the party, one that traces back decades, but like a dormant volcano, did not erupt until many events made it inevitable—the financial collapse of 2008, the housing crisis, the student debt epidemic, and the culmination of a thirty-year stagnation of wages for the majority of American workers. Racist appeals to the majority white electorate typically emanated out of the Republican Party, which has an over 90 percent white membership, but simultaneous with feelings of class revolt, many black Democrats, even after the tenure of Barack Obama, began to feel that the party both took advantage and took for granted their support. A consistently bashful approach to discriminatory biases in criminal justice, and devastating racial gaps in public education and economic outcomes, made powerful Democrats appear insensitive to the struggles and needs of its most loyal constituents. If the 2016 election is allegorical, certainly one of the morals is that a political system cannot consistently favor the rich at the expense of everyone else, while one party continually encourages paranoia and contempt for racial and religious minorities, without the expectation of disaster.

Historian Morris Berman, who has written an extraordinary but sobering trilogy on the decline of American society, often reminds readers that when empires begin to fall, they never listen to the prophets who offer warning, and they rarely consider reform. Instead, they double down on the very behavior that is causing their problems.[3] One of the motivating factors of Trump's success was the widespread, and not incorrect, feeling that the "system" was not working for average Americans. The solution? Elect a billionaire who will give massive tax breaks to the wealthy, reduce social services, and appoint members of his social circle to cabinet positions with the intention of undermining their respective governmental agencies. Teachers look especially prescient and sterling when learning happens at a snail's pace.

Joan Didion, one of America's great essayists, described Jesse Jackson's presidential campaigns as crashing into the "sedative fantasy of a fixable imperial America." In the Reagan-dominated 1980s, and even the 1990s, American politicians of both parties demonstrated a rhetorical obsession with the largely white "middle class," while in policy, they were equally fixated on the rich. Throughout these years, there were few national figures, and only one who sought the highest office of government, who rejected, in his own words, "consensualist centrist politics." That was Jesse Jackson—a candidate whom Didion credited as presenting the only counternarrative to "what had come to be the very premise of the process, the notion that the winning and maintaining of public office warranted the invention of a public narrative based at no point on observable reality."[4]

Spanish mystic St. John of the Cross begins his poem about a spiritual crisis, "Dark Night of the Soul," with the description of his setting as an "obscure night." It was on an obscure night that the struggle for the soul of the Democratic Party began.[5]

Jesse Jackson never had the intention or ambition to run for president. It was only in reaction to a slap in the face, followed by a chant, "Run Jesse Run!," that the civil rights leader with no prior political experience entered the race alongside governors and senators.

"Out of the voting rights victory, we became part of several struggles—Richard Hatcher's election in Gary (the first black mayor of the Indiana industrial city), Carl Stokes in Cleveland (the first black mayor of a major US city)," Jesse Jackson began his answer when I asked why and how he chose to run for president in 1984,

> We kept getting deeper, and we found that the rules played such a big role that we were going to have to sharpen our focus. Meanwhile, we kept working on getting mayors elected, and in the 1983 Democratic primary for mayor of Chicago, we really felt Harold Washington (the first viable black candidate for mayor of Chicago) could win in a tight three person race with Mayor Jane Byrne and Richard Daley (son of former mayor Daley). The city was preparing a big Chicago Festival, and some people had the idea that we should boycott the festival, because it became clear that Byrne was using the fest as a campaign event. I thought it would be too difficult, because the Chicago Festival offered free hot dogs, low priced beer, and performances by great artists like Stevie Wonder. But we eventually determined we should challenge her. So, we got Stevie and others

to boycott the fest, and after that came a huge voter drive registration, and it began to appear that Harold was winning.

Washington, who was an Illinois congressman, was not only the potential first black mayor of Chicago but also the opponent of the municipal and Democratic Party establishment, both of which were evenly divided between the incumbent Byrne, and the heir apparent of the Daley dynasty. "Then we heard a rumor," Jackson continued, "that Senator Ted Kennedy and Senator Mondale, the two heavyweights of the party, were coming to Chicago to respectively endorse Byrne and Daley. We thought, there's no way that is true. Why would they come here in a city primary, outside their own states? Black voters had been very much invested in Kennedy and Mondale. So, what we did was put together a telegram—telegram back in the day," Jackson stopped and laughed at the consideration of the now-obsolete technology, "With 100 names, everyone from Willie Brown, the first black speaker of the California legislature, and Coretta Scott King, saying, 'Please don't interfere. Let us have the primary.' They came anyhow. So, our response was, 'Someone has to run nationally to challenge the liberal wing, because it has become morally bankrupt. If this is what liberal number one and liberal number two will do to black voters, we need to move in a different direction.'"

Black Americans often occupy a political no man's zone, caught in the crossfire of the abuse of the Republican Party, and the benign neglect of the Democratic Party. A typical tactic of outreach to the same white, middle class that so rightly aggravated Joan Didion is the establishment of distance from black voters, interests, and "causes." Because of the latent racism of a large percentage of the white electorate, candidates for national office believe that if they identify too closely with the black constituency, whites will reject them as traitors to the race. Even Barack Obama, when lambasting black families in a black church, much to Jackson's infamous chagrin, adopted this morally dubious political strategy. In the case of Harold Washington's campaign for the mayoral office of Chicago, Jackson's outrage was more than understandable. Due to personal connections, party favors, and a narrow national agenda, "liberal number one and liberal number two" mutated their benign neglect into malignant interference. Jackson's inspired idea to run a black candidate in the national primary attracted the support of black politicians and intellectuals in the abstract, but no one, especially not an elected official, wanted to risk alienating the donors and leaders of the party. "I first took the idea to Maynard Jackson (no relation), who had been a great mayor of Atlanta, and he insisted that he could not run," Jesse Jackson remembered. "So, I thought that Andrew Young"—the former aide to Martin Luther King and ambassador to the United Nations in the Carter administration—"would be the most logical choice. He refused."

Jackson explains that he had little interest in running for elected office, because he always believed that he could best activate and exercise his considerable gifts as an organizer and orator in a role of external agitation. The encouragement of the same people he hoped to inspire and introduce to politics enabled him to develop an effective method for transfusing his outsider tactics within an increasingly anemic system of party politics. He launched a "Southern Crusade" to register black voters across the former states of the Confederacy, aiming to prevent Dixieland from becoming uncompetitive right-wing territory. The crusade was not only the most successful voter registration drive of the decade, with Jackson overseeing the addition of millions of voters to the rolls, but also the womb out of which an unconventional and historical presidential campaign was born. "The dialogue had leaked to the public that we were considering running a black candidate," Jackson told me, "And to my genuine surprise, at all of these voter registration stops, the crowds were chanting, 'Run Jesse Run!'"

Jackson emphasized with a finger in the air while speaking to me that he was not only attempting to prevent the party from taking black voters and candidates for granted but also "the issues": "The issues!" he repeated in a half shout, still demonstrating anger over the necessity of such a campaign even thirty years subsequent to its launch. "We were contemptuous that supporting Nelson Mandela was not on the agenda nor was the issue of a single payer health care program, the issue of a sensible urban policy, the issue of a new approach to the so called, 'drug war.' The party did not really have a social justice platform. So, we carved it out for them."

Jackson was able to make indentations on the surface of American politics, because he knew how to sharpen a knife. Delineating a connection between Breadbasket and his presidential campaigns, Jackson asserts that the success of any movement against adversarial odds and decision-makers is dependent on the accurate identification of a power source, and the advantageous manipulation of that source. "In the private sector, I never felt powerless," Jackson said, "Because the incentive of the system is toward profit so if you can leverage consumer power, you can succeed. In the public sector, it comes down to the leveraging of voter power."

Throughout Jackson's career, there is an observable synthesis between grand ambition and grounded execution. The right wing in America is particularly skillful at maintaining and manipulating power, because they have spent more time within the system and, as a result, have a greater understanding of how it works. The left, typically moving outside the system, is often disorganized and impractical, and because of its cultural orientation, as evident in its presence in the arts and academia, acts as if it can gain political dominance through mere "messaging." Jackson once reminded me that theology, his field of graduate study, is analysis of "religious systems," the study of which prepared him to understand the systemic workings of society—rules, policies, incentives, and power. "I was a member of an oppressed class," he said, "So, I had to think to survive." "Those who think the most deeply about power," he then speculated, "are often those who lived under the threat of power. Many younger activists don't think as deeply about structure, because they never had to."

"Eight Democrats running for the nomination," Jackson told a hot, sweaty, and crowded church in Philadelphia not long after his presidential campaign announcement in 1984, "This time around, you got a chance and you got a choice. Do you want somebody who marched for you to get the right to vote? You got a choice. You want somebody who challenged corporate America to hire you and give you contracts? You got a choice. It's choice time."

Jackson was at his most dramatic and charismatic in his oratory, speaking with political sophistication in a Pentecostal refrain, offering passionate fire as stark contrast to the antiseptic mediocrity of most American political discourse. Perhaps even more interesting than the man at the podium was the men and women in the pews: black, and having long collided with closed doors at the cloth napkin banquet halls so often serving as the setting for presidential campaign events. The city where the liberty bell is on display, an emblematic crack running up the middle, distorting its high note into a low taunt, was one of many campaign stops for Jackson. With the climactic symbiosis of Jackson's two passions, evangelism and activism, he created a dynamic hybrid of theological inspiration and political ideology—simultaneously diagnosing and disrupting America's diseases of avarice, injustice, and anti-intellectual sloth. To borrow Bruce Springsteen's description of his best songs, Jackson was singing "blues verses and gospel choruses."

The cracked floors, creaky walls, leaky roofs, and off-the-map addresses of many of the churches, community centers, and labor halls gave colorful illustration of Jackson's message. He was preaching to the lost sheep—the citizens who the shepherds forgot to count. The effectiveness of his tactic, however, lay not in its possession of the poetic grandeur of democracy, but in its simple exercise of arithmetic.

"Don't cry about what you don't have, use what you got," Jackson shouted with a smile, "Reagan won last time, not by genius. He won by the margin of despair. He won by the margin of the fracture of our coalition." Jackson shifted his intense gaze from the first few rows in front of him up toward the heavens, as if he was searching for his climactic insight:

> I close with a story. There was a little shepherd boy named David. Everybody in town was scared of Goliath. Little David! Little David! Took off his unnecessary garments, little David. He took what God gave him—a slingshot and a garden biscuit, a rock! In 1980, Reagan won Massachusetts by 25,000 votes. There were over 100,000 students unregistered, over 50,000 blacks, over 50,000 Hispanics: Rocks just laying around. He won in 1980, three million high school seniors unregistered. Now they are registered for the draft. Rocks just laying around. Millions of college students unregistered who could have chosen jobs over jails, peace over war. Now they are crying! Rocks laying around. In 1980, Reagan won eight Southern states by 180,000 votes, while there were three million unregistered blacks in those same states. Rocks just laying around! 1980, Reagan won Pennsylvania by 300,000 votes. 400,000 students unregistered. More than 600,000 black unregistered. Your time has come! Pick up your slingshot! Pick up your rock! Declare! Our time has come![6]

Having become acclimated to their own democratic utility, the crowd rose to their feet in a frenzy, giving an ecstatic ovation to a candidate preaching the essence of democracy.

The rearview mirror is unflattering to the Democratic Party and to many liberal commentators. As the distance between Jackson's campaign and the present grows greater, those who dismissed his political strategy look even more obtuse for their absence of imagination. In the aftermath of Donald Trump's flatulent ascendency to the White House, countless pundits and prognosticators demonstrated a foolish earnestness in their emphasis on Democrats' need to "win back the white working class." How Democratic organizers and candidates are to appeal to a bloc of voters all data indicates are primarily motivated by hostility toward immigrants, and resistance to the inevitable depreciation of the "white majority" in many cities and states, without making debilitating compromises, remains mysterious. There is a consistent advocacy that for liberals to succeed in America they must offer voters a decaffeinated version of the Republican brew. Jesse Jackson's clever application of the biblical David story to modern politics, with the advantage of supportive evidence, displays sounder and wiser political thinking. Rather than getting down on all fours to crawl around the mud alongside right-wing politicos in search of a few scattered seeds, why not stiffen your back, and collect the rocks accessible at the moral higher ground?

There were plenty of rocks laying around in 2016. The gardens of Milwaukee, Detroit, and Philadelphia were full of biscuits—black turnout had fallen significantly, allowing Trump to claim three states that typically elude Republican candidates for president. Every college town across America, including Madison, Tallahassee, and Chapel Hill, had countless rocks fit for the slingshot—students who might have reacted with excitement to a debt forgiveness proposal. In the full exposure of the simplicity of American political thought, there were even rocks ready to launch in those rural outposts often excluded from the progressive cartography. "When I visited the coal mine towns of Kentucky with Bill Clinton," Jackson once told me, "He was upset that they were all shaking my hand, hollering 'Good to see you, Jesse,' and he wasn't getting much attention. Clinton asked me, 'Why are they happier to see you than me?' I told him because they know me. I was there in '84 and again in '88."

There is a significant percentage of the far right electorate that, having spun themselves into a cocoon of ignorance and delusion, will forever remain untouchable to any candidate projecting a platform that does not include racial resentment. There is also the potential for conversion among those whose intellectual barricades might have begun to crack. A candidate with the correct combination of competence, charisma, and compassion can aim a light through the sliver of space and begin to illuminate that which was once dark. In 1984, Jesse Jackson was the first black candidate for the presidency to give political pundits a healthy jolt of reality, when he won a third-place primary finish. While most journalists and Democratic Party managers expected his candidacy to end with an embarrassing asterisk, Jackson won 18.1 percent of the popular vote in an eight-man race. Nearly one in five Democrats selected the civil rights leader as their nominee for the chief executive of the federal government. Those voters, even if they represented a rainbow coalition and offered a highly functional compass for the future direction of the oppositional party, found themselves wandering a wilderness of political dislocation. They found their political will denied by an anti-democratic rulebook. The Democratic primary contradicted its name by awarding delegates, who rather than actual voters make the nomination selection, according to a winner-take-all system of allocation, meaning if candidate A wins 49.9 percent of the votes in Texas, and candidate B wins 50.1, candidate B will receive every delegate from the state, effectively muting the voices of half the electorate. As a result of the suppressive system, Jackson received only 8 percent of delegates in the 1984 contest. He won the states of Louisiana and Mississippi, but his close finishes in several other states underwent the nullification of disproportionate delegation. The mathematics and mechanics of primary regulation might have allowed the first- and second-place candidates to pass Jackson with political ease, but the thunderous call for justice, diverse representation, and progressive economics that Jackson had amplified and awakened was not something party leaders could easily ignore, especially considering that it was rumbling right over their rooftops.

The Reagan years, not unlike the subsequent presidential tenures of George W. Bush and Donald Trump, constituted a historical moment under siege of right-wing reduction of social services, criminal accusation against the poor, and subtle encouragement of white anxiety concerning blacks, immigrants, and ethnic minorities. Trump might have magnified and mastered the latter tactic of sowing social discord, but Reagan, a Hollywood actor who, with his campfire charm and flashbulb smile, earned the nickname "The Great Communicator," made the most effective spokesman of the far right agenda. In 1984, he ran for reelection with the slogan, "Morning in America." After the dreadful and dangerous night of the Vietnam War, Watergate, and economic recession, Reagan and his supporters claimed that they ushered America into a sunlit, crisp, and clean-aired morning. Anyone unable to take advantage of the bright new day was the victim of their self-imposed exile—"welfare queens" swindling the system because they were too lazy to work, nihilistic blacks who bitterly refused to step out of the shadows of past grievances, and slothful youth who never learned the necessities and virtues of "personal responsibility." The systematic reduction of social services, including the widespread closure of mental health facilities, and Reagan's uniquely aggressive posture toward labor unions, culminating in the termination of every federally employed air traffic controller, left many people in the shadows. Reagan's American triumphalism, despite the effects of his policies, appealed to a large swath of the electorate, and his capitalistic rhetoric aligned with America's exploding consumer culture.[7] The Democratic Party's rebuttal to Reagan's self-glorification and slander of their voters was, characteristically, pathetic in its meekness. Walter Mondale, the 1984 nominee, and other party leaders, with the exception of Ted Kennedy, spoke in soft tones, mainly about the "middle class," and when they did criticize Reagan's reduction of public services, they did so in a style that evinced embarrassment, almost as if they were speaking under duress. Most infamously and inanely, Mondale boasted in 1984 that he would raise America's taxes, but did so without presenting a vociferous case for progressive economics. Instead, he sabotaged his own case by making it turn on a Republican issue—the deficit. It is little wonder that Mondale lost in one of the worst landslides in American history. The morning after the election, if a surveyor devoted himself to the task, he would have found countless rocks just laying around.

Jesse Jackson's 18 percent in 1984 animated an alternative vision of America—one where the sunrise could not stretch into the exploited precincts of poverty, the scenes of racist assault on black and brown opportunity, and the stressful conversations taking place at countless kitchen tables of working families who find that the bills are getting bigger while their paychecks stay the same. Winning nearly one out of every five votes also allowed Jackson, who was largely learning on the go, to pour the first gallons of mortar and lay down the first few bricks in what would become the infrastructure of a new Democratic Party. He did so not only because he was the first viable black candidate for the nomination but also because he articulated unforgiving truths about the American experience that his competitors refused to acknowledge. When Jackson was preparing for his first televised debate in 1984, he was aware of his shortcomings. Sharing the stage were senators and governors who had years of governmental experience and had already won several campaigns. "I called my old mentor, Dr. Sam Proctor," Jackson told me in reference to then university president of Jackson's undergraduate alma mater, North Carolina A&T State University, "and I asked for advice. He said, 'Always take the moral high ground, because they can't touch you there. They are all compromised. You are not.'"

Jackson's rhetorical reach for higher ground exposed a dramatic conflict between political expediency and moral efficacy. The former had long held fast to dominion in political campaigns, and with his presence, Jackson was, in ways figurative and literal, crashing the party. The policies that Jackson aggressively advocated in 1984—thirty-six years before the election of Alexandria Ocasio-Cortez and other democratic socialists to Congress, thirty-two years before Bernie Sanders ran for president, and twenty-six years before Occupy Wall Street opened a channel for class analysis of public policy to flow into the mainstream—provide political affirmation of the biblical scripture teaching that a prophet is without honor in his own time and country. The Jackson agenda of 1984 included many positions that, at the time, were "extreme" or "radical," but have since become mainstream: universal health care and childcare, acceptance of gays and lesbians with equal rights as heterosexual citizens, an urban Marshal Plan to combat "drugs in, guns in, jobs out," an end to a "no talk policy" in the Middle East and working toward a two-state solution to the Palestine-Israel conflict, taking Nelson Mandela off the CIA terrorist list, raising the minimum wage to a living wage, lowering the Pentagon budget by 25 percent, appointing women to more positions in the federal government, and addressing the crisis of dysfunction in poor, public schools. On the issue of education, Jackson also proposed tuition-free community college, and presciently warned against the reduction of state subsidies for public universities, a destructive policy just beginning in the 1980s that has culminated in a student debt crisis in which the average college graduate leaves commencement with a bachelor's degree and nearly $40,000 in unpaid loans.[8] On the general issue of lending, Jackson demonstrated public policy creativity that eluded his peers, and could have rescued America from the subprime mortgage crisis, its attendant recession, and the resulting miasma of shame that still hovers above American politics after voters received painful instruction in how its governing institutions favor the fortunate, and exploit the ordinary.

Speaking to the National Conference of US Mayors, Jackson described a partnership he would enter with municipal governments if he were to become the executive of the federal government. "Try to think of yourselves and, say, the country's top ten union leaders," Jackson said,

> as an urban cartel—the OPEC of investment capital. That's what you are. The 25 largest pension funds in America have $500 billion in assets. Together, public officials and public employees, taking just 10 percent of these assets, we can act to rebuild America. I am not calling for pouring the hard earned savings of America's public workers down the drain or into fly by night projects. Instead, I am calling for providing the trustees and investment managers of these pension funds with a wider range of opportunities to use the assets productively.

Not content to castigate parents for pathologies of poverty, Jackson connected the self-destructive behavior of many impoverished youth with the social destruction of a morally bankrupt system of governance:

> Too many of our young people are losing hope. They do not see a future for themselves—no chance of getting a decent education or a good job. If we do not, as a people, take the lives of our children seriously, how can they? If we do not, as a nation, invest our resources in our children's future, what can they look forward to?

Jackson's sweeping and radical program to focus on the "five R's"—reinvestment in infrastructure, retraining of workers, reindustrialization of cities, research for commercial development, and recovery from a military to peace economy—could have transformed the entire country. Americans often brag of living in the "richest country in the world." Jackson's policy positions, and their lack of application at the legislative level, provoke the question: What good is wealth if it is not spent wisely, and instead wasted on war?[9] Such an inquiry has the capacity to unite seemingly disparate constituencies; a project of particular relevance in a country suffering from cultural and sociopolitical divides between its metro areas and pastoral villages. "The best urban policy," Jackson told Iowa voters in 1988, "is the best rural policy," before delineating a kinship between family farmers facing foreclosure, and homeowners facing foreclosure in the working-class neighborhoods of cities like Chicago, Milwaukee, and Detroit.

The Jesse Jackson campaign provided an exhibition in authentic, left populism. The latter term was the subject of linguistic abuse in 2016 when a billionaire pledging to provide no services for the general public managed to co-opt the "populist" agenda by playing in the off-key notes of his base's base instincts. Donald Trump's predecessor would often claim, to awestruck applause, that "only in America" could he win the presidency. The inspiration and racial breakthrough of Obama's triumph aside, the claim of uniquely democratic victory is not true. Obama's beginnings were humble, but by the time he ran for president, he was an Ivy League–educated US senator—not exactly a member of the Joad family. Noam Chomsky, shortly after the election of Obama, conceded the historic nature of a black man in the White House, but described the genuine exercise of populist, participatory democracy taking place in Latin America, identifying Lula da Silva, former president of Brazil, as the genuine article. Lula did not learn to read until he was ten years old, acquired his first job in a warehouse, and gathered public affection throughout many years as an effective labor organizer, leading important movements for worker's rights and environmental security.[10] Evo Morales, the former president of Bolivia, can also boast of a political trajectory that dramatizes democracy. The first indigenous president of his country, he spent his formative years as a peasant farmer and, like Lula, elevated his political profile through activism and local leadership, particularly on issues of agriculture.[11] For the term "populism" to maintain any meaning, it must apply not to politicians who pander to popular impulse, no matter how divisive and destructive, such as Trump, but to leaders who share an essential experience with their constituents, and have earned the credibility of direct service and organization. Under that definitional criterion, Jesse Jackson's candidacy for the president is the only legitimately populist campaign for that particular office in modern American history.

As a tribune of the underclass, Jackson succeeded in winning the support of poor blacks in the inner cities, white family farmers facing foreclosure, recently arrived immigrants from Mexico and Latin America, and Native Americans struggling for sustenance on reservations. He was also able to provide a forecast of America's impending dysfunction and decay should it continue to refuse to adequately address the undercover catastrophes troubling millions of homes in major cities and provincial villages alike. "We globalized capital," Jackson told me referring to the process of international trade and financialization of markets that began in the 1980s, "But we did not globalize workers' rights, women's rights, trade unions, and environmental protection." The malignant inequality around America and abroad is the fatal consequence of the political failure that Jackson describes.

At the same time, by entering the race, and doing so with managerial competence and oratorical charisma, Jackson sent a shockwave across the Democratic Party— one that would jolt many underserved constituencies out of complacency, and into committed revolt.

"In 1984, we consistently made the argument that if Indira Gandhi could be prime minister of India, if Margaret Thatcher could lead Great Britain, and if Golda Meir could lead Israel, America should elect a woman president, and have more women in high ranking positions of local, state, and federal government," Jackson remembered in one of our conversations about his first run for the presidency. "Many white women who were reticent to support our campaign, even if they never voted for me, liked that part," Jackson continued, "It is fair to say that Geraldine Ferraro (the first female nominee for vice president, and Walter Mondale's running mate), was a result of our campaign introducing the idea." Many historians share Jackson's contention, and they also credit his 1984 campaign with activating the Democratic base—blacks, Hispanics, and progressive whites—with sufficient power and energy to gain seats in the House of Representatives in 1986, and regain control of the US Senate. Pollsters and prognosticators observed, following Jackson's campaign in 1984, a steady increase in voter registration among African Americans, and Democrats in Republican districts. In New Jersey, as an example, black registration increased so dramatically that their share of the statewide electorate jumped nearly 10 percent.[12] "What is objectively clear," Jackson asserted,

> in '84 we brought out the new black vote in South, and energized white labor and liberal voters. Two years later, Wynce Fowler won a Senate seat in Georgia with less than 40 percent of the white vote, Bob Graham won a Senate seat in Florida with less than 40 percent of the white vote, Alan Cranston did the same in California, Richard Shelby won a tight Senate race in Alabama due to a surge of black voters. These are just a few examples. The '86 victories came directly out of the increase in voter registration of '84.

Paul Wellstone, who had the most progressive voting record in the US Senate throughout the 1990s before dying in a plane crash in 2002, first entered party politics as the Minnesota chairman of the Jackson campaign in 1988.

"Jackson opened the door for so many of us," Donna Brazille, the first black campaign director on the national level for the Democratic Party who had her first political position with Jackson's campaign, said of her former boss.[13] The Rainbow Coalition colored the political skyline not only in national races but also on the state level where a new class of black leadership began to remake American politics, all operating under the influence of Jesse Jackson's exploration of common ground and cartography of moral higher ground. Douglas Wilder became the first African American governor of any state since Reconstruction in Virginia in 1990. David Dinkins, in 1989, became the first black mayor of New York City. Norm Rice became the first black mayor of Seattle, Willie Herenton became the first black mayor of Memphis, and Wellington Webb became the first black mayor of Denver. Speaking at a seminar on Jackson's campaigns, Dinkins explained that he would have never won mayoral office if not for the 1984 response to "Run Jesse Run!"—"I know what Jesse did for me," the former mayor said with absolute certainty. Former Louisiana Congress Cleo Fields, whose first political position was a student field organizer for the Jackson campaign, said that his political career would have "never happened" if Jackson hadn't inspired and hired him but also taken a crowbar to the barricades of the Democratic Party, and created an entryway for minority candidates without patrician backgrounds.[14] Even Lee Atwater, the villainous right-wing operator, most famous for race baiting on behalf of the Bush administration with the Willie Horton ad, conceded the power and influence of Jackson's 1984 campaign—"Jackson and his coalition gave the Senate back to the Democrats in 1986 and made possible a new liberal politics in the dying years of the Reagan administration."[15]

It was more than the elected apparatus of the party that broadened due to Jackson's work, as James Zogby, the founder of the Arab American Institute, a think tank devoted to producing and promoting policies protective of Arab American liberties and opportunities, exemplifies. Zogby explains that anti-Arab animus was so severe in the 1980s that many politicians would return donations from Arab organizations, and display obstinance at the mere request for a meeting. "With Jesse Jackson," Zogby said, "We felt welcome and included for the first time in a political campaign."[16] There is similar praise offered to Jackson's campaign on the integration of Asian-American issues in Democratic Party politics. Butch Wing, who was an organizer of Chinese immigrants in San Francisco, and would later become a PUSH staff member, recalls how Jackson was the first candidate for president to take a meeting with a network of Asian activists, and the first to take seriously the concerns of Chinese immigrants in a presidential campaign.[17] In 2019, Democrats running for president held their first "Native American Forum" to directly address the concerns of America's indigenous people. Thirty-five years earlier, Jackson regularly spoke on Indian Reservations and to tribal councils—a first for a presidential candidate. One of the most memorable images of Jackson's activism would form many years later at the 2016 Standing Rock protests against the construction of an oil pipeline on Native land in the Dakotas. Jackson, then seventy-five, led a march on horseback while wearing a cowboy hat that a young Native American gave to him.

Delmarie Cobb, who was Jackson's national press secretary in 1988, told me that Jackson was also the first prominent player to employ blacks, minorities, and unapologetic political progressives, in high-ranking staff positions on a presidential campaign. Many of Jackson's campaign staff proceeded to work on the national campaigns for Bill Clinton, Al Gore, John Kerry, and Barack Obama. Cobb would later work with Hillary Clinton. "Without Jackson," she said, "We would have never had the means to work in national politics." The presence of minority staff members is not merely a cosmetic issue, but one of representation and advocacy. Those with the candidate's ear, especially in private, off-camera moments, are in the best position to influence that candidate's political priorities.[18]

There were also voters who, for the first time, felt that a candidate in mainstream party politics spoke their language. Judy Tanzer, a Jewish woman who was an activist on issues of civil rights and economic justice, recalls taking her young family to see Jackson speak in Washington DC during the 1980s—"He had the ability to make you feel like he was speaking directly to you, and no one else," she said in an assessment of Jackson's charisma, but added the more politically substantive analysis that he was also the "only candidate making a real attempt to carry forward Dr. King's vision."

Due to Jackson's combative challenge to an insular political party, Democrats finally began to follow through on their pledge to represent the interests of an increasingly multicultural America. "The Republicans are the party of 'no,'" Jackson once said, "And the Democrats are the party of 'I don't know.'" Conviction and passion, Jackson's candidacy demonstrated, are not only ethically superior to equivocation and strategic moderation but also politically expedient.

The "crusade" continued in 1988 with a more seasoned campaign infrastructure, and savvier candidate, enhancing the alterations to the architecture of the Democratic Party, but also presenting a formidable challenge for ownership of the structure. Jesse Jackson explained, "In 1984, I had more supporters outside the convention than inside. There were black organizations protesting about civil rights, Latinos talking about immigration and language, the youth outside talking about education, Native Americans protesting for sovereignty. The rainbow was locked out of the convention." Jackson adopted the role as a Democratic docent. By 1988, he had brought the edges to the center. He had gathered an institutional apparatus he lacked in 1984 by gaining the support and endorsements of local officials in nearly every state, including the young, radical mayor of Burlington, Vermont—Bernie Sanders. One of the few white officials to endorse Jackson's first campaign, Sanders has often credited Jackson with providing him the inspiration, and the infrastructure to run for Congress. Nina Turner, the cochair of the Sanders presidential campaign, did not hesitate to compare her candidate with Jackson's earlier effort. "It really is the same template," she said when delineating how an outsider with passionate, progressive politics lacking major endorsements or donors can compete on the national level.[19]

Even in 1988, Jackson had little financial support for his candidacy, causing him to regularly repeat the phrase, "Poor campaign, rich message." "We slept in people's homes. We held fundraisers in church basements, community centers, and high school cafeterias," Jackson recalled in our discussion. In his effort to enlarge the political imagination, and expand the capacity for empathy within American democracy, Jackson transformed an albatross into an asset—using his unconventional campaign stops to draw attention to issues of severe social consequence, not unlike when Martin Luther King slept in the Chicago slums to spotlight the urban housing crisis. And he made many stops. Delmarie Cobb explains that, in 1988, when Dukakis was hosting two campaign events a day, Jackson would hold a minimum of five, sometimes up to twelve. When Jackson appeared in school cafeterias, he spoke about the disastrous dislocation of public education funding, resulting in wealthy parents sending their children to elite epicenters of high-tech excellence, and poor parents walking their children to dilapidated buildings without enough textbooks to provide for every student. Ronald Reagan, as president and communicator-in-chief, stood idle and mute as tens of thousands of gay Americans died from AIDS. Jesse Jackson and his staff slept in AIDS hospices in Illinois, California, and Texas. In his second campaign, Jackson also provided poetic and political continuation of his mission to connect seemingly disparate members of the underclass. His candidacy generated excitement in the inner cities, but he also accomplished what few Democrats managed—laying down the foundation for a working-class urban-rural alliance. A family farmer activist, George Naylor, explains that the massive crowds of white agricultural workers applauding Jackson in the small towns of Iowa "surprised all of the pundits." Similarly, Delmarie Cobb recalls Jackson speaking to a gathering of family farmers in Kentucky, telling the unlikely assembly of Jackson supporters, "You grow the corn. A black teenager in Chicago eats Cornflakes. You don't think that you need each other, but without your labor, he can't eat, and without his consumption, you can't make a living."

It is difficult to ascertain the complexities of the feeling that Jesse Jackson provoked in white, provincial America during his electoral efforts, but Jackson's alliance with Jim Hightower—a progressive activist and former commissioner of the Texas Department of Agriculture—and his consistent appearances at Farm Aid, with Willie Nelson once introducing him as "a dynamic American who has raised funds, raised consciousness, and raised hell for the family farmer," signal the potential for political imagination and compassion to achieve the coalescence of constituencies that conventional commentary too often insists are inalterably hostile. One farmer pitching for Jackson to his skeptical neighbors might have phrased it best when he asked, "Who would you rather have in power—a white enemy or black friend?"

Decades after his campaigns for the presidency, the *Huffington Post* asserts that Jesse Jackson is the most "important figure" in the modern history of Democratic politics,[20] the *Nation* praises Jackson with constructing the modern Democratic Party,[21] and Jamelle Bouie, columnist with the *New York Times*, argues that the Jackson campaigns offer a "roadmap" for the future success of progressive Democrats running in national elections.[22] Looking back on Jackson's campaigns in his seminal, *A People's History of the United States,* historian and activist Howard Zinn wrote that they represented a "rare moment of excitement" in mainstream politics. Former president Bill Clinton, whose relationship with Jackson, to put it mildly, oscillates between affection and assault, assessed Jackson's presidential crusades as "seminal in American history." "It was the first campaign to openly involve gays," Clinton said, "and it was the first campaign to introduce many of the issues we're still debating."[23] Confirming Clinton's memory, David Taylor, president of Manhattan's Gay and Lesbian Democrats, remarked that gay Americans "never forgot" how Jackson would explicitly refer to rights and protections for gays in 1984 speeches, including his nationally televised address on the floor of that year's Democratic Convention. Before Jackson's campaign, Taylor recalls, "we were unmentionable."[24] Butch Wing recalls one of Jackson's last rallies of the 1988 campaign taking place in the Castro district of San Francisco to a large crowd of gay activists and residents in which he declared, as a minister in 1988 when most of the country was homophobic—"Civil rights for everybody! Social justice for everybody!" Despite all of the accolades Jackson has earned, few Americans realize how close he came to winning the Democratic nomination in 1988. He won thirteen states, amassing 1,023 delegates, and took on the role of frontrunner after his win in Michigan. Overall, he won 29.4 percent of the total votes in a five-person race. Finishing a close second to Massachusetts governor, Michael Dukakis, Jackson demolished the other Democratic darlings in the race, including future vice president, Al Gore.

"If you put a size nine foot in a size six shoe," Jackson once told me when describing the importance of rules and regulations, "you're going to have some broken toes. There's nothing wrong with your foot. You just need a new structure."

Unlike in 1984, Jackson managed to secure a delegate count commensurate with his popular vote tally. In the interim period between the two campaigns, Jackson and his diverse range of supporters "fought like hell," to use one former staffer's phrase, to convince the Democratic Party to rewrite their policy on delegation. "They were naïve—didn't think they were giving up much," Jackson said of Democratic Party leadership. Because of the work of Jackson and his staff, the Democratic primary nomination process reformed its rules so that delegates were awarded in proportion to popular vote numbers. A candidate who loses a state, for example, but wins 25 percent of the votes in the state will receive approximately 25 percent of its delegates. "We democratized the Democratic Party," Jackson boasted of the triumph. The fire that Jackson set to an unfair system would eventually light the way for Barack Obama to walk into the White House.

In the most closely contested primary in Democratic Party history, Hillary Clinton won the 2008 elections in most of the large and densely populated states, including California, New York, Florida, and Pennsylvania. Had she collected all of the delegates in those respective states, Barack Obama, even while winning many smaller states in the national race, would have never won the nomination. The first black president himself made it clear that the inspirational example of excellence of Jackson in the 1980s provided him with belief in an eventual black presidency, but beyond cultural influence there exists the mechanics of political power. Jackson's reprogramming of those mechanics—"democratizing the Democratic Party"—is directly responsible for the ascendency of Barack Obama. "Without proportionality," Jackson said in his office, "Barack would have never won. Some journalists attributed his victory to his campaign's mastery of high tech, social media outreach. Others said it was his charisma. All of that is important, but even with social media and charisma, Barack would have lost if the rules worked against him."

A scavenger hunt through the pages of books on Barack Obama by America's leading historians and journalists exposes a foolish disregard for the term Jackson almost obsessively recites in any political discussion, "structure." Nowhere is there a reference to Jackson's demand for proportional delegate allocation.[25] Following the lucid nightmare of the 2016 election, Jackson is quick to note, both pundits and politicians made the same critical error in their avoidance of the Electoral College as explanatory of Donald Trump's presidency. Scribblers charging by the word wasted countless syllables and endless digital pixels with abstract impressions of Clinton's campaign errors, scrutinizing everything from her rhetoric to debate comportment, but rarely did anyone identify the anti-democratic tragedy of a candidate earning three million more votes than her opponent, and yet still losing the race. The passivity even the candidate herself showed in the aftermath of her defeat is a condition Jackson likened to a "disability." "I'll guarantee you one thing," Jackson announced in our discussion of the issue, "if that happened to me—If I won the presidential election in '88 by three million votes, but did not become president, I would have destroyed the electoral college. We would not have that system today. I would have led a movement, with all of my voters marching in the streets, pressuring their Congressmen and women, their Senators, to end it. That's what Hillary Clinton should have done."

When Hillary Clinton's husband won the presidential race in 1992, becoming the first Democratic president-elect since Jimmy Carter prevailed in the 1976 election, many commentators credited Clinton's win with his ability to "triangulate," to use the late Christopher Hitchens' characteristically brilliant pejorative—that is, the location and adoption of a position safely in between the left and right poles of political debate. Several leading newspapers, reporting in the year of Clinton's campaign, described the essentiality of significant black turnout for the Democrat to win a competitive three-person race.[26] It is hardly a secret that black voters felt personal affection for the charismatic governor of Arkansas, but as Jackson once said, "You cannot separate our bringing out the black vote from Clinton winning in 1992." The numbers show that Clinton barely won many states, such as Georgia, Louisiana, Michigan, and Ohio, and it was precisely the surge of black voters to the polls that put him over the top. While it is difficult to ascertain the personal motives of millions of people, it is equally clear that many of those voters first entered Democratic Party politics in support of Jackson's 1984 and 1988 campaigns.

President Bill Clinton's record as a progressive is, under the most generous interpretation, decidedly mixed. He vacillated between advancing New Deal programs, like increasing college aid subsidies and attempting to pass comprehensive health-care reform, and cribbing the notes of Newt Gingrich in order to undermine Republican momentum, most infamously when he "ended Welfare as we know it," to use his own damning language. Given the damage that Reagan inflicted on the notion of communal solidarity and assistance for the poor throughout the 1980s, one still must shudder upon imagining how a Republican would have governed in the 1990s. It is also important to observe that during Clinton's two terms in the White House, Jesse Jackson acted as one of the most aggressive critics of Clinton when he saw the president betraying the left. Jackson opposed Clinton's restructuring of welfare transfer payments, and vociferously denounced the 1994 crime bill, which many criminologists and historians hold responsible for the dramatic rise of the imprisonment of black men. Many of the liberals in Congress, and state and city governments, who applied pressure on Clinton to maintain some semblance of a progressive political identity, were graduates of the Jackson class of 1984 or 1988. It is not an embellishment to assert that the primary reason the American left was able to survive within the two-party system during the 1980s and 1990s was Jesse Jackson's leadership, organization, and advocacy.

Without Jackson's jeremiad, populist politicking, and revivalist crusade, the Democratic Party would not have seized control of the Senate in 1986, it is unlikely that Bill Clinton would have become president in 1992, Barack Obama would not have become the first black president in 2008, Bernie Sanders would not have entered Congress or run for president in 2016, and dozens of history-making black, Latino, Native American, gay, and liberal white officials would have never held office. The erudite conservative columnist George Will calls 1964 Republican candidate for president Barry Goldwater a "creative loser," because, despite not winning the election, he "changed the political vocabulary." Will also asserts that Goldwater actually won in 1964; it "just took them 16 years to count the votes," assigning credit to the senator from Arizona for Reagan's triumph at the polls in 1980.[27] Jesse Jackson, also a creative loser who invented a vocabulary that remains poetic and persuasive verse for Democrats and leftists, did not win the presidential nomination in 1984 or 1988, but he has prevailed and succeeded for over three decades, giving colorful illustration of his mentor's advice to invade and occupy the moral high ground. The modern Democratic Party is indeed what it was not in the 1980s—a "rainbow coalition" of black voters, Latinos, progressive women of all races, Native Americans, Asian Americans, students, LGBT citizens, and voters of all backgrounds with connections to activist networks on issues ranging from environmentalism to criminal justice. Jesse Jackson is not entirely or exclusively responsible for the transformation of the Democratic Party, but his ushering of all of these once ignored and beleaguered constituents into the mainstream organization of Democrats initiated an internal revolution that is observable in the influence of countless local officials, the steady progress of Bill Clinton to Barack Obama, and the 2018 election of the most diverse and progressive House of Representatives in the history of the country.

"Where there is no vision, the people perish," the Bible warns. It was the vision of Jesse Jackson that resurrected and continues to regenerate the movement for peace and justice in American party politics.

Chapter 4

PROPHECY

Jesse Jackson began his address at the 1988 Democratic Convention by introducing the audience to Rosa Parks. Raising her hand in the air, and smiling wide and bright, he christened her the "mother of the Civil Rights Movement." "Those of us here think we are sitting, but we are standing on the shoulders of giants," Jackson declared before reciting the names of whites, blacks, Christians, Jews, and atheists who died, from bullets flying into their bodies, knife wounds, and brutal beatings to make American democracy credible, and the rainbow coalition possible, with their work in the civil rights movement.[1]

National political conventions were once the settings of political combat and backroom calculation. In an unpredictable, and often unmoored, display of infighting, approximate in sight and sound to the floor of New York Stock Exchange, party delegates would actually select their presidential and vice presidential nominees at the convention. John Kennedy, for example, fought, lobbied, and brokered deals in order to have his name in the VP slot on the Adlai Stevenson ticket of 1956. He fell short, but did not accept his defeat until mere minutes before the delegate count. Gore Vidal depicted the high energy and intrigue of past conventions with his play about the battle for a presidential nomination, *The Best Man*. In the 1970s, due to the healthy shift in emphasis from party elites to primary voters in nomination power, conventions became little more than expensive celebrations of the hosting party. Rather than capturing the intricate machinations of realpolitik, they began to resemble cheerleading exhibitions in which the greatest reward awaited the speaker or presenter who could wave his pom-poms and perform cartwheels with the most enthusiasm. For Jackson to begin his speech, not with a triumphalist tribute to the Democratic Party, but a reminder of the bloodbath and body count that was necessary for America to construct a genuine democracy signaled a different theory and practice of convention oratory. "My audience was not those on the convention floor" Jackson told me, "It was those watching on television who never got involved in party politics before—the outsiders, the marginalized, the first time voters our campaign brought into things." Jackson had an hour on primetime television. He was not about to waste it on the bromides of bumper sticker slogans. The address was an electric and emotional hybrid of populist advocacy for a left turn in American politics, but also a fiery homily on the secular rewards of faith, and the human spirit's capacity to overcome the catastrophes of fate and the cruelties of man. Jackson weaved together political logic and data supportive of his political claims, but when he sang and shouted in sermonic delivery, he relied upon the evidence of his own experience. Transforming the Omni Coliseum of Atlanta, Georgia, into a Pentecostal temple, he gave a testimony.

Democratic nominee Michael Dukakis was reportedly nervous about allowing Jackson to speak at the convention. "When he gets through," the candidate told a journalist in tones of consternation, "none of us will be able to meet that standard." Writing in the *New York Times*, a paper previously unfriendly to Jackson's presidential campaign, veteran columnist E. J. Dionne claimed that Jackson's "rousing" performance "did nothing to dim Dukasis' prediction."[2]

The prophet, according to popular misinterpretation, is a clairvoyant who might accurately identify tomorrow's winning lottery numbers, or prevent a child from running across the street because she can envision an inevitable hit and run. Theology and history offers a much richer understanding of the term "prophecy," and makes clear that it is not synonymous with psychic power. Abraham Joshua Heschel, the rabbi who became a close friend and supporter of Dr. King, explained in his book, *The Prophets*, that the prophet does not speak for God; he reminds his audience of "God's voice for the voiceless." Heschel's theological interpretation submits that "prophecy is the voice that God has lent to the silent agony, a voice to the plundered poor, to the profane riches of the world."[3]

Theologian and religious historian, Richard Lischer, writes in *The Preacher King: Martin Luther King, Jr. and the Word that Moved America* that in ancient Israel there were two forms of prophets—central prophets and peripheral prophets. Those on the periphery moved among the poor, gave unsparing and scathing denunciations of power, and never obtained access to the monarchy. Central prophets advised and consulted with kings, struggling valiantly to persuade them to serve the will of the people and keep their covenant with God. King, according to Lischer's analysis, spent the last years of his life as a peripheral prophet, especially as his message and mission became increasingly radical. When he met with President John Kennedy, and later President Lyndon Johnson, to discuss civil rights legislation, however, he was a central prophet.[4] Jackson never amassed the official influence of King, but with the success of his presidential campaigns, he began to move from the margins to the center.

Heschel writes that he chose to rigorously study the ancient prophets of Judaism when he realized that "the terms, motivations, and concerns that dominate our thinking may prove destructive of the roots of human responsibility and treasonable to the ultimate ground of human solidarity." Prophecy offers a redemptive alternative. It is the "exegesis of existence from a divine perspective."[5]

I look at the world from a secular vantage point. Prophecy and speculation over the supernatural means little to me, and I do not believe that a God moves through any speaker, even the most extraordinary. Heschel and Lischer's theological arguments construct a helpful frame through which to look at certain moments, however, if one can take the questionable liberty of demystifying prophecy. Leaving differing beliefs in the existence of a divinity aside, perhaps one can argue that a prophetic moment is that which enables access to the highest truth of the human condition—the truth of universal human fraternity, the truth of suffering, and the redemptive power of love; the truth that has inspired much of religion, the best of art; the truth to which we aspire in our most magnificent moments. If it is possible to understand prophecy from that perspective, the 1988 Democratic Convention address from Jesse Jackson is the only moment in modern American history when prophecy conquered politics.

Mario Cuomo, the late governor of New York, is famous for his contention that an effective political leader "campaigns in poetry, but governs in prose." Jackson's rhetoric at the 1988 convention aspired to reach the heights of poetic grandeur. Its central ambition was to rescue the values of progressive unification around causes of justice from abstraction through their articulation in concrete terminology. He told a heartwarming story of his grandmother, and her tactics borne of privation and desperation, for keeping warm the children in her home:

> When I was a child growing up in Greenville, South Carolina my grandmama could not afford a blanket. She didn't complain, and we did not freeze. Instead she took pieces of old cloth—patches, wool, silk, gabardine, crockersack—only patches, barely good enough to wipe off your shoes with. But they didn't stay that way very long. With sturdy hands and a strong cord, she sewed them together into a quilt, a thing of beauty and power and culture. Now, Democrats, we must build such a quilt.

Jackson transitioned from his homespun wisdom to the most important political battles of his time, many of them still ongoing, by identifying the isolated issues of social justice as "patches." When workers fight for fair wages, Jackson thundered, they are right, but their patch alone is insufficient. When mothers petition for child care, equal pay, and paid family leave, they are right, but their patch is still too small. When blacks fight for civil rights, when Latino immigrants work toward an opportunity for citizenship, and when gays argue for equality, they are all righteous in their devotion, but their respective patches are not individually big enough.

"Be as wise as my grandmama," Jackson advised, "pull the patches and the pieces together, bound by a common thread. When we form a great quilt of unity and common ground, we'll have the power to bring about health care and housing and jobs and education and hope to our nation."

Like King making compassionate reference to the financial precarity he shared with his prison guard, Jackson identified common ground with class interest. Few within the Democratic Party spoke with adequate aggression against "Reganomics," which Jackson defined as a set of policies based on the idea that "the rich have too little money, and the poor have too much." In his address to the nation, he referred to the extreme income gains of the top 1 percent, along with the data indicating that the wealthiest Americans paid 20 percent less in taxes in the 1980s than they did in the 1970s. The middle class, working class, and poor, meanwhile, were slipping further away from domestic stability on a daily basis. Jackson implored his fellow Democrats that for the party to maintain a laudable and likable identity, it must believe in government as "a tool of democracy" working with the "consent of the governed" to improve living conditions for all Americans, but most especially those who live under the threat of illness, disability, poverty, or bigotry. After most politicians ignored rising inequality for decades, the few voices in the public square who warned of the dangers of austerity, and the destructiveness of policies giving advantage to the rich over everyone else, resound with greater prescience and profundity. The proposals of the Jackson candidacy—radical for their time and place, but pedestrian in Canada and Western Europe—are now those that dominate the platforms of most major Democratic Party leaders.

The speech soared not when Jackson spoke in the prose of politics, but when he offered the poetry of testimony. In his address, he is able to transcend the political and reach toward the prophetic. Not content to merely make a practical case for the poor, he advanced their dignity and asserted their humanity.

> They work hard everyday. I know, I live amongst them. They catch the early bus. They work every day. They raise other people's children. They work everyday. They clean the streets. They work everyday. They drive dangerous cabs. They change the beds you slept in in these hotels last night and can't get a union contract. They work everyday. No, no, they're not lazy. Someone must defend them because it's right and they cannot speak for themselves. They work in hospitals. I know they do. They wipe the bodies of those who are sick with fever and pain. They empty their bedpans. They clean out their commodes. No job is beneath them, and yet when they get sick they cannot lie in the bed they made up every day. America, that is not right.

The United States is the only free and wealthy country that denies its people the most basic of human services. It is alone in the developed world in its cruelty toward the poor, forbidding them access to medicine when they are sick, threatening them with bankruptcy if they desire to take off work to care for a dying parent or spouse, burdening them with decades of debt for pursuing an education, and making their poorest children come of age in conditions of filth and infection.[6]

Abuse, slander, and mistreatment of the poor is not only harmful public policy. It is a violation of the essence of democracy. Walt Whitman, writing in *Leaves of Grass*, identifies the "password primeval" and "ancient sign" of democracy among the "deformed persons . . . the diseased and despairing . . . the rights of those that others are down upon." The great American bard prefaces his identification of the democratic voice with the promise, "I will accept nothing which all cannot have their counterpart of on the same terms."[7] Jackson sings in Whitman verse in his 1988 address; not only advocating for the humanity of the diseased and despairing but also affirming and advancing it in real time. Just as Whitman announced on the opening pages of his epic that every atom belonging to him as good, belongs to you, Jackson articulates something far beyond representation of the dispossessed, but political, social, and spiritual intimacy.

With a simple refrain—"I understand"—Jackson could separate himself from the other mere politicians and establish a familial and experiential kinship with his audience, beginning by broadcasting the criticism of skeptics:

"Jesse Jackson, you don't understand my situation. You be on television. You don't understand. I see you with the big people. You don't understand my situation." I understand. You see me on TV, but you don't know the me that makes me, me. They wonder, "Why does Jesse run?" because they see me running for the White House. They don't see the house I'm running from. I have a story. I wasn't always on television. Writers were not always outside my door. When I was born late one afternoon, October 8th, in Greenville, South Carolina, no writers asked my mother her name. Nobody chose to write down our address. My mama was not supposed to make it, and I was not supposed to make it. You see, I was born of a teenage mother, who was born of a teenage mother. I understand.

I know abandonment, and people being mean to you, and saying you're nothing and nobody and can never be anything. I understand.

Jesse Jackson is my third name. I'm adopted. When I had no name, my grandmother gave me her name. My name was Jesse Burns until I was 12. So I wouldn't have a blank space, she gave me a name to hold me over. I understand when nobody knows your name. I understand when you have no name.

I understand. I wasn't born in the hospital. Mama didn't have insurance. I was born in the bed at the house. I really do understand. Born in a three-room house, bathroom in the backyard, slop jar by the bed, no hot and cold running water. I understand.

Wallpaper used for decoration? No. For a windbreaker. I understand. I'm a working person's person. That's why I understand you whether you're black or white. I understand work. I was not born with a silver spoon in my mouth. I had a shovel programmed for my hand. My mother, a working woman. So many of the days she went to work early, with runs in her stockings. She knew better, but she wore runs in her stockings so that my brother and I could have matching socks and not be laughed at at school. I understand.

At 3 o'clock on Thanksgiving Day, we couldn't eat turkey because momma was preparing somebody else's turkey at 3 o'clock. We had to play football to entertain ourselves. And then around 6 o'clock she would get off the Alta Vista bus and we would bring up the leftovers and eat our turkey—leftovers, the carcass, the cranberries—around 8 o'clock at night. I really do understand.

"I had a life, an experience, that most of the others (politicians) did not, because American politics had become so caught up in the affairs of the wealthy. So, on a spiritual matter, I was simply trying to say, 'I understand your pain, your difficulty, your challenges,'" Jackson told me when I asked about his refrain for the crescendo of his speech. "My grandmother almost did not vote for me," he remembered, "Because she could not read or write. It was hard for her, because she would have to admit her illiteracy. So, I understand. It was simple." Jackson continued with a practical application of his philosophy that still eludes most Democrats, especially those who in the aftermath of Trump immediately began to focus on the white working class—"Democrats were obsessed with regaining some of the votes of the white men who went to Reagan. I thought it more important to get those we never had, because they never registered, but were our natural allies, than scramble and make compromises for those we lost. That's how Barack won in 2008. He brought out the rainbow."

As Jackson reaches his soaring conclusion in the speech, he addresses those whose voices society often places on mute, those who suffer through degradation, and those whose lives, both painful and heroic, are often without advocacy in the nexus of corporate media and major party politics. His voice rising in a full-throated shout, Jackson exercised the politics of friendship, and, in doing so, demands a friendship of politics. In a culture that too often evaluates worth and character according to the narrow and shallow metrics of wealth, glamor, and power, Jackson advanced a deeper alternative of universal beauty and sublimity.

> In your wheelchairs. I see you sitting here tonight in those wheelchairs. I've stayed with you. I've reached out to you across our nation. Don't you give up. I know it's tough sometimes. People look down on you. It took you a little more effort to get here tonight. And no one should look down on you, but sometimes mean people do. The only justification we have for looking down on someone is that we're going to stop and pick them up. But even in your wheelchairs, don't you give up. We cannot forget 50 years ago when our backs were against the wall, Roosevelt was in a wheelchair. I would rather have Roosevelt in a wheelchair than Reagan on a horse.

As Jackson offers his homiletic helping of encouragement, the camera catches a man on the convention floor, sitting in a wheelchair. His face cracks into a half smile, but his eyes betray sadness. It is not presumptuous to imagine that Jackson's words about "mean people" cut his heart like a scalpel. As soon as Jackson uttered the words, "look down on you," the same man raises his thumb in the air. He never allows it to drop. Even as the crowd goes wild with Jackson's comparison of FDR to Ronald Reagan, he keeps his arm extended, his thumb pointing toward the sky. It is in the coupling of Jackson's words and that man's facial expression and approving gesture that a politics of transcendence emerges, and through that emergence one gains an ability to accurately appraise the stakes of an argument. More than taxation, regulation, and even law, political debate can, in its most ambitious moments, raise the most crucial inquiries into what a society values. If we, as a people, would rather affirm the dignity of the man in the wheelchair than tacitly provide aid and encouragement to the mean people who look down on him, we must make a series of decisions, and those decisions must go beyond personal behavior and private charity. They must implicate the very essence of our society—how we organize our institutions, and how we exercise our power.

"Every one of those funny labels they put on you, those of you who are watching this broadcast in the projects, on the corners, I understand," Jackson announced in a softer, more delicate enunciation. He then continued in the final emphasis of exactly what his campaign meant, and who it was meant for: "Call you outcast, low down, you can't make it, you're nothing, you're from nobody, subclass, underclass; when you see Jesse Jackson, when my name goes in nomination, your name goes in nomination."

Chapter 5

HOW YA LIKE ME NOW?

The *New York Times* accused him of egomania, asserting that his addiction to media coverage was running interference with his commitment to civil rights. A prominent black journalist, writing for a major magazine, upped the ante on the paper of record, claiming that his public activity, even his arrests in acts of civil disobedience, were little more than self-serving "publicity stunts." Right-wing reportage cast him as an anti-American traitor, but even the liberal press, as on display in nearly every large circulation newspaper, argued that his refusal to know and keep his role as advocate for black America, rather than issuing denunciation of American foreign policy and corporate capitalism, made him, at best, an unhelpful figure or, possibly, a harmful actor in political culture. According to the common and off-key refrain, he was, through a chameleon trick of transformation, simultaneously an unrealistic radical who did not comprehend the pragmatic mechanisms of political reform and an arrogant camera chaser who lived only for the glory of seeing his own name in headline ink.

The pronouns do not conceal the name of Jesse Jackson, but his friend and mentor, Martin Luther King, Jr.[1] Before the federal government created a national holiday in his honor, with most Republicans voting in opposition, and prior to countless cities naming streets and schools in his dedication, King, who sources ranging from Michael Eric Dyson to the editorial page of the *Jewish Standard* consider the "greatest American of the 20th Century," was hated, reviled, and even called "the most dangerous man in America."[2] It was not merely the FBI, Republican Party, and other institutions of conservatism that denounced him, but also at the hour of his death King had a disapproval rating of 63 percent. Nearly two-thirds of Americans saw King as a reckless agitator, and even a large percentage of blacks turned against him in the belief that his unsparing jeremiad against the Vietnam War would alienate the Johnson administration from the civil rights movement.[3] "In the final year of his life," Jesse Jackson told me, "King could not book a speech in a large black church or college campus. He could not get a book deal. Both parties attacked him. His allies attacked him. He moved into depression. It was the burden of leadership."

King receives the adulation of a saint in contemporary America, but the painful irony is that the reverence for his memory actually undermines his legacy, or as Jackson put it in 2020, "I detest the way King days are commemorated, making him appear superficial. We've neutered him in death." Meanwhile, mendacious politicians manipulate his message into a disguise with which they can smuggle any position—no matter how contrary to King's vision and mission—through customs. Mike Pence even invoked the name of King—on Martin Luther King Day—to argue on behalf of President Donald Trump's goal of constructing a wall along the southern border of the United States. America claims to love King in the morning, but by the afternoon it has moved in the direction opposite of King's philosophy. Many Americans also routinely cast mockery and ridicule on living civil rights leaders and activists who are organizing and advocating for precisely what King believed throughout his life.

Speaking on the canyon separating America's hollow and hypocritical celebration of the mythic King, and the politics and leadership of the actual King, Jackson offered an analytical summary: "We honor martyrs not marchers." "Martyrs," he continued, "comfort us. Marchers challenge us. Martyrs only require that we look back, while marchers demand that we move forward."

In 1968, only 37 percent of Americans had a positive view of Martin Luther King. In 2019, a mere 31 percent of Americans, according to a YouGov poll, had a positive view of Jesse Jackson.[4]

Santita Jackson, the civil rights leader's eldest daughter and a radio talk show host in Chicago, recalls that when her father ran for president in the 1980s, he wore a bulletproof vest every day. "If they aim for the head," one particularly morbid secret service officer said, "there's nothing we can do."[5] One cannot help but wonder if Jackson was assassinated in the 1980s, would universities, libraries, and highways bear his name? Would elected officials, of both parties, cite his legacy as justification for the advancement of their own agendas? Would the silence of the grave have ingratiated Jackson to otherwise hostile Americans, just as it did for King?

"How ya like me now?" asks the graffiti at the bottom of a painting of Jesse Jackson with pale skin, blue eyes, and blonde hair. The artist, David Hammons, and Richard Powell, the curator for the exhibit in Washington DC where the painting made its official debut among threats of vandalism from white and black locals, aspired to deliberately provoke the audience with the questions, "Are our likes, dislikes, and expectations of people based on race? How would Jackson fare in the media, and our elections, if he was white?"[6]

Frank Watkins, a longtime friend and advisor to Jackson, believes that the answer is obvious: "If Jackson were white, he would have been president." "He had greater skill than any of the people running, a sharper, natural instinct for politics, and his oratory was without parallel," Watkins went on to explain. Speculation over counterfactuals and alternative realities is nearly impossible, but it is safe to assume that if a white aide to one of America's greatest grassroots leaders, who spent years negotiating hiring agreements and trade union admission for previously excluded groups of people, secured the release of American hostages abroad, and had registered millions of citizens to vote across southern states where they were once prohibited from exercising the franchise, declared his candidacy for president, the *New York Times* would not have put the word "serious" in scare quotes when describing his ambition to become a "serious" candidate.[7] A meticulous study from the faculty of the Communications Department at Emerson College concluded that the coverage of Jackson's presidential campaign from the *Times*—easily the most influential newspaper of the American press—had "a proclivity to highlight Mr. Jackson's racial heritage," and that the *Chicago Tribune* was, generally, dismissive.[8] Despite all the predictable crying about the "liberal media," a comparison to the campaign of Donald Trump, another outsider without conventional political experience, is devastating to the disseminators and shapers of news. During the Republican primary, Trump benefited from approximately $5 billion of free media time, due to the major press outlets covering his every move and utterance with energy they would typically devote to a national emergency.[9] Cable news did not yet exist during the Jackson campaign years, but it is noteworthy still that in March of 2016, MSNBC, CNN, and of course, Fox News bizarrely gave thirty minutes of airtime to Trump's empty podium before he appeared to speak at a rally.[10]

Delmarie Cobb, Jackson's press secretary in 1988, brought with her a resume of vast media experience, including as a television reporter in Indianapolis. Her savvy not only was essential to Jackson's success—providing insider media knowledge that not even a candidate with Jackson's natural skills could intuit—but also gave her an intimate vantage point for how the national press acted on a bias against his mere existence in the race. "The racism was so front and center," Cobb said when I asked her about her impressions of the major media's reaction to Jackson. "The running theme was that Jackson was in the race for a personal agenda, whereas white candidates never get that treatment—not even Trump." Journalists offered subtle distinctions in their framing of candidates to underscore their suspicions. "The press called all of the other candidates' voters, 'supporters,'" Cobb remembered, "They called Jackson's voters, 'followers.'" Her experience working in broadcast journalism and politics places her in a unique position to analyze the reflexive procedure of the press:

> It is a follower's world. It takes a special person in the media to take a different angle, and go against the crowd. You're not going to be popular—your job might be insecure—if you try to make a difference. So, we saw one or two reporters who looked at Jackson fairly, but most just followed the leader, which was the big, national outlets.

Fox News is eye-level fruit for observers seeking evidence of a corporate tilt in media coverage of consequential issues, but an upward gaze and extension of the arm makes accessible exactly how severely the mainline media—the so-called "liberal" media—protects the system in which it thrives. "He was the first successful candidate," Cobb said, "to bring a real 'rainbow coalition' into national politics." The rainbow coalition is in direct contrast, and opposition, to the demography and ideology of the corporate board.

The first time that I interviewed Jackson, I asked him a question that would make even the toughest character uncomfortable—"Why do you think so many people hate you?" I briefly described how associates and relatives of mine can hardly tolerate the sound of his name without collapsing into convulsions. Jackson's first rhetorical move was to disarm the potential tension of the question with dry humor: "Well, you should answer that. Why do you people act the way that you do?" Then, he provided a serious and introspective answer. "Sometimes in my quietest moments I think about just what you're asking," he said, "And I think our impact was traumatizing to them." Speaking in the plural so as not to exclude his committed staff and supporters, Jackson elaborated, "Many of them thought when they finally got rid of King in '68, and we floundered because we were so disoriented, that they were through with us on the national level."

Jesse Jackson, as the embodiment of black leadership and advocacy in American politics, never received a hero's welcome, but there were moments when his intellect and charisma allowed him to triumph in ways not even his most vicious critics could deny. Few could question that his rousing renditions of "gospel populism" at the 1984 and 1988 Democratic Conventions stole the shows with high moments of oratory and inspiration that none of the other speakers— most especially the respective nominees, Walter Mondale and Michael Dukakis— could replicate. In the early 1990s, there was a movement to draft Jackson to run for mayor of Washington DC, and in 2000 Bill Clinton awarded Jackson with the Presidential Medal of Freedom. So, the most salient question is: What changed? How did Jesse Jackson morph in the public eye from a power player whose leftist and populist perspective was not always welcome but respected, by most, to an object of derision, even from many liberals?

The demotion of Jackson from a highly visible outsider-leader to persona non grata gives profound and disturbing insight into the process of exile by which an effective organizer, who despite his own failings helps to reshape America into a country that is more democratic, becomes restrained. In a political culture hell bent on the preservation of extreme wealth inequality and racial hierarchy, any player who proves himself too successful must be ejected from the game. The ejection of Jackson, along with his steady demonization, demonstrates the awe-inspiring power of propaganda and the coalescence of conservative media with mainstream media to dramatically alter public perception. In the song "Local Hero," Bruce Springsteen sings, "First they made me the king / Then they made me pope / Then they brought the rope . . . ." The rise and fall in mainstream acceptance of Jesse Jackson illustrates how assassination of reputation is equally, if not more, effective than physical elimination.

Jackson's diagnosis of conservative, white America with posttraumatic stress disorder is necessary for understanding the beginning of misdirecting public opinion. One imagines such ghastly figures as Mitch McConnell and Newt Gingrich waking up with night sweats from visions of black women taking the oath of office. The story of Republican media manipulation, however, is not nearly as amusing. "The right wing," Jackson once explained to me, "hates anyone who even gestures toward justice." Bill Clinton is not exactly Eugene Debs, or even Franklin Roosevelt, but conservatives treated him as if he was a Bolshevik emissary. Jackson argues that antipathy toward Clinton is an example of white hostility toward the mere hint of reform. "There are confederate monuments throughout the South, streets named after slaveholders, but you'll find only three statues of Abraham Lincoln," Jackson said. He also offered a reminder that Martin Luther King has only two memorials in the Southern United States, one of which is a marker at the site of his death.

"We want omelets without eggs," Jackson said, and part of the culinary confusion is an American naivete that celebrates multinational corporations with headquarters in former segregation states, and multiracial college and professional sports teams, without expressing a full measure of political gratitude for the civil rights movement that made progress possible. There might exist an official commemoration of Martin Luther King, Jr., but it is important to remember that the campaign of slander that has succeeded in lowering the public appraisal of Jesse Jackson first transpired against King. Jackson has also delineated a distinction between peace and quiet, arguing that the phrase "peace and quiet" should not pass the lips of anyone with political sophistication. "Quiet is the absence of noise," he said, "but peace is the presence of justice." It is safe to say that, just as Americans want omelets without eggs, they also want quiet without peace, and harmony without justice. As a consequence, anyone who "gestures toward justice" will eventually become, according to mainstream treatment, a pest in need of swatting.

The poignancy of David Hammons' whitewashed rendering of Jesse Jackson is that his question "How ya like me now?" signals the double standard in operation throughout American culture. Jackson himself attacked the double standard when a reporter asked if he was "offended" by Hammons' creative portrait. "It's not the painting that is the insult," Jackson answered, "It is the reality behind the painting that is the insult."[11] A black public figure must move within a political closet—always bumping into walls limiting what he can do and say—while a white leader, no matter how boorish or reckless, is free to roam around the whole house. Hammons' question also probes deep into the subconscious of millions of Americans. Few would willingly admit that Jackson with blonde hair, fair skin, and blue eyes is a more attractive figure to them, but the evidence indicates otherwise.

The Kirwan Institute for the Study of Race and Ethnicity at Ohio State University defines "implicit bias" as "the attitudes or stereotypes that affect our understanding, actions, and decisions in an unconscious manner."[12] Implicit bias is not merely an interesting subject for Freudian speculation, but a social crisis with fatal manifestation in medicine, where black patients are routinely denied care and treatment options that whites take for granted, and most notoriously, in law enforcement, where unarmed, and often even unthreatening blacks, are shot down or harassed by police officers who see danger when none exists.

Implicit bias operates with more subtlety and nuance in the processes of democracy. Voters are often unable to overcome their own subconscious aversion to a candidate based upon secondary characteristics. The intellectual pollutant chokes the air out of politics, inflicting even greater damage on the electoral respiration system, when the media uses its power to influence rather than inform the electorate. When scrutinizing the Jackson candidacy and the steady shift in public perception of Jackson's leadership, it is irresponsible to ignore the deleterious role of race.

Sociological studies of the labor market reveal the continuation, even in northern cities with Democratic mayors, of hiring biases against black applicants. According to the groundbreaking work of Devah Prager, even when black job seekers are more qualified than their white competitors, they will not receive invitations to interview if their names are "stereotypically black."[13] Throughout the allegedly meritocratic world of business, there is an underlying assumption of racism that black candidates for jobs are, by default of their identity and ancestry, unqualified. Centuries of programming create an implicit bias that blacks, regardless of evidence to the contrary, are lazy, irresponsible, and unfit for the serious tasks of leadership, decision-making, and institutional management. The abysmal record of everything from the absence of black CEOs in Fortune 500 companies to the dearth of black coaches in the NFL, where 77 percent of the players are black, demonstrates how in America, authority must have a white face. Perhaps, a face with blonde hair, blue eyes, and pale skin. All but the most naïve must realize that the answer to the question, "how ya like me now?", changes radically according to pigmentation. Even sympathy for those who suffer rises and falls with levels of melanin. Jackson, in one of our conversations, praised the savviness of Lyndon Johnson for launching the "war on poverty" in Appalachia. "He whitened the face of poverty," Jackson said before explaining that when John Kennedy spoke about poverty in Harlem, the media and majority of white voters dismissed the speech as a "publicity stunt."

It is rather predictable and cliched to hear endless commentary every election cycle about how a presidential campaign is the "ultimate job interview." A hiring bias worked against Jesse Jackson in his job interview for the ultimate political authority in the federal government of the United States. As one of the nation's most effective civil rights leaders and negotiators, his "lack of experience" became fodder for endless chatter—chatter largely absent from debate about the third-party candidacy of Ross Perot, who earned 19 percent of the vote in the presidential election of 1992, and, most absurdly, the Republican nomination of Donald Trump, who failed to prove that he could score a "C-" on a middle school civics exam.

Jackson was not entirely blameless in the presentation of his candidacy as a threat to American stability. The conservative factions of the Republican Party, their Democratic counterpart, and the mainline media were salivating at the thought of Jackson committing an error that might confirm their slanderous portrayal of him as a subversive radical. In 1984, during the middle of his first run for the presidency, he fell into the trap. Speaking off the record with a New York journalist about why he alone among the Democratic candidates was advocating for American opposition to apartheid in South Africa, and why reporters were consistently asking Democrats about the Palestine-Israel conflict, and not any other issue of international affairs, including the ongoing South African human rights travesty, Jackson uttered a racial slur and flirted with a worldview that has a hideous record of oppression and genocide. He referred to New York City as "hymietown," and insinuated that the disproportionate amount of Jews in the New York media account for the discrepancies of coverage. The reporter saw an opportunity to enhance his own career with an incendiary story, guaranteed to elicit high-profile attention. Worse than the journalist's violation of his code of professional ethics was Jackson's undermining of the beauty and purity of the rainbow coalition. Relations between Jews and blacks in America are complicated. During the civil rights movement, Jews were the most active and loyal nonblack supporters of public accommodation and voting rights for the victims of Jim Crow. Rabbi Abraham Joshua Heschel led many marches with Martin Luther King, and there were many Jewish students, most infamously Andrew Goodman and Michael Schwerner, murdered for providing assistance to black freedom riders in the South. Jackson had maintained friendly associations with Jewish intellectuals and progressive Jewish organizations, but in the 1970s and 1980s black and Jewish relations began to fracture. The use of a slur by America's then most prominent black civil rights leader was something of a culmination.

Jackson initially worsened the offense with his insistence that he meant to cause no harm with the remark, denying the hurtful edge of the slur and instead claiming it was merely a "colloquialism." After two weeks, he issued an apology, while continuing to assert that he did not utter the words with meanness in his heart, but rather was irresponsibly and foolishly repeating a holdover phrase from his streetwise youth—a rough and tumble period of American life when epithets against all ethnic groups were in the common vernacular. America has an odd and often-contradictory conception of moral offenses, typically placing more weight on words than deeds. For example, an Islamophobic remark will usually provoke much greater condemnation from pundits and politicians than a president invading or bombing a predominantly Muslim country for specious reasons. All the same, Jackson has apologized multiple times for the contemptible remark, most memorably in his 1984 DNC address:

> If, in my low moments, in word, deed or attitude, through some error of temper, taste or tone, I have caused anyone discomfort, created pain or revived someone's fears, that was not my truest self. If there were occasions when my grape turned into a raisin and my joy bell lost its resonance, please forgive me. Charge it to my head and not to my heart. My head—so limited in its finitude; my heart, which is boundless in its love for the human family.[14]

More troubling than the slur is the flirtation with the anti-Semitic conspiracy theory regarding Jewish control of the press. It was particularly unhelpful to Jackson to have the vocal endorsement of Louis Farrakhan, the demagogic leader of the Nation of Islam who regularly spits out anti-Semitic, anti-white, chauvinistic, and homophobic bile at his audiences. Jackson's initial hesitation to disavow Farrakhan and distance himself from the Nation of Islam solidified suspicions, to many critics, about Jackson's prejudices. Without hesitation, Jackson made it clear that he "deplored" most of Farrakhan's message, and even made comparison that measured the distance between his vision for America and that belonging to the Nation of Islam. In doing so, he also emphasized how his campaign was not only political, but pastoral. "My whole life is about redemption," Jackson said, "I have reached out to George Wallace, even though some people got killed because of him. I've reached out to some of the lowest-down bastards you can imagine." In the 1970s, Jackson rebuked the tactics of the Black Panthers, condemning violence of all kinds, but refused to condemn the organization itself. Operating as an independent civil rights leader has a different set of implications, however, than running a political campaign. The replication of his 1970s approach with Farrakhan was, according to many journalists, more damaging than the "hymie" slip. There is, perhaps, no greater proliferator of anti-Semitic conspiracy theories in the United States than Farrakhan. The association, fairly or unfairly, coalesced with Jackson's gaffe to present an unflattering picture. Eventually, Jackson would fully distance himself from Farrakhan, but some reluctance might have resulted from loyalty to his constituency. Black support for Farrakhan remains high, even with the pathologies and bigotries he represents. Jackson once said to me that there is no more effective tactic of negotiation or ingratiation than "appealing to someone's sense of goodness," and elaborated to say that such appeals of conscience are only possible with assimilation, not rejection. Jackson believed that bringing Farrakhan into the mainstream might have a redemptive influence on the charismatic leader. He was wrong, but one cannot blame him for trying, and one cannot help but observe a poisonous, and racial, double standard at work in the American media.[15]

When Jackson announced his intentions to launch a second presidential run in 1987, the *New York Times* led with a story on how "Jackson is haunted by the anti-Semitism of Farrakhan."[16]

The placement of Jackson within an anti-Judaic frame is an example of how the major media outlets, especially when reporting on the plans and movements of dissident figures, search for evidence to affirm their assumption, rather than form conclusions out of data and observation. While visiting a family friend in a New York hospital in 1984, Jackson met a Jewish family whose matriarch was near death. In honor of the family's request, Jackson missed a scheduled campaign appearance to pray with the family until the elderly woman drew her last breath. A *New York Times* correspondent, acting on assignment to report Jackson's campaign maneuvers and activities, failed to even mention Jackson's act of pastoral charity until the primary had ended.[17] Such a story might have eroded the claim of Jackson's anti-Semitism, revealing his offensive "hymietown" slur as aberrational, and his acquaintance with Farrakhan as inconsequential to any judgments of character. On the latter, it is significant that Jackson's relationships received scrutiny that few other candidates—from Nixon to Trump—ever have to counter. The single exception is Barack Obama, who had to continually answer for the rhetoric of his firebrand minister in Chicago. What might Obama and Jackson have in common? It is not a defense of the Nation of Islam, or the hateful ravings of its leader, to observe that the most prominent news publications and networks—to the detriment of progressive and dissident candidates—never interrogate white conservatives for their radical associations.

John Hagee, a prominent megachurch minister in Texas, was a friend and advisor to George W. Bush, often making appearances at official Republican events. The relationship between Hagee and Bush, and the infrastructure of the

GOP, extended far beyond the loose association of Jackson and Farrakhan, and yet the media largely ignored the pungent presence of the fire and brimstone preacher. Hagee had called the Catholic Church the "great whore," argued that Muslims uniformly believe that they have a religious duty to kill Christians, and predicted that the legalization of gay marriage would destroy the United States.[18] Bush also accepted the endorsements of Jerry Falwell and Pat Robertson, two religious arsonists who claimed the 9/11 attacks on the United States was God's revenge against America over abortion, gay rights, and the removal of prayer from public schools.[19] Donald Trump, as candidate for president, spent considerable time courting the support of Jerry Falwell Jr., who presides over Liberty University, where psychology courses teach students that homosexuality is a mental disorder and where administrators refuse to include sexual orientation in its anti-discrimination bylaws.[20] Another clerical hatemonger, Franklin Graham, son of Billy, recited a prayer at the inauguration of Trump without audible objection from the press. Graham has called Islam "an evil religion," and for several years provided prominent amplification to the bigoted birther theory, questioning Barack Obama's American citizenship.[21] The damage of the racial double standard is as clear as the regressive culture and gilded governance it protects. The popularity, charisma, and organizational success of Jesse Jackson constituted a threat to the mechanisms of white authority, corporate hegemony, and an increasingly pacified Democratic Party. There were many reasons to put a political target on his back.

The reach of radiation into the American environment, often originating at a right-wing ground zero and extending far beyond into mainstream precincts, is responsible for the reputational devastation of many potential reformers. Even moderate figures suffer from the attacks of right-wing misinformation efforts. In the 2016 race, Steve Bannon, before he became an official part of the Trump campaign, commissioned a book on the "corruption" of the Clinton's, and eventually succeeded in securing servile coverage for it in the *New York Times*.[22] The sad and bizarre success of another slanderous book, *Shakedown: Exposing the Real Jesse Jackson*, is revelatory, providing indispensable insight into exactly how right-wing propaganda rises from the doldrums of conservative thought into the American political atmosphere. To study the slander of Jackson, which began in the 1980s not for random reasons, but because his organizational success presented a serious threat to the management class of both America's duopoly and corporate authority, provides profound insight into what tactics the right wing, and, contrary to the "liberal media" myth, an obsequious and unimaginative press will employ to destroy future movers and shakers of progressive politics.

Shakedown sold over 200,000 copies, and became a media sensation in conservative circles. Kenneth R. Timmerman, the book's author who also wrote a searing expose on how the French "betrayed" America by refusing to participate in the catastrophic invasion and occupation of Iraq, provides an instruction manual for right-wing sabotage of democratic knowledge in his book on Jesse Jackson. Offering polemical winks and nods in the direction of stereotyping, he argues that Jackson is a criminal whose primary pursuit in life is to enrich himself through whatever means necessary, and earn as much TV time as possible. Timmerman also performs a favorite trick of conservative illusionists with the argument that Jackson, rather than an opponent of racism, and unlike the white power structure he condemns, is the "real racist."

Even a cursory glance through the pages of *Shakedown* offers exposure different from Timmerman's intentions. He begins with the claim that Jackson "pretends" as if he was a victim of racism to secure moral authority in American politics.[23] It is impossible to imagine any black man born in 1941, and raised in the Jim Crow state of South Carolina, not being a victim of racism. A capsule review of Jackson's childhood includes attendance of segregated schools, inability to patronize public businesses or receive any public accommodations, and getting arrested at the age of nineteen for attempting to check a book out of the Greenville Public Library. It is not merely the absurdity of Timmerman's opening lie that is worthy of study. It is also its ideology. The right wing constantly seeks to discredit stories of injustice by casting doubt on the plaintiffs. If they can successfully convince Americans that there are few, if any, genuine victims, then they can preside over a political debate in which there are no victimizers.

The self-congratulatory pronouncements of a "post racial" age after the presidential election of Barack Obama displayed an all-American rush to erase the past, and neglect any substantive recognition of how historical injustice continues to define present circumstances. Even more fantastical was the widespread notion, counter to all data, that Donald Trump won the presidency merely because working-class whites had grown frustrated with "bad trade deals." Jackson, and those like him, are inconvenient, because they function as living, breathing reminders of an American reality that most would prefer to forget or deny. They are the medicinal treatment for a nation that the late Gore Vidal once dubbed "The United States of Amnesia." To begin with the lie that Jesse Jackson is not a genuine victim of racism, Timmerman advances the dangerous idea that America operates as a real meritocracy—a central tenet to the bipartisan myth of the American dream, which receives its most eloquent articulation not from the fringe right, but the center-left.

Jackson has often insisted that "excellence and effort are important, but inheritance and access are more important." The provocative question, "how ya like me now?", probes even deeper into America when one considers how the excellence and effort of Jesse Jackson might have received even greater reward if he had equal, or even comparable, inheritance and access as wealthy white Americans. United for a Fair Economy, in 2012, studied the *Forbes* list of America's 400 richest citizens, and found that only 35 percent did not inherit a significant amount of wealth. In fact, 21 percent of the magnets on the list inherited all of their wealth.[24] Race enhances the essentiality of inheritance and access to the American economic story, because up until only recently blacks were robbed of the opportunity to build and transfer wealth from one generation to the next, due to housing discrimination laws that prevented black families from buying homes, and the systemic economic racism that Jackson fought in the 1970s. Lack of inheritance resulting from centuries of deprivation accounts for why, even as the racial income gap has begun to close, the average white family still has ten times the wealth of the average black family.[25] If Jesse Jackson's claim of injustice is illegitimate, as Timmerman asserts at the beginning of his polemic, then his indictment of America is invalid, and his calls for reform, insidious. Rather than airing and aspiring to correct a true grievance, Jackson becomes a manipulator who is responsible for "division and polarization" in American culture.

Noam Chomsky explains that discussions of "Americanism and harmony" act as weapons against dissent, because if the focus in American political culture becomes unification around the American way, it is suddenly easy to vilify anyone who discusses "class struggle" and "civil rights."[26] Civil rights and economic justice activists are the problem, according to the "harmony" criterion, because they are disruptors. The system they oppose is fine. The average white American harbors resentment and distrust toward Jesse Jackson, just as he opposes Black Lives Matter, because he believes, perhaps genuinely, that the mere raising of issues related to race is what causes racial disunion. The hostility toward the phrase "black lives matter," and white insistence on amending it to "all lives matter," confesses not only a racial naivete but also a reflexive conservatism. What they are conserving, by design or not, is their own advantage and privilege. Unity works as a distraction and false god. As Jackson himself explains, "Vision is more important than unity. If everyone is united but blind, the one-eyed man becomes king."

The right wing's first move to defang and declaw a dissident is to depict him or her as the real problem, and thereby repudiate the position that American society has fundamental problems. Next, it is essential to undermine any moral authority or virtue that the dissident might appear to possess. The second lie of Timmerman's smear is that Jesse Jackson is not a "real minister." It is a claim central to the book's mission, as made obvious by its endless repetition in chapter after chapter, and the author's insistence on frequently putting scare quotes around the word "reverend" whenever using that title to refer to Jackson. By Timmerman's own account, however, Jackson received his ordination as a Baptist minister in 1968 with Rev. Clay Evans, himself an ordained minister, and Rev. C. L. Franklin, father of Aretha Franklin, presiding. At that point, Jackson had completed all but one semester of studies in a graduate program at the Chicago Theological Seminary before leaving to accept a job as aide to Martin Luther King. The seminary would eventually award Jackson his master's degree, giving him practicum credit for his experience in the civil rights movement.

At Jackson's seventy-seventh birthday party, held at Rainbow/PUSH headquarters in Chicago, Stephen G. Ray Jr., the current president of CTS, praised Jackson as one of the school's most accomplished alumni. Since Timmerman demonstrates the minimal journalistic standard of acknowledging reality—Jackson, according to all relevant authorities in the discipline, is an ordained minister—he argues that because the civil rights leader never actually pastored a church, he is a "phony preacher"—even this claim is untrue, as Jackson's first job in Chicago was as associate pastor of a Baptist church. Timmerman stretches his elastic falsity to absurd lengths not only to make Jackson seem less credible but also to scaffold a doctrinal tenet in the American religion of capitalism: self-interest is saintly, and acting for altruistic purposes is suspicious. Just as Jackson explained that the American right fulminates with rage at a mere "gesture toward justice," and just as notions of harmony work to demonize dissent, it is essential to the project of American individualism that people do not consider concepts like social solidarity, personal sacrifice for communal interests, or to use Aristotelian language, "matters related to the city." Americans are to think only of themselves, and perhaps their closest relatives. They should not bother with worry over children who do not have potable water in Flint, Michigan, or disabled widows who cannot afford health care. If Jesse Jackson is not a genuine minister with a passion for civil rights emanating out of his own experience with racism and poverty in the Jim Crow South, but instead a sophisticated con man who has crafted a lifelong scam out of fictional claims of victimhood and counterfeit ordination, it reinforces the antisocial pathology that society does not exist, and that Americans are to pursue their own private happiness in a Serengeti Plain where only the strong will survive.

Timmerman's charge might seem like it derives solely from a kangaroo court of right-wing fantasy, but it is merely an enhancement of the suspicion and derision against Jackson that had received its first airing, albeit with more subtlety, in mainstream reportage. The cover story on the Jackson campaign for president that *Newsweek* ran in 1984 featured a photo of Jackson in homiletic passion—the facial expression of mid-shout, arm extended past the podium—with the emboldened words, "What Jesse Wants."[27] The implication, especially resonant with white America, was that the campaign was not an extension of Jackson's two decade mission for racial equality and economic justice, but a self-serving enterprise of profit enlargement and status advancement. Similarly, the *Washington Post* gave its front-page story on the Jackson campaign of 1988, the headline, "What does Jackson want?"[28] George H. W. Bush, while running for president, denounced Jackson as a "hustler from Chicago," thereby giving prestigious sanction to a racist charge that a black man appearing to work for political reform is, in actuality, a self-serving con artist.[29]

The distortion of Jackson's reputation as a civil rights leader into a resume of successful swindles is crucial to Timmerman's title, *Shakedown*. Jackson, Timmerman argues with no evidence, has amassed a fortune using the tools of intimidation, corruption, and "race baiting." Beginning in the 1970s, Jackson became the nation's most effective challenger of economic apartheid, confronting businesses refusing to hire black workers, trade unions refusing to admit black applicants, and state and municipal governments refusing to offer contracts to black companies and organizations. Calling him the "apostle of economics," *Ebony* credits the advocacy, negotiation, and public pressure campaigns of Jackson and Operation PUSH with securing thousands of jobs, even more slots in unions, and millions of dollars in contracts for a racial group that the United States once prohibited from owning land and attending university. James Ralph Jr, a leading historian of the civil rights movement in the United States and dean of Faculty at Middlebury University, has called Jackson's campaign for economic opportunity and integration "one of the most important civil rights causes of the twentieth century."

"Everything we did was public," Frank Watkins reminded me when I asked about the common criticism that Breadbasket, and later PUSH, were clandestinely benefiting from their advocacy for black workers and entrepreneurs. The publicly verifiable activity of PUSH primarily included convincing corporate boards to sign "moral covenants" to hire more black workers, train more black job seekers, and invest in black neighborhoods. It is all rather banal, and the most worthwhile inquiry into the matter comes not from the conspiracy-minded right, but the socialistic left, returning to questions of efficacy beyond short-term improvements in racial equality within the corporate structure.

Jackson's campaign that underwent the most scrutiny was his boycott against Anheuser-Busch, the maker of Budweiser with a terrible track record on minority hiring and engagement. Leveraging the power of black consumers, and his considerable media skill, to apply pressure on the major company, Jackson persuaded the beer brewer to commit to hiring more minorities at all levels of its corporate structure, and create a minority outreach plan for distributorship deals. Jackson's son, Yusuf, would eventually become the owner of a distributorship on the North Side of Chicago. Critics of Jackson seized on the transaction to allege "pay for play," depicting Jackson as a hypocrite who, rather than actually advocating for black workers and business owners, was working overtime to secure a sweetheart deal for his son. The only problem with the story is that Jackson led the boycott in 1982 when Yusuf was twelve. Yusuf Jackson did not buy the distributorship until 1998. *Chicago* magazine, under the ownership of the conservative Tribune media company, reports that Yusuf Jackson met August Busch IV at the home of a major donor to the Democratic Party. They developed a rapport, and out of their friendship arose the distributorship deal. PUSH was no longer involved with Anheuser-Busch in 1998.[30] Perhaps, Jesse Jackson took advantage of some old connections with the company to ease and accelerate the partnership, which he denies, but that would only validate Jackson's thesis about "inheritance and access" having greater value in American capitalism than "excellence and effort." There is no evidence that the Jackson family did anything unscrupulous, only the innuendo that they might have benefited from the network politics of American business that countless white families—from the Bush's to the Trump's—work to their favor on daily basis without comment from the press.

The present incarnation of PUSH's economic advocacy involves hawk-eyed focus on Silicon Valley. While wearing the cloak of progressivism, leading technology companies have consistently failed to hire executives of color, and have few women and racial minorities serving on boards of directors. Timmerman looks at racial stratification in the economy, and rather than condemning racism, indicts Jackson for "race baiting." The phrase itself offers insight into a damaging worldview: racism is not a social crisis and, as a consequence, the real trouble in America is people like Jackson, who talk about racism. Economic exploitation and class struggle are not genuine in the American meritocracy. Instead, the actual villains are those who "shakedown" benevolent corporations through deceitful public relations campaigns. Sarah Palin infamously mocked Barack Obama's work as a community organizer as slothful, and possibly, sinful. The applause line whipped her audience into a frenzy not only because it worked in opposition to Obama but also because it affirmed the central tenet of America's self-aggrandizing ideology: there are no flaws in the dogma or exercise of power. Only heretics are worthy of damnation.

A relative of mine once offered rebuttal to my complimentary appraisal of Jackson's career by recalling when her husband, who was a plumber, returned home early one afternoon in a fit of rage. Jesse Jackson, leading a group of protesters, succeeded in shutting down a job on which he was scheduled to work. The protest was part of an organized effort, which eventually succeeded, to make the plumbing trade union suffer consequences for its deliberate exclusion of black workers. My relative's anecdote illustrates how the wealthy managers and beneficiaries of extreme inequality divide the working class, convincing them that their suffering is the result of each other. It also presents a binary choice. Who is to blame for the legitimate frustration of a white laborer having to return home early, with less pay and little accomplished—Jesse Jackson and civil rights activists, or the racist ownership class that created the conditions worthy of protest?

In 1987, Jesse Jackson was in a Los Angeles hospital to console an associate whose mother lay dying. He offered pastoral care, and moved quickly through the corridors of the clinic, eager to arrive at an early campaign event for his second presidential bid. His feet quickened their pace with his realization that he had a plane to catch. Just then, a voice called out to him. When he turned around, a distraught man, wearing the weight of worry on his face, pleaded with Jackson to say a prayer for his wife. "She might not make it," he added, straining to hold back the flood behind his eyes. Aides to the Jackson campaign instructed their candidate that there was no time. They were already late. With hardly a word, Jackson shrugged them off, and followed the frightened husband into the intensive care unit. Amid the deathly beeps and buzzes of hospital machinery, Jackson took her hand, and asked her surrounding family her name. "Ronnie, it's Jesse Jackson," he said gently. Then, he prayed for her healing, "We need a miracle here now, Lord. Touch this room. Touch this woman. Give strength to her family." When Jackson said, "amen," Ronnie's husband collapsed in his arms, sobbing, Ronnie, her husband, and the rest of her relatives gathered at her bedside were Jewish. "I am still disturbed," one of Ronnie's relatives would later say of Jackson's "hymietown" remark and hesitation to condemn Louis Farrakhan, "But I was not the one who was held crying in his arms."[31]

Reverend Frank Watkins said to me, "I'm more of a political person than I am a pastor. Jesse's more of a pastor than he is a political person." The bad rap on Jackson is that he is a calculating self-promotor who cannot even select an outfit from his wardrobe without considering the effect it will have on his public image. Reality is much more contradictory and interesting. For all of his skill as an organizer and orator, most of his mistakes are due to political naivete more than inauthentic calculation. There is no defense of "hymietown," but the delay in his disavowal of Farrakhan was due to a pastoral impulse of seeking ways to give wrongheaded people an opportunity for redemption. When the right-wing media, and many mainstream pundits, began to attack Jeremiah Wright, Obama's minister, the then senator from Illinois almost instantly condemned Wright, creating distance between the preacher and his family. Jackson, an unconventional politician in his two campaigns, was not as cunning, even though he clearly understood the costs of each second that passed without an unequivocal repudiation of the Nation of Islam. The different model of leadership—less tactical and more theological—is likely far outside the narrow range of understanding on display during cable news broadcasts.

On Christmas morning on 2018, Jesse Jackson made his fiftieth annual Christmas visit to Cook County Jail, giving an address to the inmates that combined motivational pathos, personal stories of his own hardships, and political instruction on issues of criminal justice bias, the connection between poverty and crime, and the right for inmates to register to vote, even while in jail. Among the entourage accompanying Jackson was a Rainbow/PUSH staffer registering inmates to vote. Also with Jackson, by invitation, was Rabbi Samuel N. Gordon from the Holocaust Memorial Council and Congregation Sukkat Shalom in Wilmette, Illinois, a northern suburb of Chicago. Gordon and I struck up a conversation before PUSH's program for the inmates commenced. "I would do anything Reverend Jackson asked," he told me. I replied by asking how long they've known each other, expecting the rabbi to describe a friendship decades in the making. "Two months," he said. I made the obvious move of asking Gordon to explain his profound admiration for Jackson. He proceeded to tell me that after an anti-Semite committed the hate crime of busting into the Tree of Life Synagogue in Pittsburgh and murdering eleven Jews in worship, just two months prior to the jail visit, he extended a statewide invitation for any faith leader—Christian, Muslim, Buddhist—to join his temple for an interfaith denunciation of religious bigotry, violence, and anti-Semitism. Jackson learned of the service, and without any entourage or prior demands for time or attention, entered the temple. Gordon, needless to say, was pleased, and asked Jackson to speak. The Christian minister and civil rights leader gave, according to the rabbi, "the most wonderful and brilliant address on the connections between Jews and Christians, referring to parts of the Torah and the writing of Abraham Joshua Heschel." He then stayed for the duration of the night, enjoying conversation with the Jewish members of the congregation.

Both major Chicago newspapers covered Jackson's jail visit, as did a handful of television news stations. Not one reporter asked Rabbi Samuel Gordon for comment.

A long and lamentable tradition of minstrelsy troubles American culture. The application of black face makeup and the exaggerated performance of racial stereotypes have provided entertainment for white Americans since the era of antebellum slavery. Although now taboo in polite society, recent political scandals involving elected officials in Virginia and Florida and the routine embarrassment of white college students attending Halloween parties in racist costumes demonstrate that there is still a predatory appetite for mockery of black Americans. It is easy for indignant commentators in the media to admonish anyone who commits the cultural crime of donning black face, but comprehending and condemning the function of black face in American political debate requires greater intellectual dexterity and moral consistency.

"Most people wanted Affordable Care," Jesse Jackson told me in reference to the Affordable Care Act, the signature legislative achievement of the Obama presidency, but "they did not want Obamacare." "By calling it 'Obamacare,'" Jackson continued, "Republicans put his black face on the program. So, many people who supported the Affordable Care Act did not support Obamacare. That shows how deceptive race can make politics." Considering that polls show one-third of Americans are unaware that the ACA and "Obamacare" are the exact same program, and that approval ratings for the ACA are higher than those for "Obamacare," Jackson's analysis is salient.[32] He strengthens his own case with recitation of historical studies documenting how white America's support for social welfare programs plummeted when they became associated with black beneficiaries. Ronald Reagan's literary and theatrical invention of the "welfare queen" as a pervasive thief of government largesse is another effective example of the application of black face to public policy.[33]

The painter David Hammons removed black face from Jesse Jackson and, in doing so, invites introspection of America's moral character. The treacherous crossroads where optics and politics meet is difficult to navigate, and often proves unpassable for the left. Even so, the right, despite its gaggle of generous donors and skillful manipulators, is incapable of destroying the left without critical aid and assistance. The image of Jackson sustained vandalistic blows from far right campaigns of slander, but it was not until powerful members of the Democratic Party picked up cans of spray paint and equipped themselves with hatchets that Jackson became a casualty of iconoclasm.

The right wing's campaign against Jackson is a familiar American horror story, but the liberal betrayal of Jackson is a tragedy much more painful to reconcile.

Figure 1 Marches for civil rights in Selma, Alabama. Alabama, Selma—March, 12, 1965. (Photo by Paul Slade/Paris Match via Getty Images.)

Figure 2 Civil rights leaders Hosea Williams (1926–2000, left) and Jesse Jackson (center) in Washington, DC, during the Poor People's Campaign, 1968. (Photo by Jill Freedman/ Getty Images.)

Figure 3 Reverend Jesse Jackson attends an Oval Office meeting with President Jimmy Carter, Washington DC, August 4, 1979. (Photo by Afro American Newspapers/Gado/ Getty Images.)

Figure 4 Jesse Jackson, Baptist minister and candidate for the Democratic presidential nomination in 1984, attends a press conference with Cuban dictator Fidel Castro during Jackson's visit to Cuba. (Photo by Jacques M. Chenet/CORBIS/Corbis via Getty Images.)

Figure 5 Jesse Jackson with Nelson and Winnie Mandela. (Photo by David Turnley/Corbis/ VCG via Getty Images.)

Figure 6 Reverend Jesse Jackson being hugged from behind by wife, Jacqueline, as children (L to R) Jesse Jr., Santita, Yusef, Jackie Jr., and Jonathan look on, at home in Chicago, Illinois. (Photo by Taro Yamasaki/The LIFE Images Collection via Getty Images/Getty Images.)

Figure 7 Presidential candidate Reverend Jesse Jackson raising linked hands with civil rights veteran Rosa Parks during Democratic National Convention. (Photo by Bill Pierce/ The LIFE Images Collection via Getty Images/Getty Images.)

Figure 8 Reverend Jesse Jackson hugging his mother Helen Burns after addressing Democratic National Convention as contender for presidential nomination. (Photo by James Keyser/The LIFE Images Collection via Getty Images/Getty Images.)

Figure 9 Cesar Chavez at mass, getting his hand kissed by Reverend Jesse Jackson who is passing a cross to him as he joins Chavez's fast on behalf of the UFW during boycott of the grape growers. (Photo by John Storey/The LIFE Images Collection via Getty Images/Getty Images.)

Figure 10 Reverend Jesse Jackson addresses a group of disabled persons during a rally on October 03, 2000, Capitol Hill in Washington, DC, to support Americans with disabilities. (MANNY CENETA/AFP via Getty Images.)

Figure 11 Reverend Jesse Jackson greets Cook County Jail detainees on August 7, 2001, at the jail in Chicago. Jackson, along with several other ministers, traveled to the Cook County Jail, Illinois, to publicly take an AIDS test in front of 300 detainees, in hopes of encouraging them to take the test. (Photo by Tim Boyle/Getty Images.)

Figure 12 Reverend Jesse Jackson has a word with Senator Barack Obama, after a congressional Black Caucus ceremony at the Library of Congress, in which members where sworn into the CBC for the 109th Congress. (Photo by Tom Williams/Roll Call/Getty Images.)

Figure 13 The image of a weeping Reverend Jesse Jackson is projected onto a large screen as CNN announces the victory of Democratic presidential candidate Barack Obama on November 4, 2008, during Obama's election night rally at Grant Park in Chicago, Illinois. (STAN HONDA/AFP via Getty Images.)

Figure 14 Jesse Jackson joins other protesters, including a group of veterans against the wars in Iraq and Afghanistan, on the first day of the NATO summit on May 20, 2012, in Chicago, Illinois. (Photo by Spencer Platt/Getty Images.)

Figure 15 US civil rights activist Jesse Jackson, Romany activist and head of the Central Council of German Sinti and Roma Romani Rose and Roma leader Roman Kwiatkowski, lay down flowers at the memorial site of the former Auschwitz-Birkenau German Nazi Death Camp, commemorating the seventy-fifth anniversary of the last Nazi killings of Sinti and Roma at the camp in Oswiecim, on August 2, 2019, the Roma Holocaust Remembrance Day. (ALIK KEPLICZ/AFP via Getty Images.)

Chapter 6

STRANGER IN MY OWN HOMETOWN

A Democratic Party "superdelegate" in 1988 anonymously told the *New York Times*, shortly after Jesse Jackson earned more votes in the Illinois primary than Michael Dukakis, that Democrats should support the Dukakis campaign because "the station's about to be blown up by terrorists and we're the only ones who can defuse the bomb."[1] Most superdelegates are elected officials, and although he or she was speaking metaphorically, it seems noteworthy that a member of high standing within the Democratic Party would compare America's first viable black candidate for president—a candidate responsible for bringing millions of new voters into the party—to a murderous maniac. David Garth, a political advertising consultant more mercurial than ideological in his willingness to work for both parties, told the same newspaper that he never saw "panic take over" a political organization like when it appeared that Jackson might win the nomination.[2] Jesse Jackson's competence and charisma, along with a vast network of committed volunteers and staffers, demonstrated the vulnerabilities of the Democratic Party. Rather than a static institution of soft resistance to austerity, union busting, and racist rhetoric, it was a malleable instrument that a campaign of sufficient strength could flex for the benefit of the American masses unserved and unrepresented—the poor and working class of all ancestral backgrounds, and particularly those who are black, Latino, and Native American, not to mention gays receiving almost no federal support at the height of the HIV/AIDS crisis, students, and activists on anti-war and environmental issues. Recognizing their own susceptibility to the influence of progressive movements, Democrats quickly developed a counterterrorism unit. The only caveat is that party insiders and decision-makers were not thwarting actual terrorists; they were working to reduce, if not eliminate, participatory democracy within their own ranks.

"Jackson's support began with black voters," Delmarie Cobb recalled, "But it expanded outward, because he, unlike most other politicians, was articulating a politics of usefulness. He was tapping into what was happening in their lives. So, white farmers, and working people of all races, were seeing the usefulness of his campaign to their struggles." Even as Jackson demonstrated growing appeal during the 1988 run, the media and party insider calculation was that he was doomed from the start because of his supposed inability to win a large northern state. Jackson had an advantage in the Democratic primaries of most southern states, because the majority of southern Democrats are black. Conventional wisdom dictated that, despite winning Vermont in 1984, Jackson could not carry a contest with a large share of white voters. Jackson's victory in Michigan—one of the largest and most industrial of northern states, with a majority white electorate—petrified the leaders of the Democratic Party, because it crashed through their protective shield. The next statewide primary in the race for the nomination was Illinois, where Jackson was polling higher than Dukakis and where his vast connections from his twenty years in Chicago would work to his favor. If Jackson were to win two large northern states in succession, it would establish him as the clear frontrunner, while exposing party leadership as unimaginative and out of step with the will of their voters.

"They were threatened by Jackson, not only because he was black, but because they knew that they could not control him," Cobb said in reference to the power players of the Democratic Party. She then offered full measurement of the lengths the Democratic National Committee would go to deplete the momentum of the Jackson campaign and, in doing so, betray their own constituents. "Paul Simon had suspended his campaign"—Paul Simon was a popular senator from Illinois whose presidential bid failed to win a single state contest—"At the time, Dukakis and Jackson were very close in delegate count. Paul Simon was told and pushed by the DNC to get back into the campaign to stop Jackson from winning Illinois." The timeline confirms Cobb's suspicions—Simon resumed his campaign and left the race shortly after winning the Illinois primary, successfully depriving Jackson of another victory. Cobb also submits that it is "more than coincidental" that the Democrats began "super Tuesday"—a single date in which multiple states host a primary election—in 1984, and increased the number of states in 1988: "It was because our campaign didn't have enough money to visit all of those states in such a short period of time." The Machiavellian maneuvering of Democratic leadership, along with the manipulative coverage of the mainstream media, demonstrates how often in American politics "democracy" is little more than a thin patina concealing a core of corporate favor.

A consistent threat to the corporate core is escalation of citizen participation. Al Sharpton remembers how before Jackson declared his candidacy in 1984, he went on an immensely successful voter registration drive in black neighborhoods, and then began registering Latinos, Asian Americans, gays, and students. "He was the only national figure working to turn the Democratic Party into a multicultural coalition," Sharpton said before elaborating, "People forget that the Democratic Party then was not the party it is now. My enemy was Mayor Ed Koch of New York, a Democrat. His enemy in the '70s was Richard Daley Sr., Democratic mayor of Chicago. Those were the opponents of racial justice." When Jackson was ushering millions of previously disaffected citizens into the Democratic Party, promising to change its demography and ideology, he was not met with gratitude. "People also forget," Sharpton explained, "that not even the black establishment—Charlie Wrangel, Coretta Scott King, and others—supported Jackson in 1984. It wasn't until 1988 that they came around, because they felt they had to. If they didn't support Jackson, they would have lost their own black support." Sharpton claims that Jackson would never go on the record with the story, because he is "all about unity," but that he was in the room, and personally witnessed elected officials discourage Jackson from registering more voters: "More voters meant that they had to work harder, and campaign for those votes. More voters meant they might face a primary challenge from the progressive wing of the party."

The hostility that Jackson faced as a candidate for the most powerful position in the US government began to take form years before he even announced his candidacy. The deceitful tactics that party managers employed against a populist tribune were elementary steps from an instructional manual of old design.

In 1975, when Jackson was leading the newly founded PUSH to integrate the economy in an effort primarily local to Chicago, the Trilateral Commission, an organization of elite liberal internationalists under the authority of David Rockefeller, issued a book-length report, *The Crisis of Democracy: On the Governability of Democracies*. Several of the intellectuals most instrumental in the analysis would later accept positions in the Carter and Reagan administrations. The "crisis," as its authors argued in Orwellian terminology, was an "excess of democracy" emanating out of the "new activism" of the 1960s and early 1970s. The civil rights movement, the student free speech campaigns, the anti-war movement, women's liberation, gay rights, the American Indian Movement, and the burgeoning environmental movement were coalescing to increase "government activity" and decrease "government authority." The distinction is profound as well as revelatory in the insight it provides into how administrators of elite institutions think. Government *activity* is the service that it provides its people. Government *authority* is the power it has over its people.[3] In the 1960s and 1970s, the United States expanded its small welfare state with the Great Society agenda, which included Medicare and Medicaid, educational aid programs ranging from the elementary to university level, consumer protection laws, rural development, and increased funding for public housing and the arts. Even Richard Nixon, a conservative with domestic policies that are now unimaginable in the Republican Party, signed the Environmental Protection Agency into law, and supported the poverty relief policies put into place by his predecessor. After many years of systemic neglect of the citizenry, popular movements were finally prodding American officials into performing the duties of their elected offices, and in the words of the Constitution, "providing for the general welfare of the United States."

Meanwhile, the revelation that leading American officials lied to justify the invasion of Vietnam, their failure to adequately care for returning combat veterans with life-altering injuries, and the Watergate scandal of the Nixon presidency, collectively struck a knockout blow to public faith, trust, and confidence in the federal government. Citizen organizations were insisting on more scrutiny and supervision of power, and young journalists, like Bob Woodward and Carl Bernstein, who famously uncovered the Watergate scandal that helped to destroy Richard Nixon, were making the media "adversarial," to quote *The Crisis of Democracy*. The report made many recommendations for the restoration of the "prestige and authority of central government institutions" relating to educational administration, media regulations, and tactics for quelling public revolt. Most of the ideas became a matter of public policy on a bipartisan basis with little, if any, pushback.[4]

Samuel Huntington, an intellectual responsible for much of the analysis of America's "crisis of democracy," wrote with nostalgia that President Harry Truman "was able to govern the country with the cooperation of a relatively small number of Wall Street lawyers and bankers."[5] The Democratic Party, as evident in, among other things, its implementation of the Trilateral Commission's suggestions, functioned with the same governing apparatus and ideology long after Truman gave his final address from the White House. It would only enlarge its political field of vision when mass movements made optical enhancement unavoidable. The Jesse Jackson campaigns for the presidency were revolutionary in intention because they went further than external agitation, and fought to give mass movements not just influence, but authority in the Democratic Party. Exercising its own smaller and more internal "crisis of democracy" management, the party institutionalized tactics to tame the unruly herd.

One year after Jackson's first run for the presidency, and in reaction to its measurable impact, Al From, the then executive director of the House Democratic Caucus, founded the Democratic Leadership Council. Most journalists would refer to the powerful advisory group as the "DLC" Jesse Jackson, the DLC's prime target for political elimination, aptly translated the initialism to mean, "Democrats for Leisure Class." "It was private," Jackson said, "Extremely friendly to business, labor was not involved, and not one prominent black Democrat was involved." At the time Jackson also offered the memorable criticism that the most prominent members of the DLC were "yuppies who parted their hair to the left, but voted to the right." Al Sharpton is direct in his assessment, suggesting that the "number one reason" that From, Bill Clinton, Al Gore, and other influential officials created the DLC was to "undermine Jackson and the Rainbow." Several years after its creation, the DLC would appoint Barbara Jordan, a black congresswoman, to a leadership position, but Jackson's analysis is cogent. When the DLC's chairman, Bill Clinton, ran for president in 1992, he advanced the idea of the "new choice" Democrat. The novelty was a Democrat, who many would say, wasn't a Democrat at all. The "new Democrat," Al From has said, "was pro-business, pro-defense, pro-police, anti-big government, and anti-racial quota." "I respect what they were trying to do," Jackson offered, "broaden the base, but they were doing so at the expense of important relationships."[6]

Broadening the base was essential on the national level. Even though Democrats controlled both houses of Congress in the late 1980s and early 1990s, they had lost three consecutive presidential elections in embarrassing, landslide defeats. Mondale, in 1984, won only his home state of Minnesota against Ronald Reagan. The success of the DLC—Bill Clinton did win in 1992, and won reelection of 1996—is undeniable, but that success only happened as a result of the voter surge of the "rainbow coalition." As president, Clinton promised to "end Welfare as we know it," and fulfilled his promise with a disastrous bill demanding that all welfare recipients work in low-wage jobs, even single mothers without access to childcare. He also deregulated the banking industry, one of many bipartisan maneuvers that put in motion the financial crisis of 2008. The Clinton administration adopted a "tough" position on illegal immigration to the extent that supporters of Donald Trump's barbaric policies at the border will often refer to Clinton's rhetoric as justification. Jesse Jackson recited Mat. 16:26 when I asked if electoral victory nullifies the need for progressive authenticity: "What will it profit a man if he gains the whole world, yet forfeits his soul?"

Jackson's sermon on the necessity of principle in politics does not mean that he is without political savvy. "Many good relationships came out of the Clinton years," he told me, adding nuance to his analysis. "Clinton appointed many of our people to government agencies, gave grants to civil rights organizations in many states," Jackson explained in a demonstration of realpolitik, "and helped start the careers, through those appointments and such, of many progressive and black officials." Often missing in the superficial consideration of electoral politics, from activists and intellectuals, is the reality of network, association, and assembly as political power. Even a conservative Democrat has an imperative to please his constituents, voters, and volunteers. That imperative will result in employment, authority, and influence for committed members of the base. The base of the Democratic Party differs dramatically, in ideology and demography, from the base of the Republican Party. "If a Democrat is in power," Jackson said in the articulation of another sports metaphor, "we can play offense. If a Republican wins, we have to play defense." The relationship between Jackson and Clinton is as fraught as it is fascinating. Under the Clinton administration, Jackson spent time working as a special envoy on policy to Africa, proving his point about networks and appointments. It is impossible to imagine Jackson, or anyone remotely similar in political philosophy, having a role in a Republican White House. Frank Watkins, Jackson's longtime advisor, is not nearly as sanguine about Clinton, recalling that when a Clinton staffer offered him a job in the executive branch of government, he replied, "I don't work for racists." The escalation toward the moments of Watkins' brutal denunciation of the incoming Democratic president provides not only high drama but also insights that should reverberate for progressives struggling to determine how to contain or cajole, depending on the situation, the slow-moving machinery of the two-party system.

"The DLC saw themselves as the future, I saw them as inherently limited," Jackson said. They were scrambling for a candidate to advance their "third way cause"—a clever name for moderation—and soon discovered the governor of Arkansas—a man of immeasurable charisma with an intellect to match. "Personality is the conduit for information and persuasion," said Jackson whose own charm and gravitas have served him well. It seems just as likely that Clinton's rare personality gifts were as responsible for his presidency than the centrist machinations of Al From. For a class of political tacticians concerned about electability, the DNC and DLC certainly made a critical error in 1988 by marching, like wooden soldiers, behind the robotic and restrained Michael Dukakis. He was "more electable" than

Jesse Jackson, but lost, just as Al Gore was "more electable" than the progressive Senator Bill Bradley, and John Kerry was "more electable" than former Vermont governor Howard Dean. Dean, like Jackson, also criticized the DLC as the "right wing of the Democratic Party." He would often say in speeches, while running for president in 2004, that he represented the "Democratic wing of the Democratic Party."[7]

The high-stakes combat between the Democratic wing and the right wing first became public in 1990 when the DLC held a conference in New Orleans, and begrudgingly invited Jesse Jackson to give a brief address. Because Jackson's pastoral style is to avoid attack, and seek "common ground," he did not insult the members of the DLC, but he did find a clever tactic for attempting to upstage and undermine them. Al From, Bill Clinton, and the other powerhouses of the upstart had the tough task of trying to move the party to the center without alienating the progressives for whom Jackson spoke. Their strategy was to articulate, through co-optation of key terms, moderate and conservative positions in the vocabulary of the left. "Equal opportunity," for example, became a phrase that they repeated with the frequency of a meditative mantra. "The problem with 'equal opportunity,'" Jackson would counter, "is that things as they are not equal. So, if we say there is 'equal opportunity,' but outcomes are not equal, the implication is that some people are inferior. The political implication of that stinks." When Jackson arrived in New Orleans, he opened his speech with a declarative rhyme: "I'm delighted to be united." He proceeded to enumerate, using the DLC's own rhetoric against them, all the positions they articulated, but had not adopted, that resembled his own agenda of the 1988 campaign. Due to his shrewd strategy, Jackson managed to dominate the stage, and steal the spotlight in 1990. The DLC would guard against their own vulnerability in 1991, refusing to invite Jackson to even attend that year's meeting in Cleveland. Never bashful in the foaming face of opposition, Jackson still flew to the Midwest industrial city, and gave the press his own tour of what Democratic Party politics might make possible if it were to exercise an authentic position for the poor, rather than couching corporate fealty in liberal oratory. After meeting with several journalists one by one in his vehicle, and instructing his driver to travel through the sections of Cleveland suffering from the blight of urban decay, Jackson spoke to a capacity crowd at a labor union hall.

"The key to winning," Jackson remarked at the time, "is a search for consensus, expansion, and inclusion. This is not consensus, expansion, or inclusion. It is the creation of two classes of Democrats."[8] The stratification of the Democratic Party contributed to the continual rightward drift of American politics. With the Clinton cabal shrewdly occupying the center, the only feasible strategy for Republican success was to establish distance from Democrats by moving to the far right fringe, and in the process, summoning all of the strength and resources of their burgeoning media apparatus—talk radio, and eventually Fox News, which made its debut in 1996, to depict even moderates, like the Clintons and Al Gore, as intent on destroying anything they associate with capitalism and Americana. The "left" has become a phantom term in American discourse with right-wing commentators, and millions of ordinary citizens, abusively using it as an umbrella to cover everyone from ecoterrorists to pro-choice centrists who sit on corporate boards. Critics of Jackson might quickly correct his 1991 rebuke of the DLC by reminding him that Democrats did win the next election, but Jackson had the vision necessary to see further onto the horizon. By resigning from arguments about class struggle and the financial precarity of American life, Democrats surrendered significant political territory to conservative demagogues ready to claim that economic hardships are the result of easily identifiable scapegoats— illegal immigrants, poor blacks siphoning essential funds from the public coffers, and the bizarre fantasy category of the "liberal elite," which apparently includes everyone from community college professors to Academy Award–winning actors.

In Cleveland, influential Democrats separated themselves from Jackson through means of neglect and, in doing so, sent a signal that they were no longer interested in assimilating the rainbow coalition into their idea for governance. After Clinton secured the nomination, Democrats would escalate by moving from avoidance to attack. "Clinton and the DLC were engaging in counterculture politics," Jackson remembered, "So, they would go to labor, and say something to insult labor to show that they weren't beholden to unions. Then, they did it to us." The "us" was not merely Jesse Jackson and his staff, or even Jackson and his supporters, but a much larger and historically significant group of people whose ostracization would indicate a method of politics much more insidious. Gore Vidal once wrote, "The secret core to each presidential election is who can express his hatred of African Americans most subtly."[9]

"A Sister Souljah moment" is a popular phrase among the mediocre commentariat. Most of those who parrot it appear to know nothing of its origins, and probably could not identify, at point of gun, Sister Souljah. The press utters the term to describe an incident in which a candidate for the presidency denounces the "extremists" within his or her own party. It is typically not something that occurs by happenstance, but is a tactical repudiation with the design of reassuring moderates that the candidate is not one of "them." Members of the media appear to derive great pleasure from calling on presidential nominees to create one of these "redemptive" moments. They did so when footage of Barack Obama's former minister making inflammatory remarks surfaced, and when there was an expectation that John Kerry would disavow his own history of anti-war activism during the Vietnam years. One might notice that the demand is never placed on Republican candidates for president. There is an understanding, as Donald Trump's campaign demonstrated with surreal theatrics, that extremism is a virtue on the right, and a vice only on the left. The original Sister Souljah incident functions as a "teachable moment," to use another popular bromide of American discourse.

Sister Souljah is a rapper, author, and activist who was developing a large following of young fans in the early 1990s. Speaking about the LA riots in 1992, Souljah presented a rhetorical question to her interlocuter, "If black people kill black people every day, why not have a week to kill white people?" The statement was, of course, stupid and cruel, but the media reaction was hysterical. Columnists and reporters spent buckets of ink and hours of broadcast time dissecting and denouncing the comments. It was as if Sister Souljah was the most important person in the history of the world. Even Republican senators, and members of the Bush administration, went on record to castigate the young rapper. The problem for Jesse Jackson was that, prior to her statement condoning the violence of the LA riots, he invited her to participate in a panel discussion on music and activism at that year's Rainbow/PUSH national convention. Several of Jackson's advisors encouraged him to rescind the invitation so as to avoid the inevitable smear that would result from any appearance Jackson might make alongside the controversial entertainer. Jackson, and his ambitious son, Jesse Jackson Jr., then a law student who would eventually become a congressman, had a different idea. The elder Jackson had navigated through black militancy deftly in the 1960s and 1970s. Learning from his mentor Martin Luther King, who preached nonviolence and peaceful resistance, but understood that conversion to his Gandhian philosophy was possible only through engagement and assimilation, rather that opprobrium and alienation, he again returned to his pastoral method of inclusive outreach. Jackson and his son arranged to meet with Sister Souljah the night before her appearance at PUSH with the intention of facilitating a dialogue, hoping to guide her into a more humane and effective ideology. The pastoral maneuver did not resonate with the American press, which is always constructing binary choices and casting heroes and villains, nor did it persuade political animals who live only for a fresh kill, and, in their Machiavellian calculations, cannot appreciate dialogue and tolerance.

The keynote speaker at the 1992 Rainbow/PUSH convention was then governor of Arkansas and Democratic nominee for the president of the United States, Bill Clinton. "Rev. Jackson prepared a wonderful introduction for Clinton," Frank Watkins told me, "But those of us in the hall heard rumors flying around, 'Clinton has something planned.' Rev. Jackson was with Clinton so there wasn't anything we could do." Paul Begala, the political operator who, along with James Carville, ran Clinton's campaign, saw his employer's lecture as not an opportunity to make an appeal to one of the country's most prominent civil rights organizations, but as a doormat to cushion his entry into presidential politics. Speaking at the podium, with Jackson to his immediate left, Clinton took a long pause—perhaps some hesitation given, if nothing else, the impoliteness of what he was about to do, and said the following in the latter half of his speech:

> You had a rap singer here last night named Sister Souljah. I defend her right to express herself through music, but her comments before and after Los Angeles were filled with the kind of hatred that you do not honor today and tonight. Just listen to this, she told the *Washington Post*, about a month ago, 'If black people kill black people every day, why not have a week to kill white people?' . . . I know she is a young person, but she has a big influence on many people. If you took the words 'white' and 'black' in that statement and reversed them, you'd think David Duke was giving that speech.[10]

Clinton accused Jackson of inviting the equivalent of the Imperial Wizard of the Ku Klux Klan to participate in his convention. Clearly intelligent enough to understand the difference between the leader of a violent, hate group and a rapper who made one horrendous remark, he disrespected Jackson and Rainbow/PUSH, at their own event, to ingratiate himself to white voters who don't want a president who is friendly to *those people*. Jackson, far from naïve, understood exactly what transpired, remarking at a press conference immediately following Clinton's remarks, "He was aiming for an audience that was not here." Mary Matalin, the director of Bush's campaign, was impressed by Clinton's coldhearted show of political instinct, saying, "We wondered from the beginning how they were going to deal with the Jesse Jackson factor. Not only did they not kowtow to him, they publicly humiliated him."[11] As much as he understood politics, Jackson still spoke in his pastoral vocabulary before the Clinton team left the conference. "Man, I was reaching her. How could you be so stupid?" he protested in vain, already feeling a knife blade three inches into his back. He wasn't so sympathetic to Begala when he demonstrated an uncharacteristic show of force, using his formidable height advantage to lean down into the political consultant's face and snarl, "You got your story," causing Begala to stare down at the floor and scurry away.[12]

The "Jesse Jackson factor" is a useful delineation of the influence Jackson was having on Democratic Party politics, and why the party's most prominent players would prefer to exclude him, despite his success in voter outreach and registration. It was not only a diversification of Democratic personnel that Jackson managed to spearhead but also the adoption of a general viewpoint of justice. The perspective of a Jackson Democrat, whether it was the civil rights leader himself, Bernie Sanders, or Paul Wellstone, dramatically differed in argument and ambition, from the triangulation of a Clinton Democrat. Even though the original Sister Souljah moment exposed a willingness to orchestrate minstrel theater for the satisfaction of prejudicial white voters, the first break between Jackson and Clinton might more accurately measure the distance between the two forms of politics they practiced.

When news broke that Bill Clinton had an extramarital affair with Arkansas pageant queen, Gennifer Flowers, many pundits predicted that it would demolish his chances of election. He was in a tight primary race with opposing Democrats, and any drop in poll numbers could have proven unrecoverable. The charisma of Clinton, and the faithful support of his spouse, Hillary Clinton, allowed him to emerge through the assault of the scandal with mere flesh wounds. At the same time, the Clinton campaign was formulating ways to fend off inevitable Republican ridicule should he win the Democratic nomination. Because Clinton had no military record, and he avoided conscription into the Vietnam War by studying abroad and writing a letter to a recruiter expressing his opposition to American aggression in Indochina, he and his handlers worried that they were vulnerable on national security issues, and that he might make an easy target for a favorite right-wing attack—that is that liberals are so delicate that they cower at an incoming gust of wind.

Ricky Ray Rector was a black man who murdered an Arkansas policeman. The judge in his trial sentenced him to death, despite the fact that immediately after his crime Rector attempted suicide by shooting himself in the head. The bullet effectively lobotomized him, leaving him with the cognitive capacity of a small child. The ACLU, the NAACP, organizations serving adults with disabilities, and many local advocates of civil rights in Arkansas all petitioned Clinton to exercise his power of governor to stop the execution. At the time, 80 percent of Americans supported the death penalty, but regardless of one's convictions on capital punishment, to allow for the state-sponsored killing of a man with brain damage so severe that he had no recollection of his life, much less his crimes, seemed barbaric. When the protests of a coalition of civil rights, religious, and death penalty abolition groups failed to move Clinton, Jesse Jackson called the governor personally to make his own, intimate appeal. "Now, Bill just on a moral, humanitarian basis . . . ," Jackson reports saying to begin their conversation. He then told him that "Rector obviously was going to be harmless and institutionalized for the rest of his life, and to kill him anyway would serve no defensible purpose." Enlarging his argument with religious language, he also said, "We should always be mindful of the biblical injunction against harshly punishing our fellow human beings. The more blessed is mercy." Eliciting no denial from the Clinton camp, Jackson told the press that Clinton replied, "I've been researching various ways to get around it, but it just couldn't be done."[13] As governor, Clinton could have stopped the execution in five minutes. Clearly, he wasn't researching legal options, but those of political cover and expediency. At the height of the Rector controversy, the director of the University of Arkansas's Governmental Studies Institute posited, "The death penalty is about as good a way to get Willie-Hortoned as there is," referring to the infamous Bush attack ad against Dukakis, depicting the governor of Massachusetts as irresponsible for giving a "weekend pass" to a convicted rapist. Clinton was thinking and reading the same thing, because he not only allowed the execution of Rector to proceed but also flew back to Arkansas for the killing. "Never has a contender for the nation's highest elective office," the *Houston Chronicle* wrote at the time, "stepped off the campaign trail to ensure the killing of a prisoner." Moments before his execution, Rector set aside half his slice of pie, telling his guards that he was "saving it for later." Christopher Hitchens wrote that the Rector execution demonstrated a "creepily sadistic attitude and willingness to bid for the racist subconscious of the electorate, to say 'don't call me soft, I can snuff this black guy who doesn't know what the charge against him is.'"[14]

The American press devoted far more hours to covering Clinton's extramarital dalliance with a former beauty contestant than the Rector execution, but the horror of the Rector story stayed with Jackson. He wrote a book arguing for the abolition of the death penalty, making Rector's brutal annihilation the central example of his argument, the thrust of which is accessible through the polemic's title, *Legal Lynching: Racism, Injustice, and the Death Penalty*.[15] The issuance of a moral rebuttal to political calculation in the Rector case offers as clear definition as possible of what Mary Matalin might have, intentionally or not, captured with her phrase, "the Jesse Jackson factor." The Jesse Jackson factor was the elevation of ethics above expediency, the advocacy of fair and just policy over profit, and loyalty to the poor rather than the ruling class.

The first term of the Clinton administration, more than most people realize given that those years lacked a recession or major war, was a turning point in American life. By neutralizing the left, governing from the center, and pushing the Republicans further to the right, the "Democrats for Leisure Class" strategy of triangulation won a short-term victory, but helped put into motion a long-term tragedy. In a 1995 interview with Charlie Rose, while reviewing the first term of the Clinton presidency, Jackson questioned the stability, and even the sanity of authorizing trade deals that "export jobs rather than products," while reducing aid for the poor, and lowering taxes on "inheritance and capital gains." Rose countered that Clinton was searching for a way to lead the country, and finding it in the "center," to which Jackson offered the challenge,

> Well, let's define what the center is. If I am leading a march of 10,000 steel workers, auto workers, and chemical workers in Decatur, Illinois who are fighting to keep their jobs under a fair contract, that's not left. That's moral center. If I'm fighting for a plan to lift our children up through education, not lock them up in jails, that's cost efficient and morally right. It's moral center. If I am fighting for a plan to reinvest in American cities, and put more Americans back to work rebuilding the country in order to offset the pain of this economic downsizing, that's not some lunatic fringe. That's where our country must go to be strong. We are not strong when there is the greatest gap between the top ten percent and the bottom ten percent of any developed nation in the world. That is not good, and it is not right.

Failing to get a handle on Jackson's criticism of American policy and priorities, Rose obtusely returned to the conventional idea of the "center," and asked Jackson about the "deficit" and the need to "balance the budget." "Well, let me say how we got into this hole. Let's put this in context," Jackson insisted in his answer,

> Mr. Reagan came in and proposed a $750 billion tax cut for the rich, which was compromised into a $600 billion tax cut, under the assumption that if the haves have even more money, they would reinvest. Instead, they flew the cattle out of the economy. How did we get into this deficit? The S&L thieves, not guarded. The banking thieves we had to bail out. I would submit that the banking thieves, who received this tax break, must pay for the lion's share. You cannot expect those who did not have the party to pay for the party. We need to destroy this idea that the rich are too poor, and that the poor are too rich.[16]

Jackson was hardly alone in his articulation for a left alternative to the disastrous policies of the American government. Progressive senators, congressman, and mayors—many of whom rose to prominence due to Jackson's presidential campaigns—were also highlighting the extreme inequality of American society, and challenging the bipartisan consensus—the only difference was seemingly the degree—that the rich deserve economic aid, while the poor must learn character by fending for themselves. Jackson, however, was one of the most prominent advocates of the authentic left within the mainline of American culture. In the first half of the 1990s, fifteen years before the financial crisis, Jackson gave an accurate forecast of how deregulation of the banks, and the financialization of the American economy, would liquidate the wealth of average Americans. He successfully led marches and assisted in the labor negotiations on behalf of many unions, ranging from health-care employees in California to clerical and technical workers at Harvard University.

The most dramatic of Jackson's interventions on the behalf of labor was his promotion and continuation of the hunger fast that Cesar Chavez and the United Farm Workers suffered to protest the unsafe working conditions for California grape pickers in 1988. In concert with the hunger strike, Jackson helped to organize a boycott of grocery chains that stock grapes from the companies that were refusing to meet Chavez's demands.

In the 1990s, Jackson spent six years as the "shadow senator" of Washington DC, the nation's capital that, because it lacks status as a state, has only a "non-voting delegate" as representation in Congress. The almost-half-black city of 700,000 people is essentially disenfranchised, one of many instruments of voter nullification in the United States. Jackson lobbied for statehood, and took seriously many calls for him to pursue the mayoral office of DC. Recognizing that the office is powerless, because Congress controls the budget for the capital, he declined, but Jackson did lead protest marches against Clinton's "welfare to work" reform. When most Democrats, including black officials, supported the 1994 crime bill, Jackson testified to Congress that "spending more money on draconian policing measures, and building more prisons is not the answer to crime."[17] Jackson testified as a victim of crime—his DC home was subject to a break-in—but also observed that in his neighborhood there was not one after school program, arts center, or job training site. Due to the obvious consequences of mass incarceration, many politicians and pundits act as if they played no role in the creation of the conditions that led to imprisonment as reflexive policy in response to the increasing crime rates of the 1980s and 1990s. Now that crime has considerably decreased, many commentators rebuke anyone who voted in favor of the crime bill. They do not recognize that most Democrats supported the bill, including Bernie Sanders and the first African American woman in the Senate, Carol Mosley Braun. To justify his signing of the bill, President Clinton brandished a letter he received from many of the nation's most prominent black ministers encouraging him to do so. The majority of the Congressional Black Caucus also voted in favor of the bill. Jackson was one of the few figures of national repute to predict the consequences of "tough on crime" tactics. Reflecting back on the debate, he told me, "I didn't care if it had white support or black support, it was wrong. It was wrong because it would lead to blaming our kids for the urban crisis."

On the impending financial crisis emanating out of extreme inequality and deregulation, the forceful and inhumane institutionalization of countless black men, and the eradication of organized labor as a civilizing presence in American life, Jackson was prescient. Jackson also foresaw the radicalization of the right wing in its earliest stages, telling Charlie Rose, "Conservatism is becoming a big cover for becoming more racist, more hostile, more mean spirited. You can put under the cover of conservatism a whole host of anti-social behaviors." Rose countered that there are "extremes on both sides." Jackson would have none of it: "Wherever it is it needs to stop, but you cannot name the others you are talking about who have 250,000 radio stations like Rush Limbaugh and G. Gordon Liddy do. Hate has become a commodity. It is being sold as 'conservative,' to make it socially acceptable."[18] The election of Donald Trump as president of the United States validates Jackson's early admonishment that "antisocial behaviors" were becoming central to politics on the American right.

His relationship with Clinton—the first target of paranoia from the newly powerful right-wing media machine—remained conflicted, even as the two men had some genuine affection for each other that, to the surprise of many, survived their earlier battles. Jackson told me,

> The first time I met Clinton, he had me at the Governor's Mansion in Arkansas in 1988. We were supposed to talk for an hour, and we talked all night. Hillary came down and said, "You two have been talking all night. Aren't you ever going to go to bed?" We had a lot in common. Despite my differences with him, I generally hold him in high regard, and I hold her in high regard.

Clinton appointed Jackson to the position of Special Envoy to Africa, where the civil rights leader would help negotiate peace treaties and trade deals. When Jackson accepted the position, he told Clinton, "This does not mean I will not criticize you." "In many ways we remained adversaries," Jackson confided in me, "But we never became enemies." When Clinton's affair with Monica Lewinsky became public knowledge, the president personally asked Jackson to counsel his heartbroken daughter. Clinton and Jackson settled into a cease-fire two years before the adultery scandal. Jackson told me that before Clinton's bid for reelection, the Democratic president

> put out feelers that he was going to end affirmative action. So, in response, I put it out there that I would run in the Democratic primary to challenge Clinton from the left in 1996. After Welfare, NAFTA, and the crime bill, affirmative action was too much to bear. Well, that terrified the Clinton White House, and they promised to back off that position, which they did. So, I did not run.

Given the stakes of the arguments beginning to form in the 1990s, and Jackson's accurate appraisal of those stakes, he might have led from a stronger position if he had not remained friendly with Bill Clinton. Proximity to power always carries the risk of deluding the credibility of a dissident. Jackson sees it differently. "I never have high expectations of power," he told me, "We did not have a Democrat in the White House for twelve years, and went through twelve years of regression. I knew Clinton was better for us than the Republicans. So, we got what we could out of him, and challenged him where he was wrong."

Jackson patting Clinton on the back with one hand, and slapping his face with the other, allowed him to become more mainstream in American politics, but it did not ingratiate him to the press. When Jackson's off-the-cuff remarks about "cutting Obama's nuts off" hit the airwaves, many political analysts claimed that it was providential for the Obama campaign. Many even called it a "Sister Souljah moment," but argued that it was even more beneficial than Clinton's theatrics, because it did not require Obama to do anything to make it happen. The unavoidable implication is that for the last two Democratic presidents to have achieved electoral success, establishing distance from Jesse Jackson was a necessity. The obvious question is "why?"—Why is it essential for a presidential candidate to prove to the American people that he is not too cozy with America's most effective living civil rights leader? "The Jesse Jackson factor," once again, offers profound insight into the pathologies of American politics.

It is easy to notice that the mere mention of Jesse Jackson's name often makes white people uncomfortable, occasionally provoking anger and disgust. The aghast reaction of white America to Jackson illustrates "white fragility," a useful concept that Robin DiAngelo, an academic and social theorist, defines in her book of the same name:

> Socialized into a deeply internalized sense of superiority that we (white Americans) either are unaware of or can never admit to ourselves, we become highly fragile in conversations about race. We consider a challenge to our racial worldviews as a challenge to our very identities as good, moral people. Thus, we perceive any attempt to connect us to the system as an unsettling and unfair moral offense. The smallest amount of racial stress is intolerable—the mere suggestion that being white has meaning often triggers a range of defensive responses. These include emotions such as anger, fear, and guilt and behaviors such as argumentation, silence, and withdrawal from the stress-inducing situation. These responses work to reinstate white equilibrium as they repel the challenge, return our racial comfort, and maintain our dominance within the racial hierarchy. I conceptualize this process as white fragility.[19]

There are few living Americans responsible for more conversations on and challenges to racism than Jesse Jackson. For that reason, he functions as a walking and talking trigger of white fragility. It is likely due to white fragility that one of the most popular attacks on Jackson is that he "cares only about the camera." Certainly, Jackson is a shrewd navigator of the media, and he's proffered his skills in public relations to the advancement of civil rights, economic fairness, and social justice, but when white Americans decry Jackson for seeking fame, perhaps they are actually confessing to a discomfort in having to see Jackson, because when they see Jackson, as DiAngelo might explain, they feel "racial stress" and an implication of connection to "the system." Most Americans appear to have no objection to celebrity. "Reality television stars" and "social media influencers" have created lucrative livelihoods out of nothing more than selling their celebrity endorsements to the highest corporate bidders. The pursuit of fame for personal profit and pleasure rarely elicits outrage. The pursuit of fame as a tool to promote the common good, and broadcast opposition to injustice, seems to cross the invisible threshold of white fragility. There are few things more absurd than a culture that has made the Kardashian family into multimillionaire, household names, and Donald Trump president, disparaging a civil rights leader for seizing his opportunities to appear on television.

When Bill Clinton engineered the Sister Souljah moment, he was signaling to white America that he would not challenge them. He would protect their fragile sense of racial identity. Dan Balz, a *Washington Post* columnist, wrote of Obama's good fortune after Jackson's slip of the tongue,

> Being attacked by Jackson was more than enough to get across the point. Whatever people may know or think they know about Obama, they can no longer mistake him as a direct descendant of old-style black politics . . . . If Obama were looking for a way to endear himself more to those white, working class voters who were resistant to his appeals in the Democratic primaries, nothing is likely to help more than a condemnation from Jesse Jackson.[20]

It is critical to note that "old-style black politics" translates into the protest methods and aggressive activism of the civil rights movement, and "white working class voters" identifies a portion of the electorate too fragile to deal with direct appeals for racial justice. Eduardo Bonilla-Silva, a Duke University sociologist, coined the phrase "racism without racists" to diagnose the societal condition of progressing far enough for condemnations of racism as an abstraction to become routine, but inspection of racist ideology and action among those working within the system, or benefiting from the system without compunction, to remain beyond the limits of polite, political discourse.[21] The American press captured the reality of "racism without racists" when it acknowledged the overtly racist rhetoric of the Trump campaign, but largely refused to entertain the possibility that Trump's supporters were racist. In one of my conversations with Jesse Jackson, he remarked on the "absurdity" of the phrase "American values" as a contradictory force against Trump's leadership. "They should call those moral values," Jackson said, "American values are slavery." Even white Americans who recognize that the system is askew, as DiAngelo asserts, want reassurance that their moral resume is pure. Jackson's work doubles as a reminder of the corruption, cant, and cruelty of American mythology.

Alongside race, central to the American mythos is class. "The Jesse Jackson factor" was representative of the thin vestige of resistance in 1990s mainstream culture and politics to corporate dominion over the Democratic and Republican parties. "Old-style black politics" prioritized labor unions over the corporate board, the poor over the rich, social services over private profits, and democracy over plutocracy. To political operatives like Al From, and political publicists like Dan Balz, Jackson's amplification of conscience was a capital crime, rendering him fit for punishment and exile.

Jackson's victories exposed the vacuity of the American political consensus. An alliance of the two parties and the press imbued cynicism in the public by convincing millions that there was no audience for an authentic left in America. Jackson's campaigns brought millions of new voters into the Democratic Party, and he nearly won the nomination with under half the campaign funding of the eventual nominee. "I got 1,020 delegates with $19 million," Jackson told me with a grin, "If I had $40 million, I would have won another thousand delegates." The uninterrupted propagation of meritocracy through politics, film, and television told Americans that if they did not succeed in the "free market," they were unintelligent, indolent, or worse. Jackson's Breadbasket movement, and later work with labor unions, shined a spotlight on the structural flaws of America's economic architecture. The problem of poverty is not a consequence of widespread personal failure, but rather the moral failure of America to care for the poor, give respect and opportunity to workers, and honor its promise of racial equality. Beginning in the 1960s when the oppressive barricades to voting were obvious, and moving to present day, Jackson's dedication to demolishing the obstacles federal and state governments place in front of the franchise underlines the fatal flaws of America's engagement with its own citizens. To use Jackson's own phrase, he and Rainbow/PUSH "democratized democracy."

The dissent of Jackson goes beyond domestic debate and development. He is an internationalist, having spent a lifetime making connections between the internal and external of American public policy—the missing elements of social democracy in the United States, and the missiles flying from US military bases. On issues of war and peace, he would also find himself in combat with the imperial apparatus of American power.

Chapter 7

THE THREAT OF PEACE

"There is no international. There's only local somewhere else," Jesse Jackson said to me to punctuate his explanation for why and how he became an unofficial ambassador of an American anti-war, cooperative, and mutually beneficial method of diplomacy. "When Dr. King spoke out against the Vietnam War," Jackson remembered, "Almost everyone—even blacks—said 'don't do it.' The idea was that any challenge to American foreign policy would slow down the progress of the civil rights movement. King said, 'I will not bifurcate my sense of justice.'"

It is impossible to separate injustice internal to American society and the external aggression, interference, and violence of the "world's last remaining superpower," as nationalistic boosters love to phrase it, a country with the largest, most advanced, and most active military in the history of the world. Since the conclusion of the Second World War, the United States has invaded seven countries, dropped bombs on dozens more, and conducted covert missions, often ending in the destruction of democracy and establishment of lethal dictatorships, in every precinct of the planet. There is almost no corner of earth without the presence of the US military; 800 military bases and 41 naval carriers challenge the geographic autonomy and national sovereignty of countless countries.[1] While its infrastructure cracks and crumbles, its infant mortality rate continues to increase, and many of its schools descend into failing levels of dysfunction, the US federal government spends over 50 percent of its discretionary budget on the Pentagon, rendering it little more than a garrison state.[2] Ernest Hemingway wrote that "only the names of people and places have dignity" in discussion of war.[3] Budgetary breakdowns and enumerations of bases are instructive of America's imperial ambitions, but they cannot compete for clarity with the millions of people, from Indochina to Iraq, and many countries in between, who have died in ways unspeakably gruesome because of American orders to fire, raid, bomb, invade, assassinate, and destroy.

When President Truman presided over the creation of the National Security State by increasing funding for the military, establishing intelligence agencies, administering loyalty oaths to all government employees, and commencing the Cold War, Senator Arthur Vandenberg, then chair of the Senate Foreign Relations Committee, told the president that winning public support for

American interference in foreign disputes would require "scaring the hell out of the American people."[4] Truman, and his successors, with the sole exception of Jimmy Carter, followed Vandenberg's advice (Kennedy's policies were mainly peaceful, but his early rhetoric was bellicose). In any given year, Americans learn, from their politicians and pundits, of an existential threat, be it communists, drug traffickers, terrorist networks, rogue states, or an assortment of other exotic monsters.

The lack of geographic knowledge in the general public, along with ignorance of international affairs, is so dismal that a 2003 US task force on education deemed it a "national security threat."[5] The gravest threat emanating out of American obliviousness, as history teaches, is to other nations, typically those that are poor and populated by nonwhites. The transformation of America from a republic into an empire, and the repetition of costly and deadly wars, is made possible only by the widespread perception that foreign leaders are hostile and irrational. If compromise and negotiation are hopeless, the only realistic way of keeping Americans safe is through violence.

"They want to tell a war story. I was telling a peace story," Jackson said during our conversation about his international work. When Jackson announced his intentions to negotiate the release of Lt. Robert Goodman, a US airman who was shot down in Lebanon, and held captive in Syria, in 1983, members of the Reagan administration warned him to reconsider. "They all told me that I would fail," Jackson recalled. Despite their excoriations, failure would have better served the interest of the US government. Like with many of his other campaigns, it was success that truly threatened the American system and status quo.

"A black person in the South negotiates life's transactions," Jackson told me after I asked about how he developed a sense of mediation that he could apply to international missions. "When I was a little boy, I worked with my grandfather. He had an old truck, and he would sell wood and coal. He had me sit in the front because he wanted to teach me how to be a little man," Jackson smiled and continued,

> I'd help him count, because he couldn't count too well. One day when my mother and I were on the bus, I wanted to sit in the front like I did with my grandfather. So, I did. There were some white kids making noise behind us. The bus driver shouted, very mean, "Order on this bus." I thought he was directing it to the white children, but my mother knew otherwise. She pinched me, leading me to the back of the bus. When I told my grandfather, he said, "She pinched you, because she loves you. She didn't want you to get hurt." He was instructing me with the adjustment rationales for segregation; how to negotiate life.

Jackson explained that his next job was at a restaurant with mostly white customers: "I had to learn how to negotiate with people who want a lot of service, and will give small tips." "When I was accepted at the University of Illinois, I was excited about going to a Big Ten university to play football," Jackson said,

Then, I learned that, in many ways, the environment was as hostile there as it was in South Carolina. There was not one black coach, not one black professor, not one black secretary in the athletic building. So, again, I had to learn how to negotiate to survive in the midst of such hostility. One night when I was studying, I heard a melodious band sound, I thought it was kids playing music in the dormitory. I walked to the gym, and found out it was the Count Basie Band. They were there to entertain the white fraternities. The black fraternities only had records. I convinced a roadie to let me pretend that I was helping to carry instruments. He let me in the backdoor. I was able to hear the band. Negotiation.

When Jackson transferred to North Carolina A&T, a historically black university, during his sophomore year, he began to distinguish himself as a burgeoning civil rights leader. In his senior year, students learned that several of Jackson's women classmates were wrongly jailed, and due to the typical conditions for black people in the Jim Crow South, concerns and fears began to grow that police officers might beat the young women. "If you live under oppression," Jackson explained, "You have to learn how to live in the rain without getting wet. You have to have a discipline of spirit, and a thick skin. If you are easily offended, you won't successfully negotiate anything. You might not even survive."

A steel coating over the soul also allows one to make distinctions between battles unworthy of investment—when the "adjustment rationales of segregation" are appropriate—and those that demand full force combat. "I went to my fellow football players, and said, 'We have to be men,' and I started leading a march on campus. I was not in the NAACP or anything, but over 3,000 of them started following me." Jackson's spontaneous success demonstrates the innate aspect of leadership—a quality and ability that transcends teachability. "The students saw something in me that I did not yet see. Like when a coach sees talent in a player that the player does not realize he has," Jackson said, offering an interesting interpretation of how leaders are both born and made.

The student march led to the liberation of the coeds, but it also brought the backlash of an administration anxious over potential reprisal. The state government warned that if the A&T campus remained a hotbed of civil rights activism, they would move to pull their accreditations, effectively nullifying all of the studies of the student body. "It was an awful feeling to think that our degree might not have any value," Jackson said and then explained that he was slated to speak to a large assembly of students at a nearby black church under pressure to conciliate, "I walked to the podium, and I said, 'Demonstration without hesitation. Jail not bail. Onward march.' We took off downtown."

"Negotiation is something I learned very early in life," Jackson elaborated, "How to listen to both sides and gain their trust, and the necessity of having transparency in all my dealings—not using one side to pin the other down." In 1980, Jackson would pass the first test of his mediation skills when the Chicago Fire Department announced a strike—the only strike of its kind in the city's history—endangering residents who, in the case of an emergency, might not have any recourse. Rather than deal honestly with the firefighters in an effort to draft a fair settlement, Mayor Jane

Byrne attempted to seize upon the city's racial tensions by encouraging the formation of a black firefighter brotherhood. "It was the appearance of liberalism," Jackson said, "But she did it to try to bust the union." Many black firemen, exhausted and frustrated with mistreatment from their white colleagues and captains, approved of the racial split, while many white firemen, who preferred to have as little interaction with blacks as possible, also applauded the proposal of voluntary segregation. Jackson realized that a divided labor union could not advocate for its members, and that black workers, who were a small minority within the firefighter fraternity, would suffer the worst economic losses. He intervened to bring the black and white firemen together, leading a twelve-hour negotiation session with city hall. It ended in a settlement and new contract. "It was my first big deal," Jackson said, "The press did not know how to handle that I pulled this off. So, they ignored it; acting like it was just magic." Confirming Jackson's recollection, the only praise the *Chicago Tribune* offered at the time was to report that he "nudged both sides to the bargaining table." In 2018, a Chicago firefighters and paramedics federation gave Jesse Jackson a lifetime achievement award. One retired captain credited Jackson with "saving the union," claiming that it would have "collapsed" without his intervention. The major Chicago press outlets did not attend the ceremony.[6]

The American press would sputter even more incoherently when attempting to handle Jackson's triumphant negotiations on overseas campaigns for peace, freedom, and humane treatment of prisoners. Jesse Jackson had a lifetime of training, most of it involuntary, in preserving and protecting life from forces of violence when he first acted in the interest and under the guise of "citizen diplomacy." The "citizen diplomat" believes, according to the Center for Citizen Diplomacy, that he has a "right and responsibility to help shape US-foreign relations, one handshake at a time . . . through meaningful, mutually beneficial dialogue." Jackson's citizen diplomacy operated according to what Jacques Derrida, in his analysis of Marxism, called the "New International":

> The 'New International' is an untimely link, without status . . . without coordination, without party, without country, without national community, without co-citizenship, without common belonging to a class. The name of New International is given here to what calls to the friendship of an alliance without institution among those who . . . continue to be inspired by at least one of the spirits of Marx or of Marxism. It is a call for them to ally themselves, in a new, concrete and real way, even if this alliance no longer takes the form of a party or a workers' international, in the critique of the state of international law, the concepts of State and nation, and so forth: in order to renew this critique, and especially to radicalize it.[7]

Jackson is not and was never a Marxist, but the lower-class struggle for justice that transcends national, racial, and ancestral difference appears to animate his citizen diplomacy. "Being a leader from black America gives one moral authority in the world, because there was a sense that we were in the belly of the beast," Jackson said and continued,

Civil rights, human rights; the foreign leaders with whom I've met always felt they were on the margins, and they wanted recognition from America. I understood that. They always wanted me to go to the ghettos, relate to the poverty in their countries. I could do that. Even when they didn't have religious freedoms, they wanted me to meet with the religious leaders that did exist, and I could do that. So, the key ingredients were religion, poverty, and the need for acknowledgment from America. We shared some crucial elements of experience.

As with many formative ideas of Jackson's philosophy, Martin Luther King proves a lasting professor: "Most Americans see the world through a keyhole," Jackson said, "Working with Dr. King, you learn to see the world through a door."

The atrocity of the 9/11 attacks stunned Americans, provoking a unified sense of mourning that, for those who lived through those dark days following the collapse of the World Trade Towers, the cratering of the Pentagon, and the crash of an airliner in a Pennsylvania field, is still heartbreaking to consider. The terrorist strike also provided political cover for "neoconservative" hawks in the Bush administration who entered the White House with visions of remaking the map of the world in order to ensure American hegemony. Catastrophic policies ensued—none as bloody and boneheaded as the invasion and occupation of Iraq. George W. Bush, and his imperial architects of foreign policy, Dick Cheney and Donald Rumsfeld, were not the first federal officials to warn Americans of the danger of "Islamic terrorism." President Ronald Reagan, like Bush, was easy to convince that "scaring the hell out of the American people" was easy and necessary. His Secretary of State, Alexander Haig, and Director of Intelligence, William Casey, told their commander-in-chief that the primary foreign policy aim of the United States was to eliminate terrorist networks receiving assistance from rogue states allied with the Soviet Union. Syria and Libya were at the top of the list. The American press, dutiful as always, reported on terrorism and Muslim villains, frightening the public. Reagan adopted "no talk" policies with many foreign leaders, most rigidly with the president of Syria, Hafez al-Assad. Refusal to communicate, and bluster about American power, defined the international approach of an administration that constantly ridiculed its predecessor—the largely peaceful Jimmy Carter—of accommodation of America's enemies.[8]

In 1983, fighting broke out between Israel and Lebanon with Syrian involvement on the Lebanese side. Palestinian guerilla fighters, with aid from Syria, were attempting to use Lebanon as a headquarters in their fight against Israeli occupation, provoking a heavy shelling campaign from Israel. High loss of civilian life incited outrage, even among the strongly pro-Israeli American public, causing Haig to resign. His replacement, George Schultz, was no less aggressive in his ideology of foreign intervention. As tensions escalated, Reagan sent US military forces to assist Israel, but when a suicide bombing in Beirut killed 241 Marines, public anger led Reagan to reduce American personnel. The president blamed Syria for the loss of life, claiming that they violated a promise to end their militaristic activity in the region.

In December, the US launched an airstrike against Syrian forces. During the mission, a two-man jet crashed in Syrian territory, killing the pilot, Lt. Mark A. Lange, on impact. The copilot, Lt. Robert O. Goodman, Jr., was ejected before the crash landing, discovered by Syrian soldiers, and taken to a military prison in Damascus. The Syrians beat him badly, and Assad announced that they would not release him until the United States left Lebanon.

"One of the ways Reagan won the election was by harassing Carter, because he did not launch a strike in Iran to free American hostages there," Jackson said, "So, many of us had the fear that for political cover Reagan was going to order the military to go into Syria to rescue Goodman." The incompetence of the Reagan administration was another factor that could escalate tension into a full-fledged war. Donald Rumsfeld, then special envoy to the Middle East, met with Syrian officials, but never once even inquired about Goodman out of the fear that the young naval pilot would become a "bargaining chip" in any negotiations that would follow.[9] Jackson was incensed that Rumsfeld would not even mention Goodman's name in conversation with Syrian leaders. Exercising his right and responsibility as citizen diplomat, he sent a cable to Assad, requesting the release of Goodman for humanitarian reasons. A reply came from Rafic Jouejati, the Syrian ambassador to the United States, with whom Jackson had already established a rapport on an earlier visit to Israel and Palestine. Jouejati, a Christian Arab, invited Jackson to lead a delegation of religious leaders to Syria, indicating a willingness on the part of Assad to meet. He also offered the optimistic view that it could create conditions more amenable to amiable relations between the two countries.

The Reagan administration ordered Jackson not to travel to Syria, and publicly denounced his intentions to meet with Assad in the press, claiming that it would only legitimate the Syrian dictatorship, while also implying that Jackson was too naïve to understand that he was "being used." Having already announced his campaign for the presidency, Jackson also faced the racist criticism that he was only attempting to secure the release of Goodman, because Goodman was black, and that Jackson was looking to ingratiate himself to black voters in the Democratic primary. Jackson shrewdly countered by framing his mission in humanitarian terms, offering a peaceful alternative to the bellicose Reagan administration, and reminding the press that he was leading an interfaith delegation rather than traveling as a lone actor. Jackson did precisely the same—acting as the organizer and spokesman for an interfaith coalition—during a 1979 humanitarian mission in the Middle East.

Everyone predicted that Jackson would succeed only in embarrassing himself, but his confidence was unshakable. "I knew if I could get to Assad, actually sit down with him, I could convince him to let Goodman go," he told me. Jackson also explained that he was concerned that the disapproval from the Reagan administration would leave him and his delegation helpless and without aid if the mission were to go badly. "I talked to Goodman's mother," Jackson said, "And received her endorsement before going. When she was invested, I knew that would cover my back, because to abandon us would mean abandoning her."

Jackson and company arrived in Damascus on December 31, and expected to leave on New Year's Day. They did not meet with Assad, however, until the morning of January 2. For ninety minutes, the two men discussed everything from the conflict between their two nations and Jackson's clever self-deprecation as a "country preacher." "It was important to make him feel powerful in the presence of Americans," Jackson explained and then offered simple guidelines for hostage negotiations, "Appeal to the man's sense of goodness, and also locate his own interest in the conversation, and explain how he can serve his interest by acting according to his goodness." Jackson warned Assad that keeping Goodman in captivity would provide the US government with a rallying cry for war. "Don't let your pride end this boy's life, and create problems for you that you cannot solve," Jackson told the Syrian leader. Leveraging his "moral authority as a civil rights leader" and American dissident, Jackson respectfully presented the case for peace and mercy, and remembers growing more hopeful as the conversation stretched past an hour, "I could feel and hear him hearing me."

Jackson and the American ambassador to Syria, Robert Paganelli, jointly announced the emancipation of Goodman later that day. One would expect a parade for Jackson, and his delegates, considering that they freed an American from imprisonment in a hostile country, perhaps saving his life. "The first media question was, 'who paid your hotel bill?'" Jackson remembers. The coverage did not improve, as most journalists fell into one of two categories: those who believed that Jackson "got lucky" and those who advanced the cynical interpretation that Jackson and Assad collaborated in hopes of humiliating President Ronald Reagan. To Reagan's credit, he offered the cursory gratitude of inviting Jackson to the White House to participate in the press conference alongside Goodman. Jackson recalls two conversations in the mansion of American power, both of which present a stark contrast between the possibilities of American foreign policy and its militaristic reality. "One of Reagan's State Department staffers asked me, just baffled, 'What did you do? How did you get him out?'" Jackson told me with a smirk, "I said, 'I tried.'"

The more significant discussion would occur with the president himself. "Reagan said, 'Is there anything I can do for you?'" Jesse Jackson, a vociferous critic of Reagan's policies and rhetoric, sat in the unique position of having a presidential genie grant him a wish. "I could have asked for an appointment, or a grant," Jackson said, "But all I said was, 'Call Assad personally and thank him.'" It was a tall order, considering that Reagan had established a reputation through obstinacy. Jackson was asking for nothing less than a reversal of an official, "no talk" policy. "So, he called," Jackson said, "They talked. They never stopped talking." The creation of a dialogue led to Reagan's eventual withdrawal of American forces from Lebanon, and ended the threats of military action against Syria. The United States and Syria did not become allies, and tensions remain to this day, especially as Assad's son, the current president of Syria, demonstrates a ruthlessness that would have made even his father blush. Jackson's successful negotiation, however, demonstrated the rewards of thoughtful and humble diplomacy as a substitute for arrogance and aggression. One could imagine the dramatic transformation in America's relationship with adversarial powers if it were to follow Jackson's model, rather than exercising its own self-serving agenda, even when it risks widespread death and destruction.

The inconsistencies of American rationale for its harmful foreign policy decisions expose the public utterances of its leading officials as little more than transparently false bromides. Ever since the Cuban revolution of 1959, the United States has treated its neighbor off the coast of Florida as an official enemy, even attempting the assassination of its late leader, Fidel Castro, and launching the disastrous "Bay of Pigs" invasion during the Kennedy administration. The Cuban government was aligned with the Soviet Union, and in adherence to Cold War interests, the United States enforced an embargo against the small country. Trade, American investment in Cuba, and even the travel of private citizens to Cuba, were all illegal. Critics explained that embargoes tend to only isolate the regime of the embargoed nation, strengthening the leader, and allowing for the demonization of the country enforcing the embargo. Despite its proven failures, American officials justified the economic assault on Cuba with denunciations of the Cuban human rights record. The Castro regime often imprisoned political activists and religious leaders, failing to honor elementary free speech and free religion principles. Castro's crimes against humanity, as contemptible as they were, resemble traffic violations in comparison to the torturous oppression committed by many American allies. The Shah of Iran, who owed his reign of power to CIA support, systemized the torment and murder of dissidents. A US-led coup in Chile installed Augusto Pinochet, one of the worst human rights offenders of the twentieth century, and to this day, the United States continues to coddle Saudi Arabia, a country that decapitates gays, adulterers, and "apostates." When Jesse Jackson announced in 1983 that he would lead a diplomatic effort in Cuba, leading figures of the Reagan administration, members of Congress, and op-ed writers for America's most influential newspapers, denounced Jackson as providing aid and comfort to an enemy of the United States. It is impossible to ignore the implications that, on the latter point, American journalists were mostly mute when their own government not only had conversations with totalitarian dictators who abused their own citizens but also gave them the funding, weaponry, and diplomatic protection that made the abuse possible. The contradictions, tautologies, and hypocrisies of American foreign policy would only become more manifest after Jackson's mission to Cuba.

The first success of Jackson's meeting with Fidel Castro was that the Cuban leadership agreed, if the United States was amendable, to negotiations on issues of immigration, trade, and cooperation on hemispheric crises. Secretary of State George Schultz countered that without visible evidence of progress on human rights, the United States would not directly communicate with the Cuban government. Unlike Schultz and Reagan, Jackson was not merely bloviating, but actually acting to secure the freedom of unjustly imprisoned Americans and Cubans.[10]

While touring Cuba, Jackson met with several pastors who reported the threats and persecution they endured as Christians in their country. Later that evening, Jackson had a long dialogue with Castro, and asked him, "What do you have against the church?" Castro explained that as a young man he cherished and honored the Christian principles of helping the poor, and judging men by how they treat the "least of these," but took an adversarial position against the church when they opposed the Cuban revolution and had expressed full loyalty to the corrupt Batista regime, effectively helping him transform the country into a corrupt and exploitative playground for the rich. Castro requested that Jackson speak at the University of Havana, and Jackson said he would do so only if Castro met two conditions. First, he had to release twenty-six political prisoners, most of whom were there for practicing their faith. For example, Thomas White, a Los Angeles school teacher, had been in a Cuban prison for months before Jackson's visit because Cuban authorities caught him distributing evangelical leaflets throughout the country. Jackson's second stipulation for agreeing to appear with Castro at the university was that he attend a church service with him.

After much argument, Jackson persuaded Castro and, in doing so, guaranteed the freedom of twenty-six wrongly persecuted American prisoners, along with twenty-two Cubans imprisoned for the exercise of religion. He also escorted Castro to his first church service in twenty-seven years. Shortly after Jackson's departure from Cuba, Castro slowly began a process of granting religious liberty, allowing religious practice in prisons, and eventually hosting Pope John Paul II in 1998. Historian James A. Baer, author of *A Social History of Cuba's Protestants*, praises the Jackson visit and negotiation with Castro as the moment, "Cuba began to move from confrontation toward cooperation with religious organizations."[11]

"It was a big moment," Jackson remembered in our conversation, "As we moved into the church, there were several ministers there, and they just stared, abruptly stopping the service. They didn't know what to think. I had to tell Castro to take his hat off and put his cigar away. He laughed. Everyone stood and applauded. Castro made remarks from the podium; the first time he set foot in a church in 27 years." One of the ministers in attendance that day said that he has never forgotten that moment—"We knew we were witnessing history."[12] Five months later, Castro hosted the first of what would be many meetings with the World Council of Churches to discuss the restoration of religious liberty and equality in Cuba. Six years after that meeting, Castro lifted the prohibition on religious officials serving in government positions. "We brought tremendous religious relief to the people there," Jackson said.

One might also characterize it as visible evidence that Cuba was making progress, and was flexible for further progress, on human rights and civil liberties. Schultz dismissed the release of religious prisoners, and Castro's attendance of a church service, as a "propaganda ploy." Most of the press was equally neglectful in its coverage, so much so that Jackson's Cuban mission is all but forgotten. A reporter asked President Reagan if he would meet with Jackson to discuss the successful negotiation of religious captives, and perhaps look for opportunities to accelerate Cuban liberalization. He replied, "I don't have time." The State Department's coordinator for Cuban Affairs would eventually, and begrudgingly, admit that Jackson's visit "unlocked the door for future negotiations."[13]

Before arriving in Cuba, Jackson also met with the leadership of Panama, Nicaragua, and El Salvador—all countries where the United States was supporting violence against socialist insurgents; support that extended to the training of Latin American death squads at the "School of Americas" at the Fort Benning Army Base in Georgia. The campaign against Nicaragua, which included the bombing of airports, shopping centers, and other "soft" civilian targets, would later provoke official condemnation from the World Court. Jackson, following his diplomatic visits, released an official campaign statement: "The Democratic Party must reverse the militarization of our foreign policy and establish the clear priority of human rights and development over intervention, the sale of weapons and other forms of military assistance. This must be our guiding principle toward the Third World and other nations alike."[14]

The international sensibility and disposition of Jackson, and the efficacy of his citizen diplomacy, challenged the illogical and inhumane ideology of the American Empire, exposing its machinery of death as adversarial to the ideals it purports to serve. Syria and Cuba, according to its depiction from American leadership, were maniacal enemies who would respond only to lethal force. Jackson proved otherwise. The peace story that he managed to tell would again enter into a sonic duel with a war story when the United States mobilized forces for its first invasion of Iraq.

In 1990, Saddam Hussein, the ghoulishly violent and tyrannical dictator of Iraq, and former ally of the United States, invaded Kuwait in an effort to seize their oil fields. The immediate response of the Bush administration and the US government was to threaten war, with Bush himself aptly warning Hussein that "this aggression will not stand."[15] The American press, with visible excitement, began to declare that a successful use of military force in Iraq might allow America to get beyond what commentators called "Vietnam syndrome"—the lingering sense of defeat and despair that the Vietnam War ended in embarrassment for the United States.[16] It is, perhaps, worth noting that America dropped more bombs on Vietnam than it did in the entirety of the Second World War, and that its forces were responsible for the death of millions of civilians. Birth defects remain prevalent, decades following the end of the war, due to American use of deadly chemicals against Vietnamese ecology, such as Agent Orange and Napalm.[17] The press omitted these facts from its evaluation of the influence of the war on the American psyche. Jesse Jackson, however, accurately measured the stakes of war. He opposed the war in Vietnam, rebuked American military efforts in Central America throughout the 1980s, and personally helped to prevent war in Syria. Because it was impossible to formulate a defense of Hussein's crimes against Kuwait, Jackson joined many leftists in articulating a position favorable to defensive action against Iraq, but cautious regarding military intervention. Only after diplomacy fails, and only with a multilateral coalition of nations, should America use force to liberate Kuwait from occupation.

"Saddam Hussein was holding many foreign nationals—47 Americans—and he promised to use them as human shields," Jackson recalled in our discussion on his international work, "He thought it would scare America off the war if he could convince them that Americans would die first in the bombings. So, he planned to place them at military target sites." There was a particularly chilling image Hussein sent out to the press to illustrate his threat. The dictator sat next to a nine-year-old British boy, whose family worked in the Kuwaiti oil industry before Hussein's forces captured them, stroked his hair, and feigned interest in a conversation. The underlying message of murder was inescapable.

Jackson believed that his citizen diplomacy would again prove effective with Saddam Hussein. "I had acquired the reputation as a transparent, honest negotiator—promising nothing, no money, no deals—but getting results," Jackson said. He also remembered that as he was considering a mission to Iraq, he spoke at a union hall in Washington DC, and six white janitors cleaning the building outside the room where he gave his lecture pulled him aside to say, "You got to go over there to clean up that shit. You got to get them hostages." The Bush administration, like its predecessor, opposed Jackson making any independent attempt at negotiation. Jackson chose to listen to the janitors rather than the president.

After arriving in Iraq, Jackson met several times with the Iraqi ambassador to the United States. He was buoyed by their conversations, as the ambassador seemed eager to cooperate and optimistic about their mutual mission to avoid war. Freeing captives and liberating hostages would undoubtedly send a signal to the world, particularly the Bush administration, that despite Hussein's merciless propensity for evil, he was a rational actor who could appreciate his own interests. He did prove the steeliest of Jackson's sparring opponents, however. When they finally did meet, Hussein constantly reiterated that the Bush administration was unreasonably hostile, and that the human shields, though he did not call them that, were his only protection against war. Jackson explained that the annexation of Kuwait had "even his allies scared," and that war was inevitable as long as he remained obstinate, and especially as long as he displayed ice-cold disregard for human life. By posing with a British child, under the aura of threat, Hussein was confirming every characterization of him crucial to the American war effort. Jackson also insisted that if Hussein wanted global attention, he could seize the moment by making a "big decision." When the Iraqi dictator countered with his list of grievances against the United States and the United Nations, Jackson returned to his assertion that no one would consider his complaints if he continued to threaten and annihilate innocent life. The meetings lasted, intermittently, for several days, with Jackson feeling increasingly defeated at the end of each conversation, retreating to his hotel room to listen to Ray Charles, and read a book on liberation theology.

Then, one morning—seemingly out of nowhere—after Hussein said goodbye to Jackson, he asked, "Would you like to take the women, children, and wounded men with you?" Hussein's humane conciliation came as such a shock that Jackson was rendered the rarest of all things for him—speechless. One of his staff answered "yes" on his behalf, but Hussein wanted to hear it from Jackson, and repeated his question. With emphatic delivery, Jackson said, "Yes, we do." Hussein offered the foreign nationals staying in Iraq, but Jackson was not satisfied. "And also Kuwait," he said. After giving a perfunctory explanation that Jackson was "asking for a lot," he agreed. Forty-seven Americans and an even larger group of other citizens were freed to return to their homes. As they were waiting on the tarmac, ready to fly to Europe, Jackson delayed. Someone had given him a tip that there was an American woman of Arab descent held captive in room 306 of their hotel. Rushing up to the room, Jackson and his staff found two Iraqi military agents outside the door. He requested to see the woman, and found a frightened figure, her face gone blank and pale in horror and trauma. "Let her go," Jackson said to the agents. He repeated himself multiple times in a soft whisper almost as if he was attempting hypnosis until, finally, to the amazement of all those in the room, they allowed her to leave.

When Jackson boarded the plane in Iraq, one white woman shouted at him—not in gratitude or hospitality, but with a venomous screed straight out of right-wing radio. "What are you doing here?" Jackson remembers her saying, "There must be a camera around." Having grown accustomed to regular ration of insult, but never in similar circumstances, Jackson told me that the words stunned him: "I said, 'Ma'am, I just negotiated your freedom.' She said, 'No you didn't. Saddam let us loose.'" Marshall Frady, a journalist with the *New Yorker* who would eventually write a biography of Jackson, intervened, identifying himself and explaining that it was indeed Jackson who convinced Hussein to let her return home. She said nothing. "I feel bad for her," Jackson told me when I asked how he reflects on her attitude, "Her racism was so entrenched that she could not feel joy in that moment."[18]

Jackson connected the hostility from that woman on the plane to a more recent experience he had when visiting his dying mother in a Greenville, South Carolina hospital. A white woman, eyes swollen with tears, ran up to him in a state of panic. "Please pray for my father," she pleaded. Jackson offered to go into the hospital room where her father lay unconscious fighting for each breath. "No, I don't want you in our room," she replied. Jackson assured her that he would say a prayer for her father, and after she thanked him, she asked why he was at the hospital. He informed her of the condition of his mother, and she expressed her condolences. "She was basically a nice lady," Jackson told me, "She was fearful for her father, and she was sympathetic to my mother and me, but she was conflicted. She wanted a blessing but did not want the source."

The desire for a blessing but rejection of the source is exactly the incoherence that defines the American establishment's reception of Jesse Jackson, and its consideration of peace. Of course, the press celebrated the preservation of life when Jackson returned after yet another successful overseas mission, but with even greater bellicosity and scorn than after Cuba, they attempted to act as if Jackson had nothing to do with it. The *New York Times* denounced Jackson for "grandstanding in Iraq," a large circulation Florida newspaper announced that Jackson was "becoming a joke," and Joe Klein, a veteran *Time* reporter who up until recently received treatment from cable news as a secular god, mocked Jackson on air to his face for meeting with Saddam Hussein. "Louis Farrakhan was there, Ramsey Clark was there," Klein said before asking in reference to the scandalous televangelist couple, "What's to stop Jim and Tammy Faye Bakker from going there if they want a little press?" Jackson answered, "Nothing except courage and conviction."[19] Klein, like many of his colleagues in the media priesthood, neglected to mention that, unlike Farrakhan, Clark, and the hypothetical Bakker delegation, Jackson actually saved people's lives. One of the few journalists to express appreciation for Jackson was the legendary Studs Terkel, who asserted to his radio audience that the civil rights leader was "probably the only American who could do this," in reference to negotiating the release of prisoners and hostages from Saddam Hussein.

The Bush administration, far from praising Jackson, implied that Hussein manipulated Jackson for his own agenda. "A reporter asked me how I respond to the idea that I was used," Jackson later told me, "Notice it was that I was 'used,' not that I was thinking. Anyway, I said, 'Anytime someone wants to use me to save innocent people, I'll be used.'" Stuart Lockwood, the British child who Hussein harassed, was much clearer in his assessment of the story, writing in 2015, "The civil rights activist Rev. Jesse Jackson fought for our freedom, and we were released early because of him."[20] Joe Wilson, then emissary to Iraq, broke with his government, and the dominant depiction of Jackson, to tell Frady that the civil rights leader did "great work."[21] Wilson would again break with the American establishment in 2002 when he went on record with testimony that, based on his experience, research, and official investigation of the claim, the George W. Bush administration was lying about Saddam Hussein's pursuit of weapons grade plutonium.

In the issuance of a commentary on his experience, Jackson told reporters upon returning home, "Hussein feels ignored . . . . He feels if we can talk to Gorbachev while they're in Afghanistan with missiles pointed at our country, he deserves to be talked with. We need a political solution, not war." The reaction of the Bush administration, Congress, and the media was the mirror image of Reagan's refusal to reevaluate any policy toward Cuba after Jackson's progress on issues of religious freedom with Castro. President Bush, like his predecessor, proceeded to beat plowshares into swords as if Jackson's mission never happened. Jackson's contradiction of the US war story with a peace story was inconvenient. When America is attempting to sell the public on war, or an aggressive posture toward an adversary, the last thing it wants is someone with international fame undermining their most foundational claims.

For decades, the American government articulated and acted on a bipartisan consensus that Fidel Castro's disregard for human rights was so impenetrable that any form of communication or negotiation was tantamount to national masochism. Jesse Jackson proved otherwise merely by "trying." The United States made no attempt to meet with Castro, not even to encourage and accelerate his concessions on human rights. As the country prepared for war with Iraq, leading officials and analysts argued that Hussein's record of murder and torture, which was indeed gruesome, demonstrated that violence is the only language that could possibly persuade him to retreat from annexation of Kuwait or make any other compromises. Jesse Jackson proved otherwise, and yet the United States went to war without even trying to explore other options. American forces removed the Iraqi military from Kuwait—a laudable outcome—but never once did anyone pause to consider if the same end was achievable without large-scale loss of life, injury, and ecological destruction.

Norman Solomon, a journalist and founder of the Institute for Public Accuracy, writes in his seminal book *War Made Easy* that, from the Vietnam War to the second invasion of Iraq, "Officials have explained and justified military operations to the American people by withholding crucial information about the actual reasons, and potential costs, of military action; again and again, choosing to present an easier version of war's reality—a steady and remarkably consistent storyline designed not to inform, but to generate and maintain support and enthusiasm for war." Dialogue in the "remarkably consistent" script, according to Solomon's research, almost always includes well-tested and rehearsed lines about how "our leaders will do everything they can to avoid war" and that the despotic target of military intervention is a "modern-day Hitler." With steadfast media cooperation, the government also presents a binary choice: them or us. Anyone who expresses skepticism about the rationale for war, or argues for diplomatic overtures to the present incarnation of Adolf Hitler, has sided not with "us," but with "them."[22]

Jesse Jackson's success, not failure, made him a liability. If he failed, it is easy to imagine the press parading him as a living illustration of the errors of diplomacy, and the naivete of anti-war ideas. Because he succeeded in Syria, Cuba, and Iraq, demonstrating that American leaders were not doing everything they could to avoid war, and that America's enemies were not modern-day Hitler's, he was condemned. It was essential to scandalize Jackson, because he was showing that the real scandal was US foreign policy. In a culture that has become increasingly worshipful of the military, treating every single soldier and veteran as a "hero," there is no other explanation for the media's refusal to celebrate Jackson saving the lives of American service personnel, civilians, and foreign nationals.

"I'm on a boat talking to the Pope," Jesse Jackson once said to me. Slightly confused, I asked, "What Pope?" Jackson smiled, furrowed his brow, and said, "No, this is just a joke I'm telling." I nodded, and he continued, "We're talking and his little hat gets picked up in a gust of wind, and lands in the water. So, I grab a fishing rod, cast it, manage to hook the hat, and reel it in. The headline the next day is, 'Jackson Can't Swim.'"

Christopher Stone and Andrew Ramirez sat in a conference room in the back offices of Rainbow/PUSH in Chicago. Twenty years earlier they sat alone, in separate solitary cells, shrouded in darkness with little food or water, bleeding and feeling the pain slicing through their bodies from the beatings they suffered at the hands of the Yugoslav Army. Their fellow soldier, Steven Gonzales, sat on the filthy floor of another cell.

"After we were captured in Serbia, we were immediately beaten, and we spent thirty days in solitary confinement," Stone told me when I asked him to describe the unimaginable torment he experienced during his military service. Ramirez jumped into the conversation, picking up where his friend left off, "Out of nowhere, I was grabbed, and put in a room. I couldn't believe it when I saw Jesse Jackson sitting there." "He told us, 'your scars will be stars,'" Stone said before expressing astonishment that Jackson later succeeded in making them laugh. He also gave them letters from their parents. Before departing, Jackson said, "I'm not here just to lift your spirits. I'm here to get you out." Ramirez was skeptical—"It was no disrespect to Reverend Jackson. I knew he succeeded before, but I thought there was no way Milosevic was going to let us go. We were in the middle of a war." Two days later they were on their way home after Jackson had, once again, secured the release of Americans held hostage by a foreign dictator, in this case Slobodan Milosevic, the Serbian president who attempted to take control of the entire Yugoslav federation, even resorting to ethnic cleansing to prevent Bosnian and Croatian independence.[23]

Unlike in previous missions, the United States was already at war when Jackson led a delegation to negotiate for the freedom of captives. "The Clinton administration told us, 'we're not stopping the war,'" Jackson remembered in our conversation, "The first night we were there, the US bombed the hotel across the street." James Meeks, a Chicago minister who accompanied Jackson alongside Rod Blagojevich, who was a congressman at the time and would eventually become governor of Illinois, recalled, during a speech at Rainbow/PUSH, dialing Jackson on the phone in panic: "They just bombed the hotel across the street!" Jackson replied, "Aren't you glad it wasn't ours?"

The evening that Milosevic agreed to release the three soldiers, he bombed a nearby bridge. Jackson thought that he must have changed his mind, but the next morning they were all on a flight to Iceland, where Ramirez, Stone, and Gonzalez would undergo medical examinations and debriefing at a US military base. "We flew home to Chicago," Jackson remembers,

> And when we landed, there was no one at the airport but my wife and a few other people, one was an old, white man with bright, white hair, wrapped in an American flag, cheering us on. No press, though. The peace effort interfered with the war effort. Milosevic was humane, and that conflicted with the narrative they had put out there. There was resentment about us getting them out.

Ramirez and Stone were at PUSH for the twentieth anniversary of their release. They offered gratitude for Jackson's work, and told the press that they owe their lives to him. As Stone told his story, his wife fought back tears. Stone retired from the military in 2015, and graduated from law school in 2019. Ramirez has spent most of the last twenty years as a high school teacher. They are both fathers.

In 2012, Jackson traveled to Gambia, met with the Gambian president Yahya Jammeh for five hours, and negotiated the release of two Americans he was holding in prison for political activity, including the printing of pro-democracy T-shirts. He also convinced Jammeh to indefinitely halt dozens of executions of journalists and activists. "The press barely touched that," Jackson said. The Obama administration did not acknowledge Jackson's Gambian mission.[24]

Five years later, I was sitting in Jackson's office when his phone rang. He thanked a woman for her letter. "It was one of the most wonderful gifts I've received in my life," he told her. On the other end of the line was the author of the letter, Isabella Alexander, an anthropology professor and documentary filmmaker, who was taken prisoner while recording material for a report on human rights violations in Algeria. Alexander's mother made appeals to the US government to rescue her daughter. She never received a reply other than bureaucratic nonsense about the complexities of international relations, and transparently phony assurances about "doing everything they can." With vivid memories of Jackson's work in Syria, Cuba, Iraq, and Yugoslavia, she then shared her story with a board member of Rainbow/PUSH, pleading for Jackson's intercession.

"Her mother said, 'My baby's in jail in Algeria. Will you help?'" Jackson explained, "I said, 'Of course we'll help.'" He met with the Algerian ambassador to the United States in Washington DC, spoke on the phone several times with members of the Algerian government, and began making preparations for travel: "But then we found out that baby got free," Jackson said. Alexander answered "not good" with nervous laughter when a reporter asked her to describe her experience. Held under the charge of foreign espionage, Algerian authorities informed Alexander that she would face a sentence of five years in prison. Because of Jackson's intervention, she spent only ten days in prison. The Trump administration did not acknowledge Jackson's Algerian mission. Neither the *New York Times*, the *Washington Post*, the *Chicago Tribune*, MSNBC, CNN, or Fox News ran a report on the story. Aldous Huxley once said, "It is often more powerful to leave things out than it is to tell lies."[25]

Jesse Jackson offered the following analysis to one of the few reporters who did bother to cover the release of Alexander:

> Whenever we've gotten Americans out of captivity, whether it was in Syria, Cuba, Iraq, or Yugoslavia, it was with countries we were not on good terms with. They had earnest desires to relate to us for reasons of their own, but for reasons of our own, we decided to push them aside. Invariably, it took the courage to say, "let me talk to you." We look for our shared interest. Our interest is you have an American who is innocent, and it is not in your interest to hold her. It is also inhumane. Whenever a prisoner is set free, there is a window of opportunity for dialogue. What we find out when we go to these countries is 1) There is a no talk policy from the United States, 2) We underestimate the influence of the religious leadership in those countries, 3) There is abounding poverty, 4) There is a sense of resentment over non-communication with us, and 5) They really want to be pro-America, because it is in their interest, but they have their own internal politics. The peace mission is to bring down walls, and build bridges of communication. Most wars start when communication stops.

One cannot help but wonder where the people Jackson freed, with just a few conversations, and in the case of Isabella Alexander, a series of phone calls that the US government, with its $700 billion defense budget, was unwilling to make, would live right now if it were not for his simple, but courageous willingness to talk. It is safe to assume that many would live in jail cells, forever alienated from their families, their potential snuffed out like a cigarette on a curbside. A few others, no doubt, would live in the cemetery.

When Jackson and Alexander first met, she gave him a hug and said, "You saved me." Jackson answered back, "No, you saved me."[26]

The first time I saw Jesse Jackson speak was on September 24, 2005, in Washington DC. Several of my college classmates and I traveled from Joliet, Illinois, to participate in an international anti-war march. About 150,000 people filled the streets of the capital on a sun-soaked Saturday afternoon. Of every pigment and persuasion, those of us demanding peace included elderly veterans of the Second World War, health-care workers from Alabama, nuns marching in their habits, and anarchists hiding their faces with black bandanas. Banners advertised ideologies as divergent as "Communists for Peace" and "Republicans Against War." The sign I carried had the words, "Justice for New Orleans! Justice for Iraq!"

Only a month earlier, Hurricane Katrina had summoned all the power of the earth to batter, blow down, and drown the Gulf Coast of the United States. By the time the monstrous storm had reached New Orleans, it had lost a little of its muscle, moving down from a category five classification to category three. Mother Nature's mercy could not spare the Crescent City from the folly of man. Because the federal government ignored decades of warnings regarding the fragile condition of the levees of Louisiana, the rapid surge of Katrina's waters broke through them, flooding the streets, and destroying countless homes, businesses, and public buildings. In a cruel episode of cosmic irony, Fats Domino, an early innovator of rock and roll who made "Walking to New Orleans" an internationally renowned celebration of America's musical capital, was captured by cameras on the roof of his home, begging for assistance as the water rose higher and higher.

"National security begins in New Orleans," Jackson thundered from the podium at the rally preceding the march. He described the absurdity of a country spending hundreds of billions, annually, on "national defense," even creating a Department of Homeland Security, and failing to protect one of its greatest cities from a hurricane of average strength that announced its arrival weeks in advance. "The gulf states are a metaphor for the gulf war," Jackson said, "The gulf policy at home has failed, and the gulf policy abroad has failed." Jackson would later announce, with characteristic rhetorical flare, "We cannot afford to have guided missiles with misguided leadership."[27]

When Jackson ran for president in the 1980s, he proposed reducing the so-called "defense" budget by 25 percent. His consistent anti-war message earned him Ron Kovic's support as an official delegate to the 1988 convention. Kovic, a paralyzed Vietnam War veteran, is the author of one of the most powerful documents for peace in American letters, the memoir, *Born on the Fourth of July*. Democratic candidates for the presidency in 2016 and 2020 have adopted many of the "radical" positions Jackson advocated in the 1980s on domestic policy—socialized medicine, tuition-free universities, paid paternity leave, and subsidized child care—but not one has articulated an anti-Pentagon policy. One of the few remaining third rails in American party politics is anything associated with the military. Political expediency, as is often the case, collides against morality and economic reality. Progressives who blueprint the construction of a welfare state without the demolition of the garrison state fail to recognize the wisdom of Martin Luther King, who said, "A nation that continues year after year to spend more money on military defense than on programs of social uplift is approaching spiritual doom."[28] There are also practical considerations. Even a nation as wealthy as the United States must recognize its fiscal limits. When the federal budget allocates anywhere between 50 and 60 cents of every discretionary dollar, depending on the year, it will certainly struggle, even if there were to exist the political will, to find sufficient funds for public services, institutions, and infrastructure. Writing in 2017, Jackson condemned President Trump's "March Massacre budget" proposal, making the obvious connection that eludes most Democrats: "As long as the wealthy and military-industrial complex are protected, the rest of us are at risk."[29]

An international sensibility and orientation enables Jackson to delineate a kinship between the victims of American militarism at home and the casualties of war abroad. It also allows him to trace similar connections between movements of oppressed people within his country and in nations of every hemisphere. More than most American dissidents with a role in mainstream party politics, Jackson remains an international leader and speaker. With the maintenance of a travel schedule that would rival any rock and roll band, Jackson speaks to European, African, and South American audiences with almost the same regularity as he does to those in North America.

When the CIA was assisting the South African apartheid regime in the persecution of Nelson Mandela, Jackson condemned it, and was the first candidate in a presidential race to demand that his country support the apartheid resistance movements, and remove Mandela from the official "terrorist list." In 2015, Jackson was one of the few Americans to give a Mandela Day Speech at the United Nations. He discussed the vast gulf separating the "piety" surrounding Mandela, and the "policy" that will advance his legacy. If the world's wealthy nations have a true desire to honor Nelson Mandela, Jackson explained, it will restructure its institutions, like the World Bank and International Monetary Fund, to bring Africa out the basement of the economic architecture, aggressively address poverty, and take measures to reverse the escalation of extreme inequality.[30]

When a slavery museum opened in Guadeloupe in 2015, Jackson gave the keynote address at the opening ceremony. Elevating the profile of the descendants of slaves, Jackson offered an economic ecology in contrast to the prevalent praxis of materialism: "In the relationship between France and the islands, and in America, we are the creditors not the debtors. We must leverage our moral capital to work for a better world."[31]

The same year when the world was tap dancing on the edge of a nationalist nightmare, with Trump preparing to take the presidency in the United States and many racist movements making gains in Europe and Brazil, Jackson was sounding a warning siren. An international outlook, or as Jackson describes it, "seeing the world through a door, and not a keyhole," is an optical aid, providing the visual clarity necessary to understand global developments and crises that many provincial American pundits and politicians cannot comprehend.

As keynote speaker at a conference on Globalization and Human Rights at Kozminski University in Warsaw, Poland, Jesse Jackson sketched the resemblance between the civil rights movement and the Polish solidarity movement of the 1980s. He also drew on his own familiarity with Polish culture, making reference to the fact that, with the sole exception of Warsaw, Chicago has the largest number of Polish residents for any city in the world. Shortly before Jackson's arrival, Chicago's Polish neighborhoods and churches grieved the loss of Poland's political leadership in a plane crash. Jackson explained that when he grieved alongside them in Chicago, praying at interfaith services, he developed a "friendship of mourning," binding together in the universality of loss. "Solidarity," Jackson said, "as the Polish trade union movement taught us, is a private virtue and public policy."

Moving onto the undercurrents of xenophobia that would trouble the waters throughout 2016 and beyond, Jackson implored: "Right wing politicians in America, like political candidates throughout Europe, have grabbed the microphone to demonize and stigmatize immigrants desperately fleeing war and poverty. They are condemning the patient without addressing the disease." The "disease" according to Jackson's diagnosis is the structural inequities of global, corporate capitalism:

> Immigrants go where the grass is greener. If we want more stable borders, we must create a global economic order with a more equitable distribution of resources. Concentration of wealth in the hands of the haves leads to movement of the have nots. Mass exodus is a result of mass inequality. To address the migration, we must first address the exploitation.[32]

The stakes and risks of failing to confront the root causes of xenophobia and anti-immigrant paranoia are as severe as bomb craters, gunfire in a crowded room, and burning crosses. Jackson returned to Poland in 2017 to deliver remarks at Auschwitz at a commemorative memorial of the Nazi holocaust of Jewish, Roma, and Sinit people. Nationalism is the enemy of an international sensibility of solidarity. The last time it mutated into a global force of aggression and influence, cities became cemeteries, and genocide became an exercise of efficiency. After meeting with holocaust survivors for private and public conversations, Jackson declared to the gathering of scholars, activists, and victims of hate crimes at a conference in Krakow, "Your struggle is our struggle." "Unless we fight together for freedom and peace," Jackson said, "We will not get it. Nor will we deserve it."[33]

The international work of Jesse Jackson presents challenging questions to the American mainstream, and even elements of the American left. How can any movement expect to adequately address suffering and injustice at home without acknowledging suffering and injustice abroad, especially when a significant share of it is directly tied to American foreign policy? As the history of every global crisis or conflict indicates, the interdependence of the world demands vigilance of attention and action. The US wars in Iraq and Libya were largely responsible for the refugee outpouring, which in turn provoked xenophobic hostility among

Western populations. It was precisely that ethnic anxiety and resentment that right-wing leaders in Europe, and Donald Trump in America, manipulated to gain power. Fires burning thousands of miles away, if unextinguished, will eventually incinerate your house.

The international work of Jackson, in both its accomplishments and ambitions, telegraphs an alternative American foreign policy—one that Gore Vidal imagined when he told an interviewer that, due to Jackson's superior understanding of poverty and diplomacy, he would make an ideal secretary of state, assuming that the United States was actually interested in pursuing peace rather than enlarging its imperial presence. What would America's posture and position in the world look like if it actually adhered to its nominal principles of liberty and justice for all, human rights, and self-determination? Who has better represented these democratic principles of solidarity over the past five decades—Jesse Jackson or the rotating door of presidents, bureaucrats, military officers, and the so-called realists whose intervention overseas varies from election interference to "shock and awe" campaigns of lethal invasion? In the brandishing of itself as the "land of the free and home of the brave," who is likelier to receive a warm reception outside of America's borders—Henry Kissinger and Dick Cheney, both of whom cannot travel to certain countries for fear of war crimes prosecution—or Jesse Jackson? Kissinger, in an exhibition of absurdity, won the Nobel Peace Prize. If the prize means anything after such a dreadful misstep, Jackson is as qualified as anyone for it.

The American Council of Trustees and Alumni, a powerful and influential organization dedicated to curbing leftist activity on college campuses with founders that include former Senator Joe Liebermann and the late Saul Bellow, placed Jesse Jackson on its list of "anti-American" speakers in 2001 for telling an audience at Harvard University, in the aftermath of the 9/11 attacks, "America should build bridges and relationships, not bombs and walls."[34] That such an innocuous suggestion would earn Jackson aspersion—it also is a major point in K. R. Timmerman's slanderous hitjob, *Shakedown*—demonstrates the extent to which American patriotism, and even identity, is connected to militarism, dominance, and violence.

Morris Berman, a historian, cultural critic, and author of a trilogy on American decline, writes that there are "unconscious mythologies that govern American life," rendering most political debates more theatrical than substantive. One of the mythologies is that Americans are the "chosen people."[35] A bipartisan bevy of politicians—from Ronald Reagan to Barack Obama—ingratiate themselves to voters with ritualistic recitation of America as a "shining city on a hill," and projecting a foreign policy vision of America's mission to "export democracy" all around the world. Attendant to the myth of America's heavenly mandate is a "civil religion." "The real religion of the American people," Berman writes "is America itself."[36] Critics of American policies, like those on the McCarthyite list of the American Council of Trustees and Alumni, are "un-American" or "anti-American," because in the words of Richard Hofstadter, "It has been our fate as a nation not to have ideologies, but to be one."[37]

America, like Americanism, is an ideology, but it is one that leaves America without a secure identity. Berman also explains that Americans, for most of US history, have maintained only a negative identity; that is the identification of themselves by what they are not, and what they are aiming to defeat, rather than through positive traits and tenets. From the various tribes of America's indigenous people to Islamic fundamentalists in Afghanistan, America's "enemies" are not human beings capable of compromise, but Satanic maniacs who must die for America to preserve its own security.

Jesse Jackson, an ordained Baptist minister, is an American apostate. Over a lifetime of advocacy for peace and, most significantly, his international work of citizen diplomacy, he has rejected America's civil religion, and challenged its unconscious mythologies, by projecting an American policy that places itself in a community of nations, seeking cooperation wherever possible, and using its military only for self-defense. It is for this reason that three of America's most powerful institutions—the federal government, the military, and the national media—never celebrated Jackson's successes, even as he saved hundreds of lives.

At the twentieth-anniversary tribute to Jackson and the three soldiers he rescued from Yugoslavia, James Meeks credited Andrew Ramirez and Chris Stone for appearing in person to offer their gratitude for Jackson. He then drew roaring applause when he said, "It is a shame and outrage that the United States has not done more to credit Jesse Jackson—to give him thanks for what he's done."

Moments later at the same podium, with Ramirez, Stone, their wives, and Meeks standing behind him, Jackson made a distinction between oxygen and carbon dioxide. "You inhale oxygen, and it gives you life. Carbon dioxide is merely the exhale." He closed his remarks by saying, "Those who do things only for thanks don't deserve it. I'd rather have the oxygen of grace than the carbon dioxide of thanks."

Chapter 8

THE SIGN OF DEMOCRACY

Conservative philosophers and economists often remind utopian thinkers of the veracity of the "tragic vision." The vantage point of tragedy in human affairs teaches all observers that even the most brilliant and well-intended people are inherently limited in their knowledge and virtue. Considering that all social arrangements and structures operate under human leadership, every system will inevitably produce some harmful results. Corruption, deception, and morally benign errors of judgment will cause significant suffering under the best of circumstances. The tragic vision's application to democracy is that even the most thoughtful, humane, and just set of public policies will create gaps of dislocation, and the people who slip into the cracks will need advocacy and aid.[1]

The United States is far from a perfect democracy. One might even question if it is a democracy at all. A 2014 study from the American Political Science Association lamented, "Multivariate analysis indicates that economic elites and organized groups representing business interests have substantial independent impacts on U.S. government policy, while average citizens and mass-based interest groups have little or no independent influence."[2] If the rich want a tax break, they are likely to get it, while poor people will die of treatable diseases, or work like dogs to barely feed themselves. In the present, the United States is in desperate need of political organization and mobilization toward an authentic social democracy. If it ever reaches that destination, it will still require robust activism and public interest work from networks independent of government. The Rainbow/PUSH Coalition is one of those networks. After Jesse Jackson's second presidential campaign, he merged the Rainbow Coalition, the political interest group of his candidacy, with PUSH, the organization he founded in the early 1970s to lobby for racial equality in the local and national economy. Rainbow/PUSH differs from the NAACP, Amnesty International, and the ACLU in ways worthy of scrutiny, but like those organizations, it functions according to the simultaneous missions of long-term policy reform and short-term crisis intervention. It seeks to alter the system, while also providing a haven for those currently suffering due to inequities within the system.

Yvonne Isom, a criminal justice professor at Arizona State University and researcher of racial and sexual biases within the legal system, once told me that she found Jackson's politics "too conciliatory," but that she will forever have respect and gratitude for his work due to the simple fact that "if a young black man or woman is being treated unfairly by the police or the courts, he'll be there." There are two interpretations of Jackson's multidecade ubiquity in America's ongoing struggle with racism. The first is that Jackson is a tireless fighter for justice who makes advantageous use of media savvy to spotlight incidents of cruelty and oppression in the United States. The second interpretation, which due to a relentless propaganda campaign has become quite popular, is that he is nothing more than a grandstander who lives to see his face on television and his name in newspaper ink. The right wing, reciting from the same script they used against Martin Luther King, first formulated this attack, but even some intellectuals on the left, who should know better, provide a thoughtless echo for slander. Cornel West qualified his largely complimentary appraisal of Jackson in 2015 with the tired trope, "He has an ontological addiction to the camera."[3] Anyone who watches cable news is undoubtedly aware that West rides the airwaves with much greater frequency than Jackson, but personal disputes aside, it is not only wrong, but indicative of an American pathology to reduce Jackson's life to celebrity.

At time of writing, he is seventy-eight years old with Parkinson's disease, and yet he continues to work seven days a week, jumping flights heading to places far and wide, from Silicon Valley to Sierra Leone, to amplify a message of inclusion, compassion, and peace. Anyone who has visited Jackson's offices in Chicago can attest that they are far from glamorous. Gary Younge, veteran journalist and essayist with the *Guardian*, likened PUSH headquarters to a "badly run student union."[4] Although his Ferdinand Magellan mileage ensures he will forever have enough frequent flyer miles to fly first class, his travel arrangements are modest. Meals on the road are at diners or Cracker Barrell restaurants off the highway, and breakfast is always Greek yogurt with raisins. Due to his advanced age, and that he spends most of every day on his feet, his choice of footwear is Nike, not Gucci. If Jackson truly has a love affair with the camera, as many people like to charge, he is a masochist. All objective studies of Jackson's relationship with the press prove that the overwhelming majority of his coverage in the 1970s and 1980s was suspicious or downright defamatory. For the past ten to fifteen years, the national media has mainly ignored his work. It is rare to see Jackson on cable news, either as a subject or as a commentator. And yet he continues working without a vacation, even as his doctors recommend a lighter schedule. The "in-it-for-the-camera" criticism is actually more damning for the accuser than the accused.

Alexis de Tocqueville wrote in 1831, "As one digs deeper in the national character of the Americans, one sees that they have sought the value of everything in this world only in the answer to this single question: how much money will it bring in?"[5] The historian Walter McDougall, taking a cue from de Tocqueville in more recent years, describes the United States as a "nation of hustlers."[6] Profit, fame, and personal advancement are the pillars of American life, and its prevailing ethos is almost inseparable from greed. When Oliver Stone wrote a line for his reptilian villain in the film *Wall Street*, expertly played by Michael Douglas, "greed is good," many filmgoers densely celebrated the philosophy it articulated. President Calvin Coolidge might have described the American way of life with the most succinct honesty when he declared, "The business of America is business."[7] In 2018, the amount of money spent on advertising in the United States totaled $151 billion,[8] and according to journalist and theorist Douglas Rushkoff, children as young as twelve have become masters of "building a brand" in their aspirations to become highly paid "influencers" on social media.[9] One almost has no choice but to collapse under the weight of irony when considering that a civil rights leader faces condemnation for promoting his work in a culture that has turned self-promotion into a lifelong commitment, corrupted friendship with insistence on "networking," and replaced the notion of citizenship with consumerism. Ridicule of Jackson's alleged "grandstanding" defines psychological projection, but it is effective with a cynical audience. A public obsessed with wealth, worshipful of the rich, and addicted to the dopamine rush of acknowledgment on Facebook and Twitter will have no difficulty believing that someone else's motives are selfish.

Aristotle explained that "politics" are matters relating to the "city," meaning the collective. To a far greater extent than the countries of Western Europe and other social democracies around the world, the United States has successively failed to develop a conception of the common good not subordinate to individual rights.[10] Because Americans often think in individualistic terms, and according to an individuated criteria of judgment, it is common in cultural discourse to obsess on matters private—motives, intentions, interpersonal relations, and crimes—than on those that are public—state policy, political procedure, and institutional functionality. It is counterproductive, but not confusing, that an abundance of conversations regarding Jesse Jackson make their focus that which is largely unascertainable—his private motives and ambition—rather than what is tangible and measurable—his public work, its origins, and its impact. It is also illustrative of a certain obtuseness that most of Jackson's critics fail to understand the need for media savvy in civil rights work. Speaking on that subject Al Sharpton explained,

> For all of this talk about the camera, no one who comes to us with a story wants us to keep it a secret. They want it to become national. When Trayvon Martin's parents came to me no one knew who they were. I didn't know who they were. They wanted me to turn it into a story. Why did Martin Luther King go to Birmingham? Because Bull Connor was the right sheriff. He was someone even many whites at the time would dislike. So, King knew how to use the media for the story he wanted to tell.

Jackson, in his own role as civil rights leader, is no different.

A typical day at the headquarters of Rainbow/PUSH on the Southside of Chicago is as inspiring as it is chaotic. If Jackson is in his office, he is often juggling local, national, and international missions. During the 2019 Chicago mayoral race, for example, Jackson was working the phones, organizing events, and conducting radio interviews to lobby for Lori Lightfoot, a civil rights attorney who would eventually win, becoming the city's first black woman mayor, and one of the nation's first gay mayors of a metropolis. The day before the election, Jackson hosted Lightfoot and her opponent, Tori Preckwinkle, the Cook County board president, at PUSH to sign a pledge in front of local media, pledging to collaborate to solve Chicago's problems, regardless of the electoral results. In the weeks preceding the election, Jackson traveled to Silicon Valley to meet with black tech workers and entrepreneurs struggling for fairness in the world's wealthiest industry, he hosted separate interfaith commemorations of Martin Luther King and Cesar Chavez, and he spoke at several rallies of solidarity with the Muslim victims of a hate crime massacre in New Zealand. Connecting the anti-Muslim hatred overseas with the same sentiment in the United States, he said,

> Something is amiss in our society. When Job lost his children, his friends, his prestige, he turned to God, and said, 'What shall I do?' We are now in a dark time—its real dark—and we ask, 'what shall we do?' We must turn to each other, and not on each other. We can find the power of love and hope. It is dark, but hold on for the morning cometh.[11]

PUSH attempts to move toward morning, but it is not only due to Jackson that it can succeed in civil rights activism. The fame and charm of Jackson have also made him the public face of PUSH, while in the same building devoted staff members complete the labor of democratic engagement and enhancement. Betty Magness, who was the Midwest director of Jackson's 1988 presidential campaign, works out of the office, coordinating projects with an Illinois women's voter registration effort, and an organization fighting for more sensible and humane firearm regulations. Janette Wilson, armed with a juris doctorate and PhD in religion, directs PUSH Excel, providing assistance to struggling schools and low-income students. John Adams, the chief financial officer for PUSH, is also something of an amateur historian, helping the organizers of the Saturday morning forum determine what events of significance to honor or discuss in the weekly itinerary. Jackson's two assistants—April Branch and Alanna Ford—are ideal ambassadors for visitors, greeting everyone with a smile, warm welcome, and offer to give the grand tour. Branch's mother was a PUSH staff member before her, and Ford works without pause, not only helping to manage Jackson's affairs but also handling the PUSH accounts on social media. All activities run through the discerning mind and hands of John Mitchell, Jackson's chief of staff. Having never made it to the White House, Jackson adopted the presidential method and moniker for his highest-ranking staff member. Every minute of Jackson's heavy, and often chaotic schedule happens according to Mitchell's planner. Nearly everyone in the office has an advanced degree and has undoubtedly made sacrifices of income and leisure to devote themselves to an organization with offices open six days a week.

Without Jackson's current and former staff members—not to mention the volunteers—PUSH would have never accomplished anything, no matter how sharp and strong its leadership. Around the world there are countless rank-and-file foot soldiers of civil and human rights advocacy, economic justice, environmental protection, and nonviolence who improve the living conditions of desperate people under the cloak of anonymity. Every organization committed to work that is worthy has an Alanna Ford or a Betty Magness, working without any glory aside from the satisfaction of knowing they have a purpose, and that they have made a contribution to a cause that is both necessary and noble. One of Walt Whitman's most famous poems is "I Hear America Singing." Whitman pays tribute to the daily exercises of mechanics, carpenters, boat makers, young mothers, and others whose harmonizing makes the music of a free society audible and, at times, beautiful. The staff of a civil rights organization, even as its leader receives most of the praise and prestige, also sings.

The difference between Rainbow/PUSH and the NAACP, the National Urban League, or the Equal Justice Initiative is not the quality of their respective service and advocacy, but that the leader of Rainbow/PUSH has subsumed the organization into his identity. The agency is inseparable from its founder, not only according to public perception but also in its daily operations, whereas the leadership of other civil rights organizations are borderline anonymous, certainly not household names, like Jesse Jackson. In the 1970s, a *Chicago Tribune* reporter, Barbara Reynolds, wrote a pugnacious book against Jackson, who at the time was a rising star, that has not aged well. A veteran of the civil rights movement herself, she proffered two contradictory criticisms of Jackson's work with Operation PUSH. First, she attacked Jackson's politics for lobbying the Illinois state government, in his hunger campaign, to increase social welfare transfer payments. Reynolds argued that the dole was undermining black initiative and potential, and what they desperately needed was not the monthly sustenance of governmental largesse, but suitable employment. Jackson's primary focus in the 1970s was economic integration and opportunity for black workers and entrepreneurs, but Reynolds dismissed his Breadbasket and PUSH victories by positing that, in the absence of hard data in the form of monthly or annual reports, it is impossible to determine whether or not corporate promises to hire, train, and promote more blacks were empty.[12] Journalistic investigations and academic studies have subsequently proven that most companies did follow through on their declarations, securing thousands of jobs for blacks in Chicago and elsewhere, and allowing black businesses to survive in a decade of slow economic growth. Despite her shortsightedness on the issues, Reynolds did make one judgment of PUSH, during a radio interview with the legendary Studs Terkel, that is truthful, both then and now: "PUSH is entirely dependent on Jesse Jackson—his imagination, his creativity, his personality. Without Jesse Jackson, there is no PUSH."[13]

PUSH has gone far, often navigating tempestuous waters, with Jackson at the helm. His imagination, creativity, and personality have overseen the creation and maintenance of one of the world's most recognizable civil rights organizations, but to have an institutional image that functions almost as a mirror for its leader presents problems of longevity and legacy. It is a challenge to imagine PUSH when Jesse Jackson is no longer capable of acting as its leader and public face. Jackson has appointed his son, Jonathan Jackson—an impressive entrepreneur and professor—as national spokesperson of the organization, giving him the responsibility of delivering the main address at the Saturday morning forum more often than not. Rainbow/PUSH has a talented vice president, Todd Yeary, who is a minister and adjunct professor with a law degree, but he lives and pastors a church in Baltimore, typically flying into Chicago for PUSH events on the weekends. Jonathan Jackson and Todd Yeary appear to have the skills, education, and passion necessary to lead PUSH, but the organization has thrived for decades due to its association with Jesse Jackson—not only on his leadership but on his connections as well. Donna Brazille has gone on record explaining that when she worked for PUSH, the day-to-day routine and transitions were nightmarish in their disorganization, rapid alterations, and fly-by-night management. "They were the best years of my life. He was my mentor and my teacher, but I would never do it again," Brazille said before painting a picture of the challenges that accompanied her joys, "He'll be in a television studio or on a radio show and he'll say we're going to march in Philadelphia or Boston, and we'd know nothing about it. When you work with the Reverend you have to be two days ahead of him and two days behind him all at once."[14]

My observations are that PUSH still operates with the same improvisational quality. Without developing an inheritable order or structure, the organization will become difficult to manage when someone else moves into the leadership role. The other concerns that arise when an organization and its director are indivisible relate to its democratic substance, and its inability to distinguish itself from the leader when the leader, fairly or unfairly, experiences a setback in the public eye.

In his contrarian rebuke of Jesse Jackson's 1984 presidential campaign, *The Jesse Jackson Phenomenon: The Crisis of Purpose in Afro-American Politics*, leftist political scientist, Adolph Reed, gave the following analysis:

> In the Afro-American context the antidemocratic character of the organic leadership style has been obscured by the primacy of external linkages to white elites. Protest leadership is beset by the contradiction that certification of its authenticity normally is attained outside the black community. Nevertheless, that leadership status rests on a premise of unmediated representation of a uniform racial totality, and this premise has fostered a model of political authority that is antidiscursive and deemphasizes popular accountability. As this model descends from the realm of interelite negotiation to popular politics, it discloses a hortatory and charismatic aspect which—in the absence of restraints imposed by electoral formalism or a self-propelling, goal-oriented political movement— tends naturally toward authoritarianism.[15]

"Authoritarian" is a charge many miles too far. Manning Marble, the late historian and African American Studies scholar at Columbia University, persuasively undressed Reed's more alarmist concerns in his review of *The Jesse Jackson Phenomenon*, especially those related to how Jesse Jackson, and other charismatic leaders, might compromise fundamental principles without the restraints of electoral formalism: "That highly instrumentalist, conspiratorial interpretation has little correlation with social reality. If black leaders were so prone to external manipulation, why have so many led social protest movements and demonstrations?"[16] Marble's rhetorical question stands unscathed, but Reed's critical analysis does provide an opportunity to consider the triumphs and failures of personality politics.

Charisma is a morally neutral but, as American history teaches, politically essential quality. Academic analysts will typically downplay, or outright dismiss, the importance of charisma in modern politics, but it is certainly not a coincidence that ever since television became the primary source of news and entertainment for the American public, every single presidential race, without exception, has gone to the candidate with the more colorful personality. In addition, every effective dissident leader has brandished charm and oratorical appeal to connect with a mass audience. Martin Luther King, Jackson's mentor and model of leadership, is a perfect example. For all of his brilliance, strategical savvy, and political imagination, it is difficult to imagine his message resonating with as many Americans—white or black—if he spoke with his eyes affixed to the podium in a dull monotone. Charisma is indispensable in any attempt to attract public attention, and to ingratiate one's self to an audience. Jesse Jackson relied upon his charisma for most of his career.

Ernest House, an education researcher, has analyzed Jackson's PUSH/Excel program at length, concluding that its early failures were due to "the intransigence of the public schools toward change, interference and mismanagement by the federal government, and recalcitrant racism," but when Jackson visited schools and spoke to students in the 1970s, as a pitchman for his program, he further enhanced his articulative style of engagement, developing a unique hybrid of progressive political advocacy, religious rhetoric, and motivational, self-help encouragement. House spotlights Jackson's soaring, and celebrated, address at the 1984 Democratic Convention as an apotheosis. As the largely white audience wept, with hands raised in the air as if they were at a tent revival, House writes that "Jackson had successfully extended his charisma."[17]

The extension of Jackson's charismatic jeremiad inspired many blacks and other minorities to enter politics, and instructed many whites that their narrow, self-serving, and stereotypical view of race in America was in desperate need of reform. It is a crux of American politics that the charismatic leader is important to any movement—not only for marketing but also for order, as the smoldering out of leaderless movements, like Occupy Wall Street, MeToo, and Black Lives Matters illustrates—but that it also, as Reed suggests, replicates the undemocratic structure that protest movements seek to demolish. Noam Chomsky was particularly harsh in his criticism of Jackson on the issue of democratic versus charismatic leadership. Speaking in the early 1990s, the legendary linguist and political philosopher said,

> Jackson was in a very strong position a couple of years ago with the Rainbow Coalition, and he had a choice. His choice was, "Am I going to use this opportunity to help create a continuing grassroots organization which will keep on working after the election, or am I going to use it as my own personal vehicle?" He more or less chose the latter.[18]

Chomsky's analysis is uncharacteristically reductionist and uninformed—the civil rights, voter registration, labor union mediation, international peace mission, and criminal justice reform work of PUSH throughout the 1990s and 2000s is sufficient evidence to show that Jackson did not create a mere "personal vehicle." But there is a grain of truth to Chomsky's criticism, no matter how strident. While the Rainbow/PUSH Coalition, Jackson's civil rights organization, remains involved in important and efficacious work, and while its staff is full of intelligent, committed, and courageous activists, it is entirely dependent on Jackson's leadership, and even celebrity, for survival. A consequence of the current arrangement, as Donna Brazille suggests even in her praise for Jackson, is that it is often subject to his whims, desires, and priorities. Fortunately, his focus is consistent. It isn't as if Rainbow/PUSH interrupts its aggressive civil rights, anti-war, and economic justice work to adopt conservative positions or argue for regressive causes, but with a single person as its sole representation, it is inevitable that the organization will experience moments of distraction or compromise.

Jesse Jackson's relationship with Bill Clinton is fascinating, and seemingly complex and contradictory beyond anyone's understanding other than Jackson and Clinton. In my own conversations with the civil rights leader, Jackson has oscillated between criticizing and praising the Clinton presidency. His own decision to abstain from challenging Clinton from the left in the Democratic primary of 1996 enabled him to maintain access to the mainstream, work with Clinton toward progressive policy ends during his second term, and protect the networking advantage to PUSH and other civil rights organizations that comes with having a Democrat in the White House. The unglamorous politics of networking are real in their effects, and those that summarily dismiss them reveal that they prefer to live in a fantasy world.

It is credible to argue, all the same, that Jackson undermined some of his own moral authority by becoming too close with a Democratic administration that even he knew was failing to enact sufficiently progressive policies. Many of the crises currently troubling American life began in the 1980s and 1990s. Jackson had succeeded in pushing the Democratic Party to the left during the Reagan years, acting as a political valet to leftist whites, progressive blacks, Latinos, gays, Arabs, and Asians. The Clinton victory was largely the result of the mobilization of previously disaffected and alienated voters Jackson inspired and engineered ten years earlier. It is speculative, but one can easily imagine that had Jackson presented a more forthright and full-throated challenge to Clinton's centrist conciliation, the Democratic Party would have emerged as a more progressive force, and rather than always fighting for beneficial but inadequate reforms, such as the Affordable Care Act under Obama, won victories for the authentic social democracy in which Jackson has always believed.

Jackson demonstrated independence and prescience in his criticism of the Clinton administration for their approval of the "welfare to work" policy and 1994 crime bill, which included draconian measures, such as the three strikes provision, which created the conditions for the mass incarceration of poor and, disproportionally, black men. Finding and facilitating opportunities for cooperation with a moderate president is sensible, and seems to fall within the bounds of dissent and democratic engagement of an organization like PUSH. More worrisome than working with powerful and influential Democrats, however, is perhaps a cozy relationship with one of the most regressive forces in the United States—multinational corporations.

The United Autoworkers labor union was one of the largest donors to Jackson's efforts of economic integration, with Operation Breadbasket and, subsequently, the earliest incarnation of PUSH. It was one of the few large trade unions with black leadership, and those leaders, for obvious reasons, were sympathetic with Jackson's ambition to end the unofficial Jim Crow policies of hiring discrimination and contract bias in America's economic procedure. The autoworkers-PUSH collaboration enabled Jackson, as unlikely as it seemed for a young civil rights leader, to gain an audience with the most powerful automotive industry executives. His relationship with car and truck manufacturers remains close into the present. An annual PUSH conference takes place in Detroit to review the progress of diversification within the field, issuing reports to determine how many dealerships are under black control and in black neighborhoods. PUSH also interrogates the industry with the following line of inquiry: Do those dealerships receive the same corporate support and consumer promotion as those in white sections of town? Does the board of directors represent the diversity of its customers, and do the union officers resemble the demographic variety of its workers?

These are important issues worthy of scrutiny and advocacy. Given the extreme record of racism in America, on all matters economic and political, it is not difficult to imagine how a major industry would treat nonwhite stakeholders without the vigilance of civil rights organizations, like PUSH and others, keeping it within the borderlines of fairness and equality. One of the most profound insights of Karl Marx's dissection of capitalism is how the so-called revolutions of economy are merely changes in costume for the exploitative class. The shift from agriculture to industry, like the later transition from the manufacturing to digital economy, did nothing to unsettle or upend the radically unjust distribution of wealth in which workers battle for the capital coming out of a leaky faucet, while owners navigate an ocean of profit. Similarly, Jackson's undressing of Silicon Valley's hiring practices illustrates that racism recycles through America's various business transformations.

Eulonda Skyles, the first black attorney with Yahoo, remembers Jackson's debut as a watchdog and advocate in Silicon Valley with gratitude. "I remember when there were just a few of us out here all alone," Skyles told me in conversation, "We didn't have anyone looking out for us until Jesse came along." It is important for any political movement, most especially a progressive movement most concerned with human suffering, to not become so theoretical that its idealism acts as a freezing agent. The insistence on a form of purity that would preclude Jackson from dirtying his hands in the corporate mud would, if taken to its logical and inevitable conclusion, leave attorneys like Skyles, many more faceless autoworkers, and low-level employees desperately reaching out in the dark for a rung to climb into the middle class, "out there all alone." It is important, all the same, to consider how multinational corporations—as they pollute the air and poison the seas, while often mistreating their employees —might manipulate PUSH's advocacy for their own benefit.

One cannot help but notice that many Rainbow/PUSH services and events have a corporate sponsor. Toyota and PUSH have aligned to create a scholarship fund for black students aspiring to become engineers, Intel helped to supply the equipment in the Rainbow/PUSH tech center for children, and McDonald's has often provided financial assistance for the national Rainbow/PUSH conventions. None of these connections are nefarious, or even suspicious. The notion of "corporate social responsibility" was long prevalent in American culture before the maximization of profit mindset, attendant to the free market fundamentalism of Ayn Rand and Ronald Reagan, became dominant. Collaboration between Rainbow/PUSH and multinational corporations does present a dichotomy, however, between short-term benefits for underserved people in need, and long-term consequences of ideology. In a revealing report on the "strategic philanthropy" of corporate foundations, *Harvard Business Review* concludes, "Philanthropy is used as a form of public relations or advertising, promoting a company's image or brand through cause-related marketing or other high-profile sponsorships."[19]

Propaganda aimed at influencing public opinion, through the form of televised charity, is one tentacle of the corporate octopus, with a reach that also courts political favor. A group of economists published a study with the National Bureau of Economic Research explaining that "grants given to charitable organizations located in a congressional district increase when its representative obtains seats on committees that are of policy relevance to the firm associated with the foundation."[20] It does not require the cynical heart of conspiracy theorist to wonder if corporate cooperation with the Rainbow/PUSH Coalition is a tactical maneuver to manipulate public perception, most especially among its most prominent critics—black progressives. It is as if they might announce, "Don't worry about what you read about our contributions to climate change and the liquidation of the middle class. We support scholarships for poor children." Slavoj Zizek, the radical social theorist, has obliterated the rationale for corporate foundations with the argument that they "repair with one hand what they destroy with the other."[21]

Unlike Zizek, Jackson is not a Marxist. He is a proponent of what Western European analysts describe as a "social democracy"—a policy agenda and orientation that aspires to promote social justice within the confines of liberal democracy and a mixed economy. During one of our conversations on contemporary politics, Jackson said that he found it unwise for Bernie Sanders, whom he admires and endorsed in the 2020 Democratic primary, to showcase an "obsession with the word 'socialism.'" "He is right," Jackson said, "But there is too great a history of negative connotations with that word (in the United States). That is why FDR called it 'New Deal' and 'Economic Bill of Rights' and Lyndon Johnson called it 'Great Society.' You can play their game with language without playing games with your principles." Under Jackson's policy umbrella, there is room for large corporations, and a role for "corporate social responsibility." As nearly every other wealthy, Western country demonstrates, big business and social welfare policies, like socialized medicine and robust paid family leave, can peacefully coexist. Even still there exist points of collision where the impact threatens nothing less urgent than life on the planet.

Neil Young, the rock and roll legend who is also an avowed environmentalist and cofounder of Farm Aid, artistically expressed his disappointment with the American right and the left in his scorching anthem, "Rockin' In the Free World." The propulsive and pyrotechnic rock energy of Young's guitar-driven articulation of rage breaks down into the bridge, with Young singing:

We've got a thousand points of light
For the homeless man

. . .

Got a man of the people, says, "Keep hope alive"
Got fuel to burn, got roads to drive

The "man of the people" is Jesse Jackson, whose speech-closing slogan, "Keep hope alive," is coupled with "thousand points of light," the phrase that then president George H. W. Bush often repeated to sell volunteerism as an alternative to social welfare policies. Bush also claimed that he wanted to construct a "kinder, gentler nation," while doing nothing to combat police brutality or inequities within the justice system. Jackson, having acquired a reputation for successfully negotiating labor dispute settlements and diversification program funding with the major auto companies, appears disinterested, according to Young's protest anthem, in the environmental damage of the combustible engine, suburban sprawl, and the increase of air pollution as a consequence of heavy traffic. Young's own refrain, "Keep on rockin' in the free world," captures how the country coasts down a road of ruin. If ecological catastrophe awaits ahead, better policies toward racial and gender equality might help in the immediate future but won't amount to much when the ultimate bill is due.

Adolph Reed writes that a problem with PUSH's intervention in corporate America is that it "endorses a principle of decision making via exclusively private negotiations between corporate and advocacy organization elites . . . removed from the arenas of public scrutiny and participation."[22] The benefits of Jackson's negotiation, which are undeniable, accrue among the professional and working-class members of the corporation itself, not taking into account the social costs that permeate and pile up far beyond corporate boundaries. Because Jackson is not only the leader but also the public face of PUSH, his decisions become PUSH's decisions. As a consequence, the concerns of Reed will not become part of the internal conversation of the organization, even if Jackson lends his powerful voice to a cause with an unclear connection to PUSH's mission. For example, in 2005, Terri Schiavo—a 41-year-old American woman in Florida—was in a permanent vegetative state. Several doctors, after exhaustively reviewing her case, concluded that she had no brain activity, and would die quickly after the removal of a feeding tube. Schiavo's husband elected to let his wife die with dignity, rather than prolong her suspension between life and death. The mother and father of Schiavo, both Christian fundamentalists, objected to what they interpreted as the euthanizing of their daughter, eventually appealing to several far right organizations for public assistance. President George W. Bush expressed support for the Christian conservative campaign to override the facts of medicine, and the wishes of Schiavo's husband. While in Florida on other matters, Jesse Jackson joined a public protest, lending the prestige of civil rights credibility to the dubious—at best— effort to impose a position of religious extremism on a sad, but pedestrian health-care procedure.[23] This unfortunate, and largely forgotten episode is minor, but it does provide some validation to concerns regarding the trouble when a civil rights organization is inseparable from the identity of its leader. The NAACP did not offer any input on the Schiavo debate, and it is hard to imagine it ever doing so in similar circumstances.

The criticism from Adolph Reed, and even Neil Young, is legitimate, but it is important to also consider the scenery from their respective vantage points. A political scientist with a leftist orientation—not unlike an artist of social conscience—operates outside of power, able to bring to bear a pestilent—in the best sense of the word—perspective on those within systems of power. Jackson has an almost-singular position in American politics. His trajectory was that of a total outsider, leveraging the politics of rebellion and boycott, and steadily reaching until he had a hand in the door of power—still in the outer corridor, but in close-enough proximity for those at the decision-making desks to hear his shouts and feel his shoves. The ultimate question that all citizens concerned about peace and justice, including Adolph Reed and Noam Chomsky, must answer is the following: Is American democracy better for having Jesse Jackson as a leading advocate for the past fifty years or not? While an affirmative answer does not erase any criticism one might marshal against Jackson, it certainly puts the matter in a broader context.

No career with a trajectory as dramatic and longevity as staggering as Jackson's will be free of errors and missteps, but the lesson for the left to draw from Jackson's work, among those who express admiration and apprehension alike, is the power of one dedicated citizen, who possesses extraordinary talents, to engineer beneficial social change, and more broadly, the necessity of activism. The democratic declaration of "I am somebody" in word and deed should inspire more participation, more organization, and more protest—precisely what Jackson has attempted to inculcate in the mass of Americans implicated in his work. With the success of few others, Jackson has registered voters, convinced voters to run for office, and taken a battering ram to the doorway so that other civil rights networks and leaders can find space to operate within the political process. The abundance of activists will inevitably fill in the gaps left by each other's work, creating an organic system of cooperation and correction.

"The one flaw I observed when I was with Rainbow/PUSH," one former staffer said in an echo of a common concern about the organization, "was the absence of a permanent infrastructure that could continue the work after Rev. Jackson's transition." She added an important caveat, "Although, I'm not sure that there are too many people who can do what he does." A massive blindsight in most political commentary and academic analysis is the power of personality. It is a rare individual who can rise from Jim Crow poverty to become an internationally recognizable civil rights leader, balancing multiple commitments, offices, and agendas for decades. Because Jesse Jackson has played a major role in political conversation for so long, many people take his story for granted, neglecting to realize how unlikely it was from the beginning. It isn't as if there are dozens of leaders of Jesse Jackson's caliber waiting in the wings, just as there was not a ready replacement for Martin Luther King or, more fortunately, an easy substitution for Dick Cheney. Hierarchy, to the extent that it is fair and just, is often the result of an intractable human mystery—the same source of the indefinable feeling that causes our eyes to follow someone like Jackson, Bill Clinton, or Elvis Presley as they move across a room, even as their actions and gestures are entirely ordinary. It is an intoxicating, but potentially dangerous power to harness. One should not take it lightly that Jackson's use of magnetic charisma was for the enhancement of democracy, liberty, and equality.

"One of my failures is that I've never written my memoirs," Jesse Jackson confessed to me in the summer of 2019. "Last week, for instance, I thought about writing down some thoughts, getting started, but then the opportunity came along to bring food and hygienic supplies to the border," he said in reference to the humanitarian crisis in the US-Mexico border region. "So, I worked on that instead. I'm not a man of observation, and maybe I should be to a greater extent. I'm a man of action."

In his interpretation of the legendary bout between Muhammad Ali and George Foreman, *The Fight*, Norman Mailer writes, "In heavy training fighters live in dimensions of boredom others do not begin to contemplate. Fighters are supposed to. The boredom creates an impatience with one's life, and a violence to improve it."[24] Anyone who has spent any time with Jackson, especially on the road, observes that he cannot sit still for any extended period of time. Even in his late seventies, with Parkinson's disease, he travels multiple times a month, works six or seven days a week, and, as in the case of bringing aid to the Southern border, does not hesitate to take on projects of local, national, or international significance. "He doesn't eat like a normal person, and he doesn't sleep like a normal person," Jackson's driver once mentioned to me when describing some of the difficulties of his schedule. Jackson lives as if he genuinely believes, in ways that he can articulate and likely in ways that remain embedded in the mysteries of his subconscious, that as long as he is fighting, he has an opportunity to defeat the forces of evil that threw him down to the ground as a teenager outside the public library.

Mailer also compares Ali to an artist. While Foreman was emblematic of expert training and a technician's sensibility—the machine—"A victory for Ali would be a triumph for everything which did not fit into the computer: for audacity, inventiveness, even art."[25] Disagreements about his methods might complicate his legacy, particularly the idea that his leadership style is too autonomous, but the sixty-year record of evidence shows that, in a commitment to the enlargement of democracy, Jackson is audacious, inventive, and even artful. Democracy demands community and collaboration, but it also needs leaders who can construct new highways for those who were once immobile to move toward freedom.

Writing his own tribute to the prizefighter after Ali's death in 2016, Jackson declared, "When heroes win, people ride on their shoulders." [26]

Chapter 9

AN AMERICAN BLUESMAN

The traumas of the twenty-first century have exposed the civilizational shield of American pride as an easily penetrable patina. On September 11, 2001, nineteen terrorists armed with nothing more than boxcutters available for purchase at any hardware store circumvented the world's most sophisticated military to murder nearly 3,000 people, and cause the destruction of its architectural symbol of economic might. Millions of frightened, saddened, and enraged Americans asked, "why do they hate us?", apparently unaware that their government, in their name, has invaded, bombed, and brought down a fury of violence on countless countries in every corner of the planet. The governmental response was to disregard constitutional liberties, encroaching on the freedoms and privacy rights of millions of Muslims, torturing terror suspects, and using the National Security Agency to monitor the communication of unsuspecting citizens. Then, with bipartisan support, the United States declared war on two countries, one of which had no material or moral connection to the 9/11 attacks. In 2008, the entire world experienced a financial meltdown, but its origins were largely American. Decades of deregulation and casino-style capitalism, not to mention the refusal to address extreme inequality, culminated in the liquidation of middle-class wealth, and the consignment of the working poor to positions of underclass permanence. Resentment, bitterness, and hostility exploded into American politics, threatening to damage democratic norms. Voters, already feeling racist animus toward Latin immigrants, Arab Muslims, and their black compatriots, elected to the office of Abraham Lincoln a narcissistic confidence man whose play for power was to enhance lethal divisions through demagoguery. It is impossible to ignore these tragedies and atrocities, or view them in isolation. A spiritual sickness infects American life, as Martin Luther King warned, and it is precisely this condition that consequences the institutional infirmities troubling so many people's lives. Only one president has attempted to diagnose the root cause of America's problems, and for his efforts he was targeted for widespread mockery and malign.

President Jimmy Carter, and one of his chief advisors, Pat Caddell, looked at the American terrain of 1979, and saw growing social discord threatening to reverse the progress of the 1960s movements, economic recession, and an energy crisis in which cars were often lined up for blocks around the fuel station with drivers desperately hoping to get enough gas to cover their commute. They were also governing a public feeling, many for the first time, disenchantment with their own country. The mass slaughter of the Vietnam War, without credible justification, and the resignation of Richard Nixon in disgrace left many Americans deeply cynical about their elected leadership—a far cry from the nearly universal adulation of Franklin Roosevelt just thirty-four years earlier. Carter and Caddell believed that the crisis of America went far beyond anything measurable in economic data or lowering rates of electoral participation. Signs of visible decline were important, but they were also symptomatic. The president, and his advisor, concluded that what truly threatened America's future was a "crisis of confidence." The American people had lost confidence in their own lives, their communities, their bonds with each other, their institutions, and their belief systems. Carter decided that it was imperative upon him as president to address his county's spiritual disease, but, before doing so, he would have to educate himself, investing time in dialogue with other Americans equally concerned about the soul of the nation.

On May 30, 1979, Carter assembled a colorful and serious group of intellectuals at the White House—something that, as shameful as it is, rarely happens in the offices of government. The group included Charles Peters, a journalist who wrote searing reports and essays about the need for progressive politics to address the psychological toll that the cutthroat competition of American life was taking on average citizens. Bill Moyers, the former press secretary for the Johnson administration who became one of television's most thoughtful interviewers, was present, as was John Gardner, another Johnson official who founded an organization dedicated to the cultivation of civic virtue. Christopher Lasch, a historian and social critic, whose prescient book, *The Culture of Narcissism*, was published that same year, was also at the table. Rounding out the group that Carter's more skeptical advisors would christen "the God Squad" was a young, fiery civil rights leader and preacher from Chicago by way of South Carolina, Jesse Jackson.

According to other attendees at the dinner, and a surprise to no one who has spent time with Jackson, he was the most talkative of the illustrious guests. The conversations twisted and turned through topics as diverse as America's inability to decisively deal with racism, how "consumer culture" was corrosive to the soul, and the decline of neighborliness and communal investment that was in its infancy stages but many years later would become commonplace. The group agreed on a few ideas, namely that the president must aggressively address the problems that they had discussed, and that before taking any action, he should also consult with average citizens so that their testimonies could go into the public record. When they considered how Carter could speak to the nation, Jackson vehemently advised against media involvement. He worried that the press would distort, either through simplification or through obfuscation, his message. He also posited that an official Oval Office address would broadcast necessary drama and urgency to capture the attention of the American people. During a subsequent conversation the next month when Carter and Jackson jogged together outside the White House, Jackson reiterated his recommendation for the president to take his jeremiad directly to the public. On July 15, 1979, Carter did just that, naming the address, "A Crisis of Confidence," and speaking from his desk three years to the day that he accepted the Democratic nomination for president of the United States.

Citing opinion polls indicating the growing cynicism and dejection of the American public, Carter warned, "The erosion of our confidence in the future is threatening to destroy the social and the political fabric of America." A few moments later, he quoted Jackson directly, referring to him as a "visitor at Camp David"—"We've got to stop crying and start sweating, stop talking and start walking, stop cursing and start praying. The strength we need will not come from the White House, but from every house in America." The president then offered the rarest of White House qualities—truth and tough leadership, demonstrating a readiness to coldly look America's troubles in the face and call them exactly what they are:

> We are at a turning point in our history. There are two paths to choose. One is a path I've warned about tonight, the path that leads to fragmentation and self-interest. Down that road lies a mistaken idea of freedom, the right to grasp for ourselves some advantage over others. That path would be one of constant conflict between narrow interests ending in chaos and immobility. It is a certain route to failure.

Borrowing a key word from Jackson that first made it into a lengthy memo from Pat Caddell suggesting that Carter make this very speech, he explained that the other path is one of "restoration" of the American spirit—"That path leads to true freedom for our nation and ourselves."

The initial reaction to the speech, contrary to popular belief, was enthusiastic. Polling data showed that most Americans thought Carter accurately identified a sense of spiritual emptiness and civic decline pervasive throughout the country. An avalanche of adversarial press, nicknaming the address the "malaise speech" when it did not even include that word, constant attacks on Carter's pessimism from the right, and the president's own odd maneuvering, most especially the firing of his entire cabinet without coherent explanation, helped push America to the path of "fragmentation and self-interest."[1] One year later, the American public would elect to the presidency Ronald Reagan, who encouraged belief in American exceptionalism, sponsored death squads in Latin America, and declared ketchup a vegetable.

Thirteen years after Carter's prophetic "Crisis of Confidence" address, at the Democratic National Convention with Bill Clinton preparing to accept his nomination in front of America, the Democrats relegated the former president and Jesse Jackson to speaking at the same time as the Major League Baseball All Star Game when convention planners expected the lowest ratings, hence giving it the name "Losers' Night."[2] In 2008, they were not even fit for Losers' Night. The convention advertising the nomination of Barack Obama provided no speaking time for Carter, and not one second for the civil rights leader and former candidate who made Obama's victory possible.

"I blazed a trail. Obama followed a path. There's a difference," Jackson told me in a conversation about the former president. Jackson offered praise for Obama, calling the Affordable Care Act, the stimulus package, the climate change accords, the doubling of Pell Grants, the Iran nuclear deal, and avoidance of war with Syria, "big, big pluses." Even still, while thinking about lack of appreciation for Jackson in popular discourse, I was reminded of the words of Ralph Waldo Emerson: "Our housekeeping is mendicant, our arts, our occupations, our marriages, our religion, we have not chosen, but society has chosen for us. We are parlor soldiers. We shun the rugged battle of fate, where strength is born."[3]

The message of Jackson since the early 1960s, like the words of his mentor, Martin Luther King, and like the speech of Jimmy Carter that he helped to write, call for a strengthening of America. It demands that Americans begin to act with greater courage, develop more sensitivity and acuity, and focus on long-term progress rather than short-term gratification. A culture addicted to consumption and entertainment is unlikely to embrace anything that offers such a stark challenge to its own weakness. When the McCain camp conceded on election night in 2008, and Grant Park in Chicago transformed into a frenzy of deliverance, as thousands of people waited to hear from the new president-elect, Barack Obama, a well-placed cameraman caught Jesse Jackson weeping, holding his hand to his mouth. "I cried tears for the moment and the movement," Jackson later reflected when we revisited that celebratory evening in conversation. "For the moment, I cried tears of joy, but for the movement, I cried tears of sadness, because I thought of all those who could not be there to witness that moment—all of those who deserved to be there."

Jackson was there, but little, if any, commentary took fair measurement of the significance of his presence.

The late Albert Murray describes the "blues hero" as one whose "productive citizenship" is essential to the freedom of "individuals and communities." The blues hero, unlike the tragic or comic hero, works in "antagonistic cooperation" with the "dragons" breathing fire near his home. He demonstrates the necessary maturity and tenacity to fight the dragons, realizing that they will never die. Their presence is eternal, and through the hero's wins and losses, his heroism becomes stronger and sharper—like a sword under the flame. "Heroism, which like the sword is nothing if not steadfast," Murray writes, "is measured in terms of the stress and strain it can endure and the magnitude and complexity of the obstacles it overcomes."[4] The blues sensibility is a tragic one, however, because it confronts the pain of existence with the awareness that its source is eternal. The blues hero is wise enough to know that he will never vanquish the source, but resolute enough to carry on anyway.

The blues heroism of Jackson is measurable in the significance and diversity of his accomplishments, but also in the consistent refusal of the Democratic Party, the American press, and the general public to fully acknowledge and appreciate those accomplishments. While reflecting on his trilogy of books on the decline of the United States, historian Morris Berman said, "One of the big problems is that anything that can help the culture is now marginalized by the culture."[5]

Jesse Jackson seemed like a permanent, main stage player in the drama of American power and politics throughout the latter decades of the twentieth century. The ubiquity of his voice on issues of racial injustice and economic exploitation, the shadow he cast on political debate, and the influence, whether the management of the party liked it or not, he exerted on Democratic politics made it appear that Jackson would never fade from the spotlight. A series of events, beginning at the turn of the century, took a battering ram to Jackson's public image. His foes in the largest institutions of American power—major corporations, media companies, and the conservatives of the Republican and Democratic parties—no doubt delighted in the damage to Jackson's reputation for reasons vastly different than their indignant chest pounding would signal.

In 2001, Jackson held a press conference to confirm a tabloid report that for the previous four years, he had an extramarital affair with a former aide and political science professor who met Jackson while authoring a book on his international work. Together they conceived a child, Ashley, and Jackson was offering financial support to his daughter.[6] In Marshall Frady's biography of Jackson, his wife Jacqueline implied that their marital arrangement was unusual, telling the journalist, "He is rarely home and I give him no ultimatum on when to return. Of course I know what happens out there, I'm no dummy."[7] The timing of Jackson's confession, however, was unflattering. Merely three years earlier, Jackson acted as the "spiritual advisor," in the words of the former president, to Bill Clinton in the aftermath of his own affair with Monica Lewinsky. Given that Jackson is a Christian minister, charges of hypocrisy came from all corners.

In the 1970s, sordid aspects of the private life of Martin Luther King became public knowledge. The FBI, through illegally wiretapping his phones and bugging his hotel rooms, learned that often while on the road, the civil rights leader was unfaithful to his wife. Jay Edgar Hoover even threatened to blackmail King with the recordings. Bruce DuMont, an esteemed radio journalist in Chicago, asked Jackson shortly after the revelation of King's affairs to address similar accusations of hypocritical behavior against his late friend and boss. His answer, ironically enough, is a sufficient response to critics who attempted to use Jackson's personal misdeeds as nullification of his public work:

> I would suggest this about the question of his personal morality—What would be inconsistent is if Dr. King spent his time challenging personal morals, as evangelical types do who issue a series of don'ts. He was about changing the social conditions of our society, and he was true to that calling. I think, even now, when people raise questions about his personal morality, it is an attempt to distort what he was truly about.[8]

American culture has a bizarre bipolarity with human sexuality. It continually cheapens sex by using it to sell anything from toothpaste to tickets to NFL games, and it has become increasingly vulgar in the perpetuation of an adolescent fixation on cartoonish visual stimulation in pornography and hip-hop videos. It simultaneously refuses to overcome the zealousness of its Puritanical origins, demonstrating a reflexive condemnation of sexual activity outside the boundaries of "traditional morality." As a result, it is often incapable of divorcing private vice from public virtue. Bill Clinton, while holding the office of president, testified under oath about the prurient details of his dalliances with Monica Lewinsky, but credible evidence that his successor, George W. Bush, lied to justify the American invasion of Iraq, provoked no official investigation or sanction. In the year 2000, an assembly of American historians ranked the presidents according to several categories, ranging from public persuasion skills to economic management. On "moral authority," they ranked Clinton dead last. They ranked Lyndon Johnson at twenty-eight in the same category even though, by that time, it was irrefutable that he lied to the American people when he launched the war in Vietnam. The historians even ranked Richard Nixon, who resigned in disgrace and required a presidential pardon from Gerald Ford to avoid imprisonment, above Clinton in "moral authority."[9] Like similar ridicule of Martin Luther King, the denunciation of Jesse Jackson's sex life, distorts what he is truly about, and bears no relevance to his dedication to "changing the social conditions of our society." As even the survey of American historians on former presidents illustrates, however, infidelity weighs heavily in the consideration of many Americans, even when compared to deceit that leads to the deaths of thousands of people.

Contemptuous reports on Jackson's personal life also eliminated consideration of complicated family dynamics that include the possibility of forgiveness and reconciliation. The Jackson family is admirably tight-knit. His wife, Jacqueline, leads the women's group at Rainbow/PUSH, and often hosts events at the organization's Chicago headquarters. One of the few times that Jackson has cried publicly during a speech was when he recently thanked his wife for her many years of love and support. Their son Jesse Jr. continues to write and give public testimonies, while Jonathan is the National Spokesperson for PUSH, growing into an orator after his father's own heart. Their daughter Santita is a progressive radio talk show host, and their other daughter Jacqueline is an educational researcher and advocate for equitable public education policies. Their son Yusef is an entrepreneur. Jackson's daughter Ashley is a graduate of Spelman College. At Rainbow/PUSH, the Jacksons demonstrate a natural warmth toward each other, projecting a loving kinship that they replicate in their hospitality to visitors and volunteers.

An onslaught of disparaging press coverage of Jackson following the admission of an extramarital affair, regardless of the nuances that it ignored, pushed him into the background of American life. Not long after Jackson's sex scandal, the Obama season arrived in full force on the national landscape. Jackson's hot mic remarks harshly rebuking Obama created the perfect, and in many ways phony, dichotomy for the American media, quick to present Jackson as a passé firebrand in juxtaposition with the Democratic nominee for the presidency—the future of black America, according to press depiction, and the future of American politics. "I never had the fears and misgivings about him that he had for me," Jackson once said to me in reference with Obama. During the first black president's two terms in the White House, he never invited Jackson to an event advertising the presidential seal. Commentators, clearly delusional given the ascendency of Trump's white nationalism waiting around the corner, were quick to pronounce the Obama era as the country's entrance into a "post racial" handfasting ceremony. Jackson's rejection of the illusion, and his steadfast commitment to fighting racial injustice, made him an inconvenient character in the American story. His scandal, and the Obama banishment, also made him easy to exile. Al Sharpton, conversely, became a civil rights advocate and television commentator of newfound prominence after Obama invited him to the Oval Office for several discussions. Breaking with even his own history of issue orientation, and avoidance of partisanship, Sharpton announced that he would never publicly criticize Barack Obama or members of his administration. Sharpton subsequently received a weekly television program with MSNBC, and the status of kingmaker within the Democratic Party that Jackson, despite his larger efforts to expand the party while pushing it leftward, never acquired. A presidential anointing will enhance the professional profile of anyone in any field, but the extent to which Obama's endorsement, and lack thereof, dictated different directions for Sharpton and Jackson demonstrates that even the ostensibly "objective" American press has an unhealthy deference to political power.

Journalistic deference allows those with power to set the limits of political conversation and debate. In the summer of 2012, as with any presidential election season, the media made it seem as if Mitt Romney, the Republican nominee for president, and Barack Obama represented the full range of public policy proposals. During the same week of the Democratic National Convention in Charlotte, North Carolina, Jesse Jackson organized an alternative convention of seventy-five delegates whose activism the party had locked out of its official gathering. They met at a large community center only a few miles from the arena hosting the DNC. After giving the opening remarks, Jackson invited speakers from anti-war organizations, environmental groups, feminist lobbies, and poverty relief networks to present a more robust and transformational Democratic agenda, often criticizing the Obama administration for its drone strikes in the Middle East, its refusal to attach a public option to the Affordable Care Act, and its coddling of big business. It is important to note that the Jackson agenda—both in the 1980s and on display at the alternative convention in 2012—became central to the Democratic platform of 2020, proving that, with sustained effort, seemingly static systems are malleable.

Jesse Jackson's closest ally within the system throughout the 1990s and 2000s was undoubtedly his own son, Jesse Jackson Jr., an ambitious, charismatic, and intellectually dexterous congressman in the suburbs of Chicago. Most observers of Illinois politics, even those who were loathe to admit it, speculated that, because the former congressman's gifts were so striking, there was no ceiling on his political career. Analysts predicted that he would eventually become a US senator or governor of Illinois. After Obama's victory, some even speculated that the distinction of second black president might soon belong to Jesse Jackson Jr. Then, in 2012 just as Jackson was facing a reelection opponent, he went missing. Residents of Washington DC made claims of spotting the clandestine congressman downtown, but he was not reporting to work, nor was he making campaign appearances in Illinois. News broke that Jackson was under investigation for the misappropriation of campaign funds—a crime for which he was eventually convicted. Jackson made no attempt to excuse his behavior. He pled guilty, and served one year in prison. Appearing heartbroken and exhausted, his final words to the press after the trial were summative: "I'm sorry I let everybody down."[10] News did break, however, that the Mayo Clinic, in addition to local doctors, had diagnosed Jackson with a severe form of bipolar disorder.[11] The irrational swings from euphoria to despair that characterize the condition would certainly explain why a man of Jackson's intelligence and accomplishment would risk his entire career for bizarre personal purchases, such as Michael Jackson memorabilia. With typical insensitivity to human suffering, and intellectual slovenliness, right-wing pundits attempted to connect the son's behavior to the father's work. The guilt-by-association tactic failed to reach beyond far right circles of Jackson hatred, but the overall story did amount to more bad press for a civil rights leader that various people in power hoped for years to deport from mainstream political debate.

The political tragedy of Congressman Jackson's fall from grace is that, more than anyone else in an official position of governance, he was devoted to his father's most long-term cause of institutional reform. Jesse Jackson Sr., with profound consistency, has made voting rights central to his advocacy and activism. He first met Martin Luther King in Selma, Alabama, as a participant in the bloody and brutal struggle for black enfranchisement in the South, and the success of his presidential campaigns was largely dependent upon unprecedented voter registration—an effort that cosmetically and structurally remade the Democratic Party. Jackson also scored a victory for participatory democracy by convincing the party to adopt a proportional system of awarding delegates in presidential primaries. In the years leading up to his congressional election, Jackson Jr. spoke aggressively about the need for an amendment to the US Constitution offering a federal guarantee of the right to vote. He then led the cause in Congress to amend the Constitution for the purpose of establishing universal voting rights. Since his departure, no one else has resumed the fight. The exercise of the franchise is so foundational to Americans' conception of their political system that most citizens assume that it is included in the Bill of Rights. "I have a federal guarantee to buy a gun," Jackson has said in correction of a widespread misperception, "but not to vote."

Martin Luther King, John Lewis, Jesse Jackson, and others who marched across the bridge in Selma, and risked their lives elsewhere, were not protesting the federal government, but the tyrannical and racist measures of state laws. "State's Rights" is not an entirely dubious category of political theory and law, but it is often worthy of suspicion, because many of the oppressions of Jim Crow were only possible due to fact that the states had the power to dictate their own voting regulations without federal oversight. A constitutional amendment not only would guarantee the right to vote to every citizen of the United States but also would nationalize voting regulatory procedures, preventing the "crimes and trickery," to use Jackson's phrase, that were consequential in the 2016 election. For example, in Texas it was possible to register to vote with a concealed carry license—Texans who apply to carry a firearm in public are overwhelmingly white and Republican—but not a student ID. Jesse Jackson Jr. attempted to advance his argument into the public space of congressional deliberation, and his father has made valiant efforts to continue the campaign in recent years, adopting the strategy of convincing various state and city government officials to sign a pledge in support of a constitutional amendment. In Newark, New Jersey, and Baltimore, Maryland, to cite two examples, Jackson gained the signatures of, respectively, their mayors and entire city councils.[12] Lack of widespread discussion, and absence of urgency when the discussion does take place, regarding voting rights and regulations in the United States exposes not only the superficiality of a spectacle-obsessed media but also, even more significantly, the failure of the left to turn the first screw in the construction of its own empowerment.

Democrats have lost hundreds of local, state, and congressional seats because Republican operatives began manipulating districts in various gerrymandering scams, beginning in 2008. In states like Michigan and Wisconsin, Democrats typically outnumber Republicans in midterm elections, but Republicans manage to win more positions in the state legislature and Congress.[13] It is difficult to have any confidence in national races, because various voter suppression tactics reduce turnout among poor, black, and non-English-speaking voters—predominantly Democratic constituencies—and most infamously in 2016, the Democrat lost the presidential election, despite winning three million more votes than her opponent, because of the antiquated and anti-democratic Electoral College. Senator Elizabeth Warren and Senator Bernie Sanders, along with many young Democratic officials, including media sensation Alexandria Ocasio-Cortez, have issued calls for eliminating the Electoral College, but few prominent Democrats, or left leaning pundits, consistently discuss voter suppression. It is almost as if Democrats have agreed to play in a game when the rules almost guarantee their defeat. Meanwhile, Jesse Jackson, a man who once led one of the most successful voter registration drives in American history, is pounding the table in protest, and unable to attract an audience. While leftists, especially those on social media, contemplate a theatrical exhibition of outrage in cooperation with America's culture of spectacle, Jackson offers elementary pedagogy in the study of power. Progressives ignore the simple profundity of Jackson's instruction and example at the risk of their own ruin.

"Voting is an access card to democracy, or it is a powerball," Jackson told me in a conversation shortly after Trump's helter-skelter triumph. He continued in the issuance of a characteristic sports metaphor: "The most important person on the basketball court is the referee, because he enforces the rules. The fundamental question of democracy—voting rights—is the rulebook. We now live under the rulebook of Jeff Sessions," Jackson said referring to Trump's then attorney general, a lifelong opponent of voting protections and civil rights, "We live under the rules of not Selma, but Shelby, so that the Voting Rights Act is now undercut." Jackson's voice became deeper, and began to elongate the enunciation of his words as if a pulpit had suddenly appeared in front of his body when he uttered what is, perhaps, the most essential truth of the left's tragic inadequacy in American politics: "Without understanding the rules, it is possible for people to rule you into an unfavorable condition."

Jackson continued his self-styled soliloquy on the franchise by sketching connections between present political injustices and America's lowly origin:

> The big American contradiction is that many leaders want democracy for the power it gives them, not the opportunities it gives to other people. Leaders often allow enough democracy for them to justify being in power, but not enough for them to distribute power to other people. That's how we could have a Declaration of Independence with a call for democracy that would allow democracy and slavery to coexist. Anyone who is interested in democracy for power, and not participation and protection, will allow democracy and segregation, or democracy and voter suppression, to coexist. That is a fundamental flaw—not in democracy, but in those who would use it for their manipulative purposes.

As with any medical diagnosis, it is essential to understand the "fundamental flaw"—the impetus of a problem—in order to comprehend its symptomatic consequences. Esoteric theory surrounding the election of Donald Trump abounds, but disciplined analysis of the "the rules" and the actual mechanisms of voting receive only soft and low broadcast. Jackson reached for the megaphone:

> Let's apply that elementary truth to modern times. The 6 million Americans who deserve reentry—they've been to prison—and should become full citizens again, but their basic rights are denied; in Florida it is 1.5 million voters where Hillary Clinton lost by 120,000. The case in North Carolina—another battleground— they moved over 100 precincts from campus locations, school unions, to several miles down the road. That subtle, but significant move, along with other trickery, was so brazen that North Carolina Republican officials bragged that they suppressed the black vote by 8 to 9 percent, which would have more than made the difference in Clinton's favor.

Jackson also cited the investigation concluding that in Wisconsin, a state that Trump won by a mere 23,000 votes, restrictive voter identification laws, recently championed by Republicans in the state, suppressed nearly 200,000 votes, most of them black, Latino, and low income. Mass media was largely mute on voter rights, even as evidence of its decisive influence mounted. More disheartening was that most Democrats decided not to spotlight the dishonest strategy that Republicans are executing to overcome the demographic limitations of their electorate in critical states, and chose instead to chase the Ian Fleming story of Russian sabotage. The monstrosity of the 2016 decision, and the fumbling of the media and Democrats in its aftermath, resonated with Jackson as a painful reminder of the opposition he has faced since the 1960s. It is a story that precedes even his fifty-year involvement in the security of the franchise.

"Whenever we fought for the right to vote," Jackson confessed,

> we were naïve about the anti-vote science of, in fact, fraud—fraud as in voter suppression. So, we gain the right to vote in 1965, and suddenly the voter

registration is in some Klansman's house all the way out in the country, or you can't register without a job, and all that foolishness. In '65, we got the right to vote and we were excited, but we did not understand gerrymandering, annexation and other preventive measures. We did not understand the influence of big money in electoral politics.

The black freedom quest for equal access to the ballot, Jackson explained, was the hammer blow to the door blocking entry for many Americans' ability to participate in the political process. From the Voting Rights Act came the allowance of white women to serve on juries, Latinos and others to vote bilingually, and college campuses to establish their own polling stations. Ralph Ellison warned that history functions as a boomerang. As the object seemed to move forward into friendlier skies, it suddenly shot back with concussive force. Voting, as unlikely as it would seem, has become more difficult in many states. When I asked Jackson to account for the discrepancy between Western European nations, where voting is made easy, and America, which often constructs an obstacle course on the road to the ballot box, he was quick to navigate a struggle he knows all too well.

There were three barriers here. One barrier, clearly, was race, because so many Southern states had more African slaves than slavemasters. So, the right to vote meant that slaves would take over, and in fact, many did during Reconstruction. That is what triggered the violent era of lynching, to kill and intimidate blacks out of voting. Also, in many key states, Native Americans could not vote, because there was a white supremacist effort to block them. Class was another barrier. There were more field hands than landowners. That's why we vote on Tuesday, because the field hands couldn't get the time off to vote, but the landowner could get to the ballot to support his interest. Also, in the white male supremacy philosophy, women were historically seen as soft on war and soft on control. Now, what do I mean by that? In the Civil War, it was Julia Ward Howe who organized a women's peace movement against the war. Mother's Day was not about red roses and greetings cards for mothers. It was a women's day—mother's call—for peace. There was such hostility toward that from men, calling women all kinds of names. So, women were traditionally more in favor of peace, and more inclined toward ending slavery. Frederick Douglass joined the Women's Abolition Movement. So, women were seen as anti-establishment, white male supremacy, which meant their suffrage threatened the anti-democratic ethos.

"The anti-democratic ethos" has permeated so far into the public culture that it has poisoned the civic minds of even those who would most benefit from a maximal activation of citizenship's power and promise. As the United States has failed to provide basic services and protections for its inhabitants, and the cruelties of life in the world's wealthiest nation become more manifest—diabetics dying because they cannot afford insulin, children in Flint with cognitive disorders due to lead in the water, the crumbling of infrastructure—an anti-politics ideology has increased in popularity. Libertarians on the right wing cynically exploit the failures of government to argue against any sense of social compact to balance the marketplace, while many leftists have lost all faith in conventional political activity. One of Jackson's battles becomes the mission to destroy apathy. He issued a reminder of the potential of mass movements, the rewards of voting, and the risks of passivity.

"I understand the frustration. Someone living in Englewood," he said in reference to one of Chicago's most poverty-stricken and crime-ridden neighborhoods,

> thinks, 'I voted for 20 years, and there's still vacant lots—still drugs in, guns in, jobs out,' but change always does take place. I was arrested trying to use a public library. I was arrested trying to use a downtown theater. I was arrested trying to integrate the school board of Chicago. I was arrested with my sons trying to free Mandela. I was arrested trying to get black workers hired to work garbage trucks. So, if you look at what we've got in 50 years—right to vote, Equal Employment Opportunity Commission, contract compliance, Medicaid, Affordable Health Care, Environmental Protection Agency—there's a whole range of changes that have come our way, but you only appreciate your water when your well runs dry.

Walt Whitman worried after the end of the Civil War that "genuine belief" had left America. One cannot help but wonder if the animus toward Jackson exposes a lack of faith, or if one offers a kinder interpretation, lack of focus on the realization of authentic democracy. If few have concern for something as simple and fundamental as voting rights, concentration on more complicated, but equally consequential issues—like campaign finance laws—will remain fleeting and superficial. Jackson's clarion call becomes more urgent just as the consequences of American nihilism become more manifest in the degradation of democratic traditions, the resurgence of racism in the political mainstream, and the successive failure to create the "beloved community" of Martin Luther King's dream. Speaking at PUSH, in 2019, after he and his staff paid the bond of a mentally ill Chicago resident who a police officer body slammed into the pavement while arresting him for drinking alcohol on a street corner, Jackson implored the audience,

> What strikes me about the assault is not that the officer did it, but the silence in response. It happened down the block from a few black churches, and not one minister said anything. It happened in a ward with a black alderman, and he was silent. I fear we have become insensitive to degradation. I need you to come alive again.

"You live every day not knowing if it is your last," Al Sharpton said when I asked him to describe the experience that few can claim to share with him and Jackson— that of an internationally recognizable civil rights leader. "I've seen him deal with threats throughout his life. I was stabbed once," he explained, reminding me of the time I was interviewing Jackson in his Chicago office, and we had to evacuate out the backdoor, because one of Jackson's stalkers refused to leave the lobby. "What people really don't understand is—I'll put it this way," Sharpton said, his voice amplifying indignation,

> Do you really think we would spend nights in jail if it was for fame and money? How much would someone have to pay you to go to jail? How much would someone have to pay you to get a knife in your chest, or for your family to be threatened? There is danger and risk. We both are smart enough to do something else, especially once we made names for ourselves. But we take on the danger and risk, and we work hard. I am at my desk at six in the morning. Jesse is at work at six in the morning, and works twelve, fifteen hour days. He is suffering from Parkinson's. I have to help him get out of a chair sometimes, but he's still going, relentless.

Sharpton continued to draw a distinction between public perception and reality.

> We make a decent living, but we don't have opulent lifestyles. You've got megachurch preachers with private jets and massive estates. We don't have any of that. But we could have it. We can both preach. We raise money, and build staff. I have six offices around the country. He has about the same. Why would we be killing ourselves to make payroll every week if it was all about ourselves? Reverend Jackson did very well for years on CNN. He did very well for years on the speaking circuit. Why at his age would he worry about refurbishing the building in Chicago if he wasn't committed? Say that he has an ego—fine. Say that he sometimes said something he shouldn't have said—fine. But don't say he isn't committed.

The commitment of Jesse Jackson is most visible during the annual markers when most people enjoy a reprieve from their mandatory roles and responsibilities: holidays. Rather than relishing in the excuse to take a day off work, Jackson does his best to demonstrate the malleability of our life's rituals, using occasions for celebration as opportunities to display the communal core of left politics.

When the average American contemplates Thanksgiving, images of turkey dinners, football games, and, perhaps, pilgrims and "Indians" move through the mind. Every morning on that national holiday in November, Jesse Jackson hosts a radio broadcast in which he reminds his audience of the actual origin of the festivity. "Abraham Lincoln declared Thanksgiving a holiday for two reasons," Jackson will annually tell his radio listeners and the crowd that assembles later in the morning at PUSH headquarters, "To celebrate the abolition of slavery—to give thanks for the freedom of the slaves—and to show gratitude for the end of the war. So, Thanksgiving is not about football. It's about freedom. It's not a feast day; it's a peace day." To authentically honor the history of the holiday is not to simply gorge on mash potatoes and pumpkin pie, but to, in the words of Jackson, "act on the spirit of democracy, the spirit of preserving the Union." Every Thanksgiving morning at Rainbow/PUSH, Jackson and his staff organize an enormous brunch, free of charge for low-income families. He spends the day waiting tables alongside other Chicago celebrities and professional athletes he has persuaded to volunteer their time. I once observed a woman with two young children thank their table's waiter with such overwhelming sincerity it became evident that she might not ever experience restaurant service, and that she, along with her son and daughter, is the face animating the statistical reality of poverty in America.

About 13 percent of women in America live below the poverty line. Even more to the nation's shame, 16 percent of children are in poverty.[14] It is worth noting that many economists and sociologists agree that the standard for measuring poverty in the United States is woefully out of date, borderline absurd. For example, a household of four with a collective income of $26,000 is not impoverished, according to the official American definition from the Department of Health and Human Services.[15] Contrary to the pervasive myth of poor people's indolence, nearly ten million Americans fall through the cracks and into the category of the "working poor." The phrase that sounds like an oxymoron applies to those whose income is below the poverty line, but work over twenty hours a week at least twenty-seven weeks of the year. About 51 percent of poor Americans—a slim majority—work part-time hours.[16] In any given year, 2.5 million children experience homelessness.[17] When Rainbow/PUSH concludes its Thanksgiving meal, Jackson and staff box full dinners and drive to the bridges where homeless people regularly arrange tents or makeshift shelters from the harsh bite of the cold Chicago wind. PUSH employees and Jackson, often wearing an ankle-length coat and fedora, hand deliver the food, offer words of encouragement, and give them informational cards, explaining that the organization can help find them residential placement, job training, or more reliable social services.

On Thanksgiving, Jackson and PUSH connect the country's past with its present, advancing an argument through action that any celebration of historical triumphs against oppression, bondage, and violence must have the accompaniment of immediate assistance and identification with those that Franz Fanon called "the wretched of the Earth"—the "diseased and despairing" of Walt Whitman's *Leaves of Grass*. America's dominant culture, almost without contradiction, acts as an ongoing parade of its winners. Even Christmas, a day that according to its religion inspiration, is set aside to honor a persecuted minority in an empire, becomes a fervid exercise in consumerism. Retail enjoys its highest earnings in November and December. Shopping mall brawls, some even resulting in death, over sneakers, electronics, and children's toys have become an American tradition. The tradition that Jesse Jackson advances on Christmas morning provides stark contrast with a culture that would enable people to injure each other over discount prices while a few miles down the avenue their fellow citizens search for smokable cigarette butts under a bridge.

"I . . . do not . . . belong here . . ." Jesse Jackson spoke slowly and deliberately, demanding that thousands of nonviolent inmates at Cook County Jail, the largest in Chicago, repeat after him. Most of the men and women demonstrated infectious avidity, shouting the declaration as if it would reverberate throughout the entire criminal justice system. Jackson began visiting jails and speaking with inmates on

Christmas morning fifty years ago as a young aide for Dr. Martin Luther King, Jr. In five decades, he has not missed one year. "We are here to inspire and entertain," Jackson told me referring to the staff, band, and choir of the Rainbow/PUSH Coalition, "but also to transform Christmas day into liberation day."

At several turns in his remarks, Jackson offered exhortation of "personal responsibility," to use an increasingly dubious conservative buzz phrase, but he showcased sufficient political imagination and social solidarity to assimilate practical personal advice into the political realities of institutional bias and oppression that render such advice hollow in isolation. "I do not belong here," has a political application. With just a little philosophical and rhetorical elasticity, it covers an American issuance of justice that only rewards responsibility depending on the person. "When a sociologist from London visited America to study the penal system," Jackson informed the audience, "He asked, 'where is the jail for white people?'"

The disparities resulting from discrimination worsen after release for convicted felons. Virtually unemployable, and ineligible for federal student aid, including loans, ex-cons often feel, with good reason, that the most familiar means of earning an income, even if illegal, are the most reliable. Nearly every state has reduced or eliminated rehabilitation and job training programs in prison, under the thoughtless and dishonest "tough on crime" banner, and few offer adequate medical care or psychiatric counseling for prisoners. Therapeutic treatment is especially important to consider given that jails and prisons collectively operate as the country's largest housing facility for the mentally ill,[18] and that countless prisoners, subject to abuse and sexual assault during their incarceration, leave with severe trauma.

Jackson provided three immediate policy initiatives state systems should adopt to make their penal facilities more humane, which would have the additional benefit of reducing recidivism: medical testing and treatment—most prisons, for example, test for sexually transmitted diseases when prisoners enter the facility, but not when they leave; education and job training programs that offer instruction in marketable skills rather than the quasi-slave labor that currently passes for work in prison; and the return of the franchise to prisoners who have served their sentence. Rainbow/PUSH registered voters in the Cook County Jail on Christmas morning after Jackson reminded the crowd, "Until you are convicted, you can still register and you can still vote. You can vote for officials who will work to get you out of here."

The dynamics of Jackson's speech resembled a high-powered rock and roll song with mid-tempo verses and anthemic choruses. In an exhibition of his oratorical range, he would transition from the dry but essential political substance of public policy analysis to the gospel populism of his classic refrain, "I am somebody." The utterance of his trademark phrase seemed to straighten his back and solidify his voice. Jackson looked exhausted before the program began. He was jetting back and forth between members of his staff and some of the religious leaders and political officials who accompanied him to the jail visit. The lids of his eyes were heavy, and his steps were slow and deliberate. He requested that Rabbi Gordon say a prayer in the center of a large circle of the PUSH delegation. At the instant of the prayer's conclusion, Jackson's gait began to resemble the swagger that was unmistakable in his earlier years.

"I may be poor, but I am somebody! I may be locked up, but I am somebody!" With each recitation, the inmates would rise to their feet, raise their fists, and shout with the passion of their desire to go home on Christmas morning. Jackson, backed by the PUSH choir and with an ensemble of state officials and Congressman Danny Davis (D-IL), stood on a highly elevated stage. I was floor level with the prisoners and corrections officers, and as my eyes ping-ponged back and forth between the speaker at the podium and his enraptured audience, I could not help but return to the words of 1960s radical, Abbie Hoffman. "All prisoners are political prisoners," Hoffman announced at a rally right around the same time that Jackson first started making his annual Christmas jailhouse visit, "Because if you go to a jail, you see that ninety percent of the people there are black, and you see that ninety percent of the people are poor. You see that ninety percent of the people haven't even had a fucking trial yet!"[19] You also notice that most are young.

Taking survey of the crowd—the men in beige, and the women in blue, many of them with unkempt hair, and a hungry look in their eyes—I thought of how each person has a story. There is a rich and deep human experience behind every inmate number and filing, and it is only through exploring all of the cracks and crevices of those experiences that comprehension of crime, and awareness of justice and injustice, become possible. I have written five books, teach at a university, and am happily married, but I'm far from above speculation that with just a few different shakes in my life—many of which would have been outside my control—I could have been sitting among the inmates, waiting to hear Jesse Jackson speak before returning to my cell, rather than documenting the event as a journalist.

Jackson himself is no stranger to the criminal justice system. He was arrested in the 1960s for attempting to check a book out of the "white" public library in his hometown of Greenville, South Carolina, and has spent time in jail repeatedly for similar acts of civil disobedience. While many of the crimes of the Cook County inmates might not possess the same nobility or efficacy, one has to wonder how many people in a room full of nonviolent offenders can and should claim, for reasons personal or political, "I do not belong here."

The Rainbow/PUSH Coalition identified three particular inmates who could amplify that declaration, and paid their respective bonds before escorting them home to spend Christmas with their families. One was a woman in her thirties, a mother of four, including her oldest daughter who is a journalism major at DePaul University, locked away on charges of retail theft. Another was a young man, among many, on charges of simple drug possession, underscoring the human damage of the impractical and iniquitous "war on drugs." The third was a middle-aged, impoverished man who, because he could not make bail and was still awaiting trial, had spent 574 days in Cook County Jail on, of all things, a forgery charge. Before leaving, PUSH staffers recorded the names of all inmates enduring similar predicaments on the promise that they would research their cases, and coordinate with the Sheriff's department to negotiate bond reduction, or secure release.

"The movement needs to go national," Jackson told the observant members of the press, "In every major city, in every state, we need to use Christmas as an opportunity to set the captives free."

A simple act of seasonal compassion might reverberate with revolutionary resonance. The three inmates could express nothing but joy and gratitude for their homecoming. In addition to enabling more people to hug their children, parents, spouses, and siblings on a cold morning, setting the captives free can also spotlight the devastation of mass incarceration, racial and class biases in criminal justice, and the immorality of modern-day debt prisons. Registering voters, even in jail, legitimates democracy by showcasing that it includes the incarcerated—the nameless and faceless pedestrians of a system designed to defeat them.

When Jackson and his staff returned to the PUSH offices in the South Side of Chicago, Jackson collapsed his 6'4" frame into a reclining chair at the head of a conference table. With CNN flashing images of the day's news above his head, and local and national newspapers scattered before him, he made an admission as introspective as it was philosophical.

"I've freed hostages and prisoners in Iraq, Cuba, Syria, Yugoslavia, and Gambia," he said in a soft voice far removed from the shout he employed at the pulpit just moments earlier, "and it never hit me as deep as releasing people at home."

The press coverage of Jackson's fiftieth annual jail mission was scant—a combination of the timing, given that few people in any profession want to work on Christmas morning, but also more lamentable reasons that provide illustration of askew media priorities. The abusive co-optation of the phrase "fake news" from Donald Trump, and his fanatical supporters, has created a fundamental misunderstanding of journalistic bias. Despite its crudity, there is value to the terminology for its direct and combative capacity to unmask the agenda of the mainstream media. Jesse Jackson began making direct appeals for the application of democracy to criminal justice, the penal system, and the franchise for convicts in the late 1960s with Martin Luther King. In the 1990s, while most black elected officials breezed by warnings of mass incarceration and the militarization of the police, Jackson testified on the issue and made personal pleas to President Bill Clinton to reconsider the draconian elements of the crime bill. And yet Jackson survives in the public consciousness as more of a pop culture figure than a leading dissident of American life. Research into his work coupled with analysis of the pervasive reaction to his work reveals a conclusion that is as unavoidable as it is damning of the establishment press, and its corporate ownership.

The gulf separating the reality of Jackson's life and the perception of his life is cavernous, and, more significantly, it is not accidental. It is the predictable consequence of a pattern of reporting that distorts or discredits Jackson, providing ammunition to a general public prepared to indulge in the stereotyping, hostility, and suspicion that so often accompany racial prejudice. None of this is to imply anything so cloak and dagger as a group of powerful men congregating in a secret location to develop a battleplan for diminishment of Jackson's reputation over expensive spirits and cigars. It is a reflection of the reflexive bias at institutions emanating out of the market-driven values of multinational corporations—values that reject anything or anyone that might interfere with profits, or oppose those who protect those profits. In an exchange about corporate bias with an indignant television reporter, Noam Chomsky once explained that he doesn't believe that elite journalists and commentators have marching orders to articulate certain beliefs, but that if they did not have those beliefs, they would not have their positions in the first place.[20] One of the prerequisite beliefs of the latter half of the twentieth century in the American press, with a predominantly white commentariat, was that Jesse Jackson was unworthy of impartial coverage. He is a living and breathing challenge to the unspoken ideology of the American experience—the beliefs that profits are more important than people, that the white majority should remain uncontested in American power arrangements, and that war and domination are suitable goals in international affairs. His victories made his challenge even more urgent, and with them so increased the urgency of casting him as a villain in the minds of the American public.

That Jackson accomplished so much in the face of such sharp fangs of adversity is a testament to the human spirit; the "somebodiness" of the oppressed and the underdog. His persistence demonstrates faith in the claim first articulated by Martin Luther King—"The arc of the universe is long, but it bends toward justice."

When the festivities for Jesse Jackson's seventy-seventh birthday at Rainbow/PUSH headquarters ended, the crowd of family, friends, and supporters who spoke before the cutting of the cake—an impressive lineup of elected officials, civil rights activists, and academics—began to clear away. The few remaining members of PUSH staff worked in isolation and silence on various tasks. I was there to take notes, and when I began to say farewell, Jackson asked if I would wait for him in his office. I assumed that he had a story to share, or a new analysis of a political issue to put on the record. The private office was silent as I settled into a plush chair propped up against a wall. Periodically, a staffer will redecorate, rotating photos and awards in and out. Looking at me from across the room was Jackson, two of his sons, and Nelson Mandela in a framed photograph a few inches below a picture of Jackson and his wife standing at the doorway of 10 Downing Street, the home of the prime minister of England. When Jackson entered the room, he lumbered into a chair adjacent to mine—his deliberate and, at times, awkward movements demonstrating the effects of Parkinson's. He lowered his head, and closed his eyes as if he was about to fall asleep. Before I could say anything, he jolted himself awake, and asked, "Do you want to watch some of the game with me?" I said, "Sure." For the next fifteen minutes we sat, mostly quiet, watching the University of Michigan football team struggle against its opponent. "You were a quarterback, right?" I asked. "Yes, I was," he answered back softly. After a few pedestrian plays, Michigan's quarterback launched a long pass, over the arms of many stretching and jumping defenders, and under the pressure of a blitz. The ball sailed and safely landed in a receiver's arms, who stood in the center of the end zone. "That was a beautiful play," Jackson said.

Chapter 10

KEEP HOPE ALIVE

Helen Burns Jackson, at the age of ninety-two, was consigned to a hospital bed. Suffering the symptoms of heart failure and nearing the end of her long and fruitful life, she called her son, Jesse, every day. Even in the chaos of his tightly packed schedule, and through the cacophony of journalist inquiry, mass media commentary, and audience applause, she found his voice at the other end of the telephone. In 2015, Jackson had begun to regularly schedule speeches and meetings in South Carolina so that he could spend a few days a week with his mother. The specter of death, perhaps even more than death itself, makes love urgent. He planned on spending the entire afternoon and evening after a speech to local South Carolina officials about voting rights and health-care issues at the hospital. I was covering his tour of the Carolinas, which began with a public town hall about creating a political movement to pressure then South Carolina governor Nikki Haley to accept Medicaid expansion funds from the Affordable Care Act. When we arrived at the hospital the next day, shortly after his strategy session with mayors, city council members, and state legislators, I expected to find a private place to write before catching my flight. "Come into the room with me," Jackson ordered as he made his way toward an elevator. I mumbled something under my breath and walked with him down the hallway. Jackson's walk shifted into to a slow shuffle.

To enter the hospital room of a terminal patient is to join the company of a living, breathing human being, full of all the memories, stories, secrets, heartbreak, and laughter that accumulate to form a life just as it is all about to permanently vanish. Hospice workers explain that when we find ourselves in these peculiar and painful situations, we often look for an immediate task to perform. If we can pour water for the patient, fluff the pillow of the ill, or find another blanket to lay down on the cold body of the dying, we feel useful. Utility provides an odd comfort. The true task and the real gift is simple presence—to sit in the room, hold a hand, make conversation, stare out the window in silence. Much to our frustration, this is the best we can do. This is all that we can do.

We reached the room. Jackson peeked his head around the wall and pointed at his mother. A tiny, petite woman, wearing eye makeup with a silk red scarf tied around her head, smiled with her lipstick colored lips so large that her eyes almost shut. "My baby!" she shouted. "Baby's here," Jackson answered as he moved toward her fragile body wrapped in blankets and bedsheets. He leaned down, kissed her forehead and her cheek.

I sat down in a chair at the opposite end of the room. Jackson sat next to his mother. "Give me another kiss, baby," she said. "Baby's here, momma," Jackson spoke in the voice of a child as he kissed her forehead. In a transparently inauthentic attempt to conceal her joy over her son's arrival, Mrs. Jackson asked Jesse, "Why are you here? You should be working. You have important work to do."

Jackson laughed and said, "Who's the boss?" His mother said, "I'm the boss!" "No, no, no," Jackson shot back, "Who's the boss?" "Ok, you're the boss," she conceded. "Well, if I'm the boss that means baby stays here. I'm not going anywhere," Jackson whispered as he squeezed his mother's hand.

"Besides, I've been working. This is a writer, David," he said pointing in my direction. "He is my friend." I stood up, and took Helen Jackson's hand, kissed the back of it, and told her that it was an honor to meet her. Her response caught me by surprise and put a lump in my throat: "Thank you for being a friend to my son."

The love between a parent and child, especially when the physical manifestation of that love is inching toward the exit, animates the cliché of singularity and oneness into life. Jesse Jackson, a man of great fame, power, and influence—all the prestige and profit to which millions aspire and we ascribe to the names in history books and newspaper headlines—became a helpless little boy in the hospital room. He lowered his face down toward the bed and pressed his mother's hand to his forehead. I gave them their privacy.

I leaned against the wall near a window in the corridor outside of Helen Jackson's hospital room. As I reviewed the notes for my article, Jackson emerged from the hospital room with tears in his eyes. He told me that his mother wished to go to sleep, and that he would return to the room in an hour. There was a heavy rain outside, the wind making the drops pelt against the nearby window. Jackson lifted his large body and lowered himself onto a ventilator. Sitting back against the window, with the rain falling down and providing percussion, he returned to the role in which he has always excelled, and that, perhaps most especially in this moment, provided him comfort. He gave a speech: "My mother gave birth to me as a teenager. She was a hair stylist by trade, but a social worker by faith. Her calling, unofficially, was Christian social work."

Jackson recalled memories of an illiterate First World War veteran who lived on their block struggling to complete forms for government assistance. She not only helped him complete those documents but also slowly taught him how to read. Whenever women in the neighborhood needed their hair to look pretty for a job interview, family occasion, or date, but could not afford a trip to the salon, Helen Jackson would cut and style their hair in her home, without charge. "If I have ever shown desire to help those who most need it—if I've ever been successful in that mission," Jackson said with luminous intensity in his eyes, "It is because of my mother."

"Christian social work" maps the meeting ground of belief and practice. In analysis—favorable or critical—of Jesse Jackson, people often neglect to mention the orientation and tradition accessible through his formal title: reverend. It is a challenge to have a conversation with Jackson, or attend a speech, without hearing him reference the Bible. Jackson's theology, with generous influence from Martin Luther King, Obery Hendricks, and Gustavo Gutierez, interprets the Christian stories, doctrines, and dogmas as a collective manifesto for pacifism, poverty relief, and political intervention to correct the injustices of the ruling class. Christmas is a day to "set the captives free"—to celebrate the arrival of a liberator who faced opposition from the monarchy, the Roman Empire, and the corrupt religious establishment. "Why was Jesus killed?" Jackson asked an Occupy Wall Street assembly in London on Easter Sunday, "Because he fought and he occupied the corrupt temple. He went to the house of prayer, and found greed ruining the holy place. He asked, 'Why should the rich occupy the holy place?'" Jackson then identified the poor woman with only a bit to donate to the offering plate as the "99 percent."[1] In 2016, he provided an Easter sermon to undocumented immigrants taking sanctuary in a Methodist Church in Chicago. "Easter is nothing if not a day to embrace immigrants and refugees, especially those facing deportation," Jackson told a local news station outside, "Jesus was born a refugee facing death."[2]

Christopher Hitchens once pulverized an audience member at a campus lecture who asked, with indignation, "If you truly don't believe that there is a God, why do you spend so much time attacking religion?" The polemicist explained that he would prefer to be "left alone," but religion won't have it.[3] In other words, you might not be interested in religion, but religion is interested in you. This relationship is particularly powerful in the United States—a country with rates of religious devotion off the charts of the educated, developed world. Even beyond adherence to Christianity and other monotheisms in America, there is an inescapable religious fervor to American life. The entire country is a religious experiment, a faith claim, and a theological theory. Robert Bellah, an American sociologist, was the first to convincingly argue that the true religion of America is America. The majority of the nation's citizens ascribe borderline supernatural qualities to their country, believing, as several presidents of both major parties have declared, that it is not merely a country, but a "shining city on a hill." Soldiers are saints, the flag is a sacred icon, and dogmas, such as "American exceptionalism," teach the faithful that their society possesses divine qualities.[4] Subsequent to Bellah, many sharp analysts, from Frederick Gedicks, a scholar on religion in public life, to historian Morris Berman, have drawn upon how irrational, untestable faith in American benevolence, superiority, and power has violated authentic democracy, and created fertile conditions for bombing campaigns, invasions, and other acts of violence against countries that fail to genuflect to the "world's last remaining superpower."[5] Christianity, as a result of America's devotion to its civil religion, becomes attendant, or even subservient, to worship of the United States. A popular T-shirt throughout the Heartland and the South began appearing after the controversy surrounding former NFL player, Colin Kaepernick, kneeling during the national anthem as a sign of solidarity with victims of police brutality. The text of the shirt unintentionally, but perfectly captures the bizarre kinship many Americans imagine between "God and country"—"I stand for the flag. I kneel for the cross."

The jingoistic apparel, and the racial sentiment it represents, also unintentionally provides insight into the foundation of the religious right as an influential force in American politics. Contrary to popular belief, Christian conservatives did not enter political debate due to anger over abortion or even gay rights. It was racism. Most white Protestants supported Jimmy Carter's run for the presidency, because they viewed him as an honorable member of their own theological tribe—a white, Southern Baptist. Led by Jerry Falwell and Ralph Reed, they quickly betrayed Carter, and enlisted in Republican Party politics because, as president, Carter instructed his administration to target religious academies and universities in the South for their refusal to admit black students. The violation of civil rights law often resulted in the revocation of grants, along with penalties in the form of fines and federal supervision. The religious right became a powerful presence in right-wing activism not because of the sexual revolution, but because of its insistence on unlawfully discriminating against black Americans. Martin Luther King, conversely, introduced Christianity into the public space by using it to present a persuasive argument for racial equality. "King used the flag and the cross," Jackson once said while issuing a reminder that King persuasively claimed the mantle of patriotism, famously discussing the "promissory note" of the Declaration of Independence, the US Constitution, and the Emancipation Proclamation, when presenting his argument that it was the Black Freedom Movement—not the centurions of Jim Crow—that best represented American ideals.[6]

Jesse Jackson, a civil rights leader who was also partially responsible for the end of legal segregation, interprets the American battle over belief as rising out of the roots of Ancient Rome. Authentic application of the Gospels should lead to rebellion in the American Empire, just as it did in the Roman Empire. "Constantinian Christianity," Jackson said during our conversation on religion in reference to Constantine, the emperor who made Christianity the official religion of Rome, "makes people adjust to an unjust order. The Galilean Christians rebelled against the social order." No apologist for wars of choice and conquest, or defender of a vicious domestic system of wealth concentration, can make a claim on coherent Christian faith. Jackson's own capsule biography of Jesus Christ emphasizes the canyon separating contemporary Constantinians and Galileans:

> Jesus was born in the Jewish religion, and he died in the Jewish religion. He was born poor, under a death warrant, escaped to Egypt as a refugee, eventually became a political prisoner and victim of capital punishment. Jesus expanded the meaning of his faith to include the locked out, and to fight the two orders of his time: The Roman Empire occupying his land and exploiting the poor; and the religious order, which was cutting deals with the Roman Empire.

Because most of the leading intellectuals and activists on the American left are secular, there is a tendency in progressive politics to forfeit religious language to the right—a crucial error considering that 65 percent of the American public identifies as Christian, and 80 percent believe in God.[7] This isn't to say that agnostics and atheists on the left should present themselves with a phony faith, but it is to suggest that figures like Jesse Jackson, who could help create a robust Christian left, should have more time in the spotlight. It takes little imagination to draw a parallel between the Roman Empire, exploiting the poor, and corporate America and the government that enables it. The connection between the religious order, "cutting deals with the Roman Empire," and the most prominent forces of Christian Conservatism, including Mike Pence, vice president to Donald Trump, is equally easy to delineate.

"To admire Jesus is easy, especially in America where we make him a trophy. We see him on the cross, looking muscular. We know he performed miracles and said nice things," Jackson said, eventually bringing his own story into his sermon.

> To follow him is hard. When I went to the seminary, I learned that I had to take Jesus out of my back pocket, and I had to start following him, instead of thinking he would follow me. To follow him, you have to go into the quarantine shelter with the leper. You have to protect the prostitute. You have to challenge the prevailing government. It is risky, and that's why most people don't accept the rebels of Galilean Christianity, fighting to help the poor and to end war. It isn't just piety. It is justice and poverty.

A juxtaposition between ministers like Martin Luther King, Michael Pfleger, and Jesse Jackson with Billy Graham is revelatory as to how pious nationalism dilutes American Christianity. Jackson once told me that Graham, as the leading white evangelical in the country who claimed to believe in universal brotherhood, was asked to say a prayer at the 1963 March on Washington where King gave his legendary "I Have a Dream" address. Graham refused. Many years later, the Nixon tapes would expose him as an anti-Semite, ridiculing and mocking Jews to the disgraced former president, who himself was a bigot.[8] At the height of the HIV/AIDS epidemic, when Jackson was sleeping in AIDS hospices, Graham asserted that the deadly disease was "judgement from God." "Suppose Rosa Parks waited for white people. Suppose Dr. King waited for Billy Graham," Jesse Jackson once said to a television studio audience with the clear implication that, given the cowardice of "America's pastor," black Americans looking for equality under the law would still be standing in line. Bill Clinton, Barack Obama, George W. Bush, and Donald Trump all either attended the funeral for Graham or released official statements expressing gratitude and admiration for his "lifetime of service."[9]

Jackson did not finish the institutional academic requirements for his master's degree at the University of Chicago, because, in the exercise of justice over piety, he abandoned his coursework to accept the position of aide to Martin Luther King. The prestigious institution eventually awarded Jackson his degree, substituting the experience he acquired in the civil rights movement for the few remaining credits on his itinerary. Jackson, in agreement with his alma mater, submits that he learned lessons of greater profundity with King than he could have in any classroom.

> I learned in college and in seminary, but I learned all of this most deeply with Dr. King's ministry. Dr. King said that "our religion makes us political. Our politics

do not make us religious." A religious ethic is useless if it does not confront an unjust law. We had to be religious at the back of the bus to move to front of the bus. The idea that religion is transformative, personally and politically, flies in the face of the cultural flow.

Faith in American power and benevolence rests on a myth. A Christian left, even if Jackson would not use the word, can combat "myth" with "myth," in the most essential conception of the term—not a synonym for a false narrative but, as folklorists would explain, a story that plays a fundamental role in the shaping of society. Theologian Stanley Haurewas often asserts that the problem with American Christians is that they forget or dismiss how "odd" their religion really is.[10] Certainly, the theology, in ways he intends to imply and not, is bizarre, but weirdness in the American context might also mean not transforming the "pursuit of happiness" into an obsessive quest to maximize profit. Weirdness might mean viewing one's self not as an isolated agent in search of pleasure, but as a participant in a community with a responsibility to demonstrate care for one's cohabitants. The most elementary of social programs submit that a compact exists interlocking people of a shared society with one another, despite lack of personal connection or interest. You might not ever meet the disabled widow living on the other side of town—or the other side of the country—but your payroll taxes help to ensure that she will receive sustenance for a stable life. That perspective is logical, and has the support of evolutionary psychology, but it also might require a certain form of faith. "We live in our faith, but we live under the law," Jesse Jackson is fond of reminding reporters and audiences at public lectures. Faith—"the evidence of things unseen," to use a biblical definition— might give beleaguered activists and concerned citizens the courage and tenacity to imagine an alternative to the structures under which they struggle.

"If you and I had some dough from which a biscuit is made, and we put some in your shoes, and some in my shoes, the biscuit would look different, because the power of the shoe shapes the form of it. But, there's nothing different about the content of the dough," Jackson pointed out to me with the use of one his unique metaphors. Faith, according to Jackson, can help people see beyond the shape of the shoe—"Black religion is either adjusting to oppression or fighting it. White religion is either fighting oppression or rationalizing it."

A reorientation of the synthesis between religion and civics would also present new and more edifying imagery for the politics that faith might make possible. When Jackson provided assistance to Cesar Chavez's hunger strike, Chavez, as a show of gratitude, gifted Jackson with his rosary. A framed photo of the moment, captured by a newspaper photographer, hangs in the conference room at Rainbow/ PUSH, where Jackson holds weekly staff meetings. Both men are down on one knee, their foreheads touch, as they both place their hands on the cross. The symbolic value of that moment possesses much greater inspirational power than any picture of a celebrity minister praying with a president as the government prepares to launch a war.

One week after Jackson rescued three American military personnel from the former Yugoslavia, he intervened in a dispute much closer to home. The school board of Decatur, Illinois—a small, farm town—elected to expel seven black high school students who got into a fist fight during a football game. There were no weapons or injuries causing hospitalization. Most of the town was white, most of the school was white, and all the members of the school board were white. Jackson parlayed his power to fine use in the small town, overwhelming their officials with his media presence and stature, filing a lawsuit with the aid of civil rights attorney Karen Cecile Wallace, and eventually securing the students readmittance into the public school. One of the "Decatur Seven," as the Illinois press came to christen them—Courtney Carson—graduated from college, earned a master's degree, and now sits on the school board that once voted for his expulsion. Speaking at Rainbow/PUSH headquarters on the twentieth anniversary of the dispute, he explained that he never knew his biological father and, as a consequence, suffered from a deficit of male role models. "Jesse Jackson became my father," he said. "I could never get my own father on the phone, but when I called Jesse Jackson, he always called me back. It might have been at two in the morning, from another country, but he always called me back. To have this important man care about me the way he did—It saved my life."

When Carlson was expelled, at the age of seventeen, he already had a child and a criminal record. Few in his neighborhood, and few in his country, would have expectations of achievement for his life. Jesse Jackson had faith. "I am somebody," in some cases, is the evidence of things unseen. Al Sharpton recalled in our conversation when, during the 1970s, a black activist mocked the mantra, "I am somebody." "Why do you need to hear that?" he asked Sharpton, "I know I'm somebody. Don't you know you're somebody?" "He was the son of a doctor," Sharpton said, "Like Jesse, I didn't grow up with my father. Like Jesse, I grew up poor. Like Jesse, I was picked on in school. Some of us needed 'I am somebody.' And when Jesse said it, he was saying for it himself as much as he was saying it for us."

America also needs the evidence of things unseen, because it is has become increasingly clear that rational arguments are ineffective as they relate to more equitable and progressive public policy. The common refrain of cynicism that follows any ambition for better social policy—Medicare for all, debt-free universities, transforming the minimum wage into a living wage—displays a dearth of genuine belief. "How will we pay for it?" or "it is a good idea, but will never work" demand an intellectual argument, but also an insistence on faith. "We can go forward by hope or backward by fear," Jesse Jackson consistently declares. Political faith is an accelerant, while fear is the brake.

The American left in recent years, especially on racial issues, has embraced a paralytic ideology almost absent of any hope for reconciliation and justice. "Afro-pessimism" is the accurate title of a philosophy that insinuates an omnipotent and omnipresent white supremacy in Western culture and institutions. Without the total obliteration of the social structure that rose to prominence through racist policy, Afro-pessimists insist, progress against racism is all but impossible.[11] Ta-Nehisi Coates, a former essayist for the *Atlantic* and best-selling author who has become something of a left-wing superstar in American life, is an archbishop in the church of Afro-pessimism. The metaphor is apt not only because of the way that progressive audiences receive Coates' polemical writing like Catholics would review a papal encyclical but also because Coates is offering a substitute religion in place of the hopeful Christianity that was essential to the civil rights movement. For anyone who views the comparison to theology as overstated, consider Coates' own analysis of Donald Trump's electoral victory: "To Trump, whiteness is neither notional nor symbolic but is the very core of his power. In this, Trump is not singular. But whereas his forebears carried whiteness like an ancestral talisman, Trump cracked the glowing amulet open, releasing its eldritch energies."[12]

The polemicist is correct that Trump's racial identity is central to his politics, but for all his poetic eloquence, what follows is rather silly. It imagines white supremacy as a supernatural force animating the spooky, macabre mysteries of an Edgar Allan Poe story. "Eldritch energies" is a phrase of self-exposure, revealing an inability to negotiate the material world of public policy and empirical evidence. Coates is an atheist, but in his nonfiction and literary work, he betrays an obsession with magic, witchcraft, and sorcery. He wrote a graphic novel about the comic book hero, Black Panther, and his adult novel, *The Water Dancer*, features a protagonist in the antebellum South with a mysterious power to teleport slaves into the Underground Railroad by manipulating time and space. The magical realism of Coates is inalienable from his historical analysis and political commentary. Veteran journalist Salim Muwwakil, reviewing Coates' work for the Chicago leftist publication, *In These Times*, writes that the young intellectual counters former president Obama's "audacity of hope" with a delineation of the "absurdity of hope."[13] Without supernatural intervention, Coates seems to argue, justice and healing have no chance against the indestructible poltergeist of white supremacy.

Since Coates is irreligious, he would believe that such an intervention is impossible, leaving his readers only with fantasies in the genre of fiction, and in journalism and historical review, a fatalistic eschatology. The ecstatic and adoring reaction Coates has provoked on the American left, and within academia, demonstrates that his religious rejection of faith in future progress has many adherents. He is the winner of a National Book Award, a MacArthur Foundation Genius Grant, a three-time *New York Times* best-selling author, and public speaker whose college campus events attract thousands of attendees. *The Water Dancer* was an Oprah Book Club selection. In Coates' defense, he is a skillful writer, and much of his work, particularly the lengthy essay connecting redlining and housing discrimination in Chicago to a case for reparations, has opened the American conversation on its own history in ways that are beneficial and illuminative. The nature of his influence, despite his admirable qualities, is dubious. Imani Perry, a Princeton scholar, writes in her book on race in America, *Breathe*, that "a terrifying specter is haunting Blackness: the white imagination."[14] It is revealing and damning that a scavenger hunt through Coates' books, along with Perry's, for the words "vote," "voting," "public policy," "law," "protest," "boycott," or anything else that actually determines how society operates, and how change becomes possible, comes up empty.[15] Albert Einstein offered a warning that resounds in the contemporary era, "It is the theory that determines what we observe."[16]

If the theory posits an indefatigable and unbreakable white supremacist stranglehold on America, the observations that will naturally follow will render progress impossible, hope naïve, and political defeat inevitable. Jesse Jackson once told me that his study of theology helped him prepare, perhaps counterintuitively, for the dissection of social structure, rules, and regulatory procedure. "Theology is the study of belief systems," he said, "It is not a great leap to apply those tools to the study of legal, political, and economic systems." For his sincere faith and devotion in Christianity, Jackson evinces a more rational and logical worldview than Coates and his young congregants. His theory does not resemble "Afro-pessimism." It is participatory democracy, and as a result, observes the victories of protest movements, exercise of the franchise, and social solidarity. Despite his beginning in a society far more unjust and oppressive than anything Coates experienced, he cites the biblical command to "count your blessings"—"You have eyes to see, ears to hear, legs to walk. Once you count all that you have, you run out of numbers. We've gone from the bridge in Selma to the White House." When I asked him how he maintains hope, he did not delve into abstract theory, but offered the rational description of his own experience: "I was arrested for trying to check a book out of a library. I saw Martin Luther King assassinated on a hotel balcony. Sometimes when you are digging yourself out of a hole, you become so fixated on how far you have left to climb that you forget to look back to see how far you've already come."

It is not a speculative theory, but an evidential conclusion, to say that Jesse Jackson helped to universalize voting rights in America and was responsible for registering more voters than nearly anyone in the twentieth century, led the transformation of the Democratic Party from a friendlier version of white, corporate favor seeking into a representative force of multicultural America that addresses the financial precarity of American life, punctured the forcefield of American capitalism to enable countless black workers and entrepreneurs access to opportunity and consumer protections, and saved hundreds of lives in an ongoing mission to make American foreign policy more humane, cooperative, and respectful of international law. And yet Jackson remains oddly neglected in American discourse. Once when I talked to James Lee Burke, one of America's greatest crime novelists, he was aghast over the lack of accolades his fellow mystery writer, Ron Hansen, has received: "It is like Babe Ruth is at bat at Yankee Stadium, and everyone in the crowd is waiting in line to get a hot dog."

Now that he has reached his elderly years, one of the tasks that occupies his time is speaking at funerals. Mortality has struck out with a series of cruel blows in the past few years alone. He has buried his friend Aretha Franklin, his longest-serving PUSH staff member, Willie Barrow, and his beloved mother. During a commercial break in his weekly radio program, he confessed to his daughter and cohost, Santita, that he "still calls mother every day. She never answers." While preparing for the Saturday morning forum sessions, he has also said that he still expects to find Willie Barrow in his office, and when speaking at the service for

Franklin, he addressed his own mortality, pain, and physical struggle with the merciless hand of time. "I'll never stop marching," he said, "If I can no longer march, I'll still be there somehow."

Parkinson's disease has taken its toll on Jackson. His steps are heavier and slower, his words don't soar and thunder with the eloquence and power they once possessed, and his schedule includes periods of the one thing he never knew or liked to do—rest. Tears still fill his eyes when he remembers the gruesome scene of April 4, 1968, and even though he had some expectation of it, his assistant told me that the morning after Donald Trump became president-elect of the United States, she had never seen him "so disappointed." No matter his personal grief or agony, and no matter the struggles of American democracy, Jackson continues to end every speech, asking his audience to repeat after him, with the words, "keep hope alive."

For hope to survive the inevitable tragedies and traumas of life, whether they are personal or political, tangible tools of hope must exist. It is impossible to have hope in healing from a disease if medicine and health care are inaccessible. Similarly, political hope can thrive only when people understand and acquire the means of healing social ills. Leaders, like Jesse Jackson, play a profound role in directing the energy and investment of ordinary citizens searching for a method to manipulate unjust institutions into beneficial transformation. As educators, orators, and mediators, leaders can ensure that activists achieve synchronicity in their struggles according to the old and indispensable principle of social movements: organization. The macabre and magic of literary theories regarding the "white specter," and social media campaigns that obsess over the trivialities of pop culture, contribute little, if anything, to organization. Meanwhile, Jesse Jackson, in his elderly years, even as his body betrays him, and even as his crowds diminish in size and his media profile fades, dedicates himself to organization—contributing his experience, wisdom, and leadership to assisting people in the necessity of collaborating with intelligence toward the laudable goal of enhancing democracy in American life.

Whether he is serving food on Thanksgiving to destitute families, meeting with a foreign despot to convince him to free an innocent scholar, or arguing for racial and gender inclusion at a corporate shareholder meeting, Jackson is practicing Christian social work. Flying halfway across the world to liberate political prisoners, or walking into a boardroom to negotiate better wages and benefits for workers, is not altogether different in spirit than Helen Jackson teaching an illiterate veteran how to read or, despite her own financial desperation, waiving the fee for a friend who needs her hair styled before a big job interview. Christian social work endures in its immediate impact on the recipients—the people who can vote because of the work to which Jackson contributed, the thousands who were able to secure employment and start businesses in a racist economic structure, the hostages who made it home to hug their families, the children at PUSH who learn computer programming skills at no cost. It also persists in the influence that it has on those who, even if they do not directly benefit from it, can see it—Barack Obama saying to himself, "this can happen," as he watched Jesse Jackson get the best of his competitors in the Democratic primary debates of the 1980s.

Albert Camus wrote that people who live in an unjust society must refuse to become either victims or executioners.[17] Leaders like Jackson often begin in roles of victimhood, but they overcome the adversity of their circumstances to acquire significant power. They then use that power to inspire others to refuse victimhood. "I am somebody" becomes not only a slogan but also a call to action for revolt against anything that denies your humanity and dignity. They also inspire those who share some immutable characteristic with the executioners to not become one themselves. Because of the work of Martin Luther King, Ida B. Wells, Jesse Jackson, and so many others, I do not have to live as an executioner, an occupier, or an oppressor. As much as people with little imagination, and less empathy, might insist, our interests are not opposed. As Jackson taught his audience at the 1984 Democratic Convention, "we must all come up together."

Disappointments and defeats are inevitable. Finding common ground and moving to the moral higher ground is much harder than it sounds. If it was easy, Jackson wouldn't need to dedicate himself to the cause at his age and in his condition. Protest movements are unnecessary in utopia, and utopia is not locatable on any map. Another police officer will shoot someone without justification, another good person will die because she cannot afford medicine, and more bombs will fall on cities full of people far removed from the international conflict that led to war. The hard-won triumphs of history will teach people of conscience how to deal with the traumas of tomorrow.

On Independence Day of 2015, Jesse Jackson celebrated not the dominant America, but the alternative America: the America of Martin Luther King's dream and Woody Guthrie's song. Hustling for profit and power was, from the beginning, at the center of American culture, but warring in the wings were always those voices and visionaries who could see a better possibility, an alternative promise—a "land made for you and me." Jesse Jackson used a different song as soundtrack to his faithful articulation of the outside tradition: "Testimony"—a simple but powerful gospel number lifting the spirits of those who testify the truth even when under pressure to lie. The Rainbow/PUSH choir, assembled in a line behind Jackson, singing with all the might they could summon from the lungs and the gut, gave a riptide backing to the sermonic stream of Jackson's populist rhetoric, pulling the crowd into the world that his words sketched. He proclaimed, "Rosa Parks had a testimony. Martin Luther King had a testimony. Nelson Mandela had a testimony." Then, he spoke in the first person, enunciating with clarity and bravado the veracity of his own testimony.

"I once was young, but now I'm old. I've seen loss. Bitterness. Meanness. But when I look back over my life, there's power! There's joy! There's hope! There's healing!"

AFTERWORD

OF JOY AND JUSTICE

The rainbow coalition shot through the streets of America in the summer of 2020. Derek Chauvin, a white police officer in Minneapolis, suffocated George Floyd, a handcuffed Black man, over a period of nine minutes, by placing his knee firmly on the neck of Floyd, who was flat on the pavement. The assault resulted in Floyd's death—a homicide by any ethical or legal consideration. Horrified onlookers captured cell phone video, while they pled for Floyd's life. They quickly released the footage to the public. Millions of Americans watched what amounted to a modern lynching and, in the middle of a deadly pandemic, marched through major cities and small towns, organized protest rallies, and demanded justice—not only for the deceased and bereaved but for Black Americans, who, as statistical studies demonstrate, are often targets of racial profiling from law enforcement, victims of police brutality from officers who typically enjoy immunity, and subjects of hate crimes from perpetrators who share not the costume but the ideology of the Ku Klux Klan.

The rebellion that followed—visible in not only predictable precincts, like New York and Chicago, but also in the bucolic villages of Minnesota and Indiana, and everywhere between Alaska and Florida—was the largest protest movement in American history. Floyd, his family, and anyone committed to the activation of social justice in the United States also witnessed allies throughout Europe, Asia, South America, and Africa organize their own marches, rallies, and signals of support. When I sat down with Jesse Jackson in the offices of the Rainbow/PUSH Coalition of Chicago during the days of hope and rage that summer, he did not exactly state the obvious: that the Black Lives Matter rebellion projected and promoted the societal vision and mission he spent and risked his life to make possible. The closest he came was the articulation: "To have young Blacks, Hispanics, Asians, and whites together, shutting down highways in major American cities, because a Black man was murdered says a lot, and it is a lot." He could have added straight, gay, trans, Christian, Jewish, Muslim, atheist, middle-aged, elderly, rich, middle-class, and poor. It was a true coalition, and it rang true internationally. Jackson's domestic work has always aimed at equity and dignity for Black Americans, while also emphasizing hospitality for anyone and everyone to participate, and procure benefits from movements for a beloved community. Jackson's diplomatic work, from Iraq to Cuba, and South Africa to

South Korea, emanates out of opposition to violence, and uses the desire for peace and harmony to forge mutually profitable relationships between people of different faiths, politics, and economic standing. As has happened, time and time again, the world that Jackson asked audiences to imagine throughout previous decades—the world that cynics, fascists, and fools claimed was a fever dream—suddenly came alive in three-dimensional Technicolor right in front of our eyes.

The George Floyd Rebellion can claim major achievements: thirty-one state governments, and dozens of municipal governments, passed police reform legislation into law following the protests. Many activists ran for local office in Minneapolis, Chicago, and other cities, and won, bringing their perspective to official proceedings of governance. The voter registration that took place during that summer, particularly with young voters throughout the country, Latino and Native American voters in Arizona, Latinos and Blacks in Pennsylvania, and Blacks in Georgia, helped to secure the presidential victory of Joe Biden and Kamala Harris — a Black and Indian woman whose entrance into electoral politics was as a volunteer for the Jackson campaigns in the 1980s. Months later, in a run-off vote for the Senate, the same multiracial coalition of voters in Georgia would send Raphael Warnock, a Black minister and civil rights activist, and Jon Osoff, a Jewish former intern of Congressman John Lewis, to the US Senate. The Black Lives Matter protests also shifted the cultural conversation, imbuing debates regarding educational policy, pop culture, and professional sports with sensitivity to racism, both its historical and contemporary iterations. A jury of his peers convicted Derek Chauvin of murder. He will serve twenty-two years and six months in prison.

Among all the debates that ensued from Chauvin's murder of Floyd, and the movement it ignited, few journalists or pundits, on the right or left, remarked on the historic diversity of the crowds shouting "Black Lives Matter!" There is a tendency in American culture to forget, ignore, or dismiss the soft revolution of the Civil Rights Movement, and how it continues to culturally and politically reverberate. When I talked to Jackson in December of 2022, he offered a succinct summary of the societal transformation that too many people take for granted, highlighting only a small sampling of the countless illustrative examples:

> The civil rights revolution— not only for Blacks, but also women, the disabled, gays—came through nonviolence, democratic participation, and voting. We take much of our progress for granted. When I was with Dr. King, we confronted a hostile government in almost every city we visited. In 2020, during the Black Lives Matter protests, there was a Black woman mayor in Atlanta, a Black woman mayor in Washington, D.C., a Black woman mayor in Chicago, and a Jewish progressive in Minneapolis. Dr. King had to fight against unfriendly media. Now, there are people like Don Lemon, Ari Melber, and Rachel Maddow on television. Academia looked down on the movement. Now, Harvard has a Black woman president. There are scholars at every major university who study the movement. We changed the country, and we can continue.

A few weeks after I conducted that interview with Jackson, the NFL Super Bowl took place in Glendale, Arizona. Both starting quarterbacks were Black. When Jackson won a scholarship to the University of Illinois in the 1960s, because he was a spectacular quarterback in high school, he quickly felt the bitter pain of rejection. The coaching staff at the University of Illinois made it clear that they could not have a Black quarterback, because it is a leadership position, and Blacks, according to the ignorant and prejudicial assumptions of the time, were unfit to lead. Every day honest observers can count the ways that the Civil Rights Movement morphed the United States from a white patriarchy into something resembling the "liberal city" —a place where all are welcome and can assemble based not on ties of blood and ethnicity but on shared interests, desires, and mutually gainful, voluntary transactions—something resembling a multiracial democracy.

Despite the triumphs he helped engineer, and despite his own struggles with Parkinson's disease at the age of eighty-eight, Jackson is not ready to retire. His mentor, Martin Luther King, Jr., once implored an audience to live according to "divine dissatisfaction." "Let us be dissatisfied until slums are cast into the junk heaps of history," King said during a speech in Chicago that Jackson attended and helped organize. "Let us be dissatisfied until integration is not seen as a problem but as an opportunity to participate in the beauty of diversity."

There are plenty of reasons for dissatisfaction, divine and otherwise, in the United States. Just as the later months of 2020 evinced the triumph of Jackson's "rainbow coalition" philosophy, the early days of 2021 demonstrated the extremity and severity of the forces devoted to its destruction. Martin Luther King spoke about "the beauty of diversity" in the 1960s. In 2021, the reactionary right let its fascist flag fly by summoning a violent mob, many of them carrying Confederate Flags and other emblems of hate, to storm the US Capitol, assault police officers, and attempt to murder elected officials, all in the hope to overturn a free and fair election. Their success would have meant the end of American democracy. Their mere ambition and execution revealed the extent to which Republicans work alongside hate groups, like the Proud Boys and Oathkeepers, and the lethal lengths they will go to achieve their political objectives. Because the vision of Martin Luther King, Rosa Parks, Jesse Jackson, Harvey Milk, and other revolutionaries is triumphing, and because the right wing realizes it is outnumbered, especially with voters under the age of forty, it is has turned against democracy itself. Jackson spent years warning against the increasingly hateful and vengeful turn of the American right, usually to dismissal, mockery, or accusations of "alarmism" from the mainstream press. He once said that many American leaders are interested in democracy as a "power ball," meaning that they want "just enough democracy" to "legitimate their power" but not enough to create meaningful participation and shared prosperity among the public. The Trump presidency, the Republican alignment with hate groups, and the insurrection of January 6th demonstrated exactly what happens when the "power ball" is no longer useful to those who would prefer to use it, not as a tool of freedom and justice but as a weapon of white supremacy, patriarchy, and homophobia. Many of the foot soldiers within the mob, along with great numbers of the American right more broadly, believe in the "Great Replacement Theory," which posits that Jewish globalists are using racial minorities within the United States to dilute, and eventually destroy, white prominence and power. From June 2020 to January 2021, within an eight-month period, everything that Jackson, his mentors, his supporters, his volunteers, and his allies fought, worked, bled, and often died to achieve rose to new heights, and faced new dangers.

Articulating his own divine dissatisfaction, Jesse Jackson paused his praise for the Black Lives Matter movement by adding, "Freedom from barbarism is not social justice." "Police patrol," Jackson added during our conversation in 2020, "they don't control." Making his analysis even clearer, he said, "Police reform is necessary and right, but police brutality is the epidermis. Racism cuts bone deep. If tonight every cop transformed into officer-friendly, tomorrow we will still have health-care disparities. We will still have educational disparities. We will still have wealth disparities. We will still have disparities in land ownership, hiring practices, and economic inheritance and access."

Jackson sees the Black Lives Matter movement, and its success in securing a cultural megaphone, as an opportunity to challenge broader inequities and injustices within the system. "Whites see a police officer murder George Floyd," he said, "and they are embarrassed. They think, 'that's not our culture.'" "Really?" he asked with his eyes open wide, "After the Indian Removal Act, after Jim Crow, after corporate apartheid. This is the system. Whites benefit from the system. You can't swim without getting wet."

To reform an unjust, and often self-damaging system, Jackson suggests starting with the most elementary mechanism that too many people, particularly on the far left, often neglect. "The vote is a militant apparatus," Jackson said. "People downplay the vote. If it wasn't important, Republicans would not expend so much effort to suppress it—to keep Blacks, to keep college students, to keep Native Americans from voting; to stop people from voting bilingually and by mail."

In the 2020 presidential election, the vote secured the victory of Joe Biden, a party elder—former senator and vice president to Barack Obama—who, by most accounts, for most of his career, was hardly on the cutting edge of Democratic progressivism. Most of his supporters and detractors view him as closer to the center than the young, Democratic members of Congress, and governors, who more accurately and charismatically represent the party's future: Alexandria Ocasio-Cortez, Lauren Underwood, Ayana Pressley, Gretchen Whitmer, and Katie Hobbs—all women, mostly of color.

Underscoring the importance of the vote, and emphasizing the success of social movements, Jackson offers a different understanding of the Biden presidency: "Biden is a boat in a multicultural, progressive ocean. The movement of the boat is often determined by the flow of the ocean and the wind in the sails." President Biden has invited Jesse Jackson to the White House on multiple occasions, giving him a front-row seat for speeches on voting rights and thanking him during his introductory remarks for Ketanji Brown Jackson, his appointee to the Supreme Court who is now the body's first Black woman justice.

The camaraderie and affection that Biden regularly shows in the presence of Jackson signifies a sea change in Democratic Party politics. In 1988, during Jackson's second historic run for the presidency, one of his opponents was the then senator from Delaware, Joe Biden. Jackson finished in second place to the disastrous nominee, Michael Dukakis, while Biden was little more than a footnote. Even if his vote tally was abysmal, Biden represented the ideology of party leadership—party leadership that looked at Jackson with a combination of fear and disdain. Biden was among the elected officials who castigated Jackson's policy proposals as unrealistic and too far on the fringe of the left. Those policy positions included tuition-free community college, establishing universal health-care coverage through an expansion of public programs, paid family leave, capping the cost of essential prescription drugs, an enlargement of the child tax credit for poor and middle-class parents, and a massive infrastructure improvement program. Those are now all policies that President Biden has either signed into law or rhetorically championed. In order to win the Democratic Party nomination, secure the presidency, and manage the divisions within his party, Joe Biden has had to adopt the platform of his former opponent.

Biden is not alone in his appreciation of Jackson's achievements and influence. The Congressional Black Caucus honored Jackson during the first night of the Democratic National Convention in 2020. Secretary of Transportation Pete Buttigieg and former president Bill Clinton participated in the ceremony.

Unlike many American civil rights and humanitarian leaders, Jackson's work is international. He has received honors from British parliament, the South African government, and many European, Asian, and African organizations, but none might measure the reach of his accomplishments more than the highest honor of merit from the French government: the Legion d'Honneur. During the award ceremony in 2021, French president Emmanuel Macron explained that Legion d'Honneur was a token of appreciation for Jackson's "long walk toward emancipation and justice." "From your earliest years," Macron said, "you were hungry for knowledge and justice, and you are a special friend to France, a brother for us."

When Jackson gave the eulogy for Rosa Parks—one of the best of his countless speeches—he posited that, for all its accolades, Jeffersonian democracy has no "export value." How many suffering and bound people around the world could celebrate the arrival of a governmental system that includes slavery and the subjugation of women? If American leaders are to discuss democratic society with any powers of persuasion, they must mean, according to Jackson, "Parks-King democracy." In accordance with the same criteria of personal liberty and social justice, Jesse Jackson is a superior representative of the American dream and promise than most presidents and most elected officials—a philosophical fact of patriotism that Macron understood and emphasized when he said, "The values promoted by Reverend Jackson are universal, and reflect those of the French Republic." The French president projected the honor of Jackson as emblematic of "the historic alliance between the French and American peoples for a democratic and just society."

Macron and Jackson, standing side by side with their arms raised in the air, illustrated the bountiful gifts of democracy at precisely the moment that fascist movements around the world were dedicating themselves to its demolition. After the far-right Polish government eradicated its independent judiciary, scholars and activists concluded that Poland no longer qualifies as a democracy. The same travesty transpired in Hungary, where its authoritarian leaders also ushered in a new wave of homophobic policies and sentiment. Less than a year after Jackson received the Legion d'Honneur, Vladimir Putin initiated a genocidal invasion of Ukraine. In the Russian attempt at conquest, Putin has ordered the deliberate slaughter of civilians, separated Ukrainian children from their parents, and threatened to use nuclear weapons. Macron, Biden, and Jackson have continually declared support for the cause of Ukrainian self-determination, with the two presidents sending monetary and military aid, and Jackson's organization, Rainbow/PUSH, raising funds for Ukrainian refugees who have relocated to Chicago.

Influential elements within the Republican Party, including Donald Trump, opposed American aid to Ukraine, even expressing a form of sympathy for Putin with claims that the United States and North Atlantic Treaty Organization (NATO) cornered him into lashing out against the West by proxy. An American volunteer for a Ukrainian aid organization told me that Republican support for Putin is "straight up white power politics." That doubles as an accurate description of the internal movement in the United States to strike down voting rights, ban books about Black history and LGBTQ people from schools and libraries, and legitimate violence as a form of political discourse. Thousands of school board members, local officials, and even librarians have reported receiving repeated death threats from fascist maniacs who swear allegiance to Donald Trump and the GOP. The Proud Boys, a hate group partially responsible for the January 6th insurrection and known to brutally attack Black Lives Matter and LGBTQ protestors in the streets, has twelve members on the Republican Party Committee of Miami-Dade, the most populous country in Florida. Jackson went through a baptism by fire in the 1960s fighting for not the preservation but the establishment of multiracial democracy. He has told me stories about speaking in a church, only to have the lecture interrupted by streams of tear gas entering through the vents. The Ku Klux Klan was responsible. He and his associates and allies endured assassination plots against themselves and their families, faced down police prepared to beat them, and, during marches, dodged bricks and stones. Martin Luther King, like Medgar Evers and many others, did not survive. He became a fatality in a soft civil war bursting out in state after state all so that legally born citizens with darker hues of skin could cast votes, live where they choose, earn a living wage, and take advantage of the same public accommodations that whites never once questioned for themselves. Jackson implores equal vigilance now that the achievements of his generation are on the line. "We need to come alive again," he said during an early 2022 speech in Chicago. Voting, marching, petitioning, and supporting organizations like PUSH, the NAACP, and the Brennan Center for Justice have acquired newfound urgency.

It is important to remember, even while working for the protection of liberal democracy, Jackson's exhortation that "freedom from barbarism is not social justice." When the streets exploded into action during the Black Lives Matter rebellion, Jackson reminded me that social justice demands a reshaping of societal priorities—a reshaping that echoes his 1988 campaign rhetoric: "If we leave the racial battleground to find economic common ground, we can reach for moral higher ground." "Comprehensive health care benefits everybody," Jackson said. "Equality in education benefits everybody. We should fund schools based upon a child's worth not his or her surrounding property tax base. A living wage benefits everybody. A clean environment benefits everybody."

Identifying the human rights and needs that can, finally, cut through the success of divide-and-conquer culture wars affirms the message and mission that Jackson first articulated, under the influence of his then recently deceased mentor, Martin Luther King, during the Poor People's Campaign of 1968. It was there that Jackson first shouted what would become his signature call-and-response affirmation: "I am somebody!" It is the message of a great imagining of society, but one that starts with the most elementary of truths: if sick, a gay, white atheist needs medicine as much as a straight, Black Muslim. A Jewish woman needs to breathe clean air no more or less than a Christian man.

Now that Jesse Jackson has reached his elderly years, there is a poetic symmetry to his current and early work that reveals the consistency of his commitment and the constancy of American struggles for individual and communal dignity. Voting rights are more important now than at any point since the 1960s, because they are under greater assault than at any point since the 1960s. In the year preceding the 2020 election, Rainbow/PUSH registered voters, and worked with then Chicago mayor Lori Lightfoot to allow polling places in city and county jails. Opposition to racist policy and rhetoric is more significant now than at any point since the 1960s, because contemporary Republican politics have injected hatred into the mainstream, the likes of which few have seen the success of Nixon's "southern strategy." Even still, it was a quality of life issue that brought Jackson to a familiar place in January of 2022.

* * *

At precisely the moment when the country was paying tribute to the heroism of Martin Luther King, Jackson hosted a press conference at the Martin Luther King Legacy Apartments in Chicago. On what would have been King's ninety-third birthday, Jackson stood alongside representatives from the Chicago Coalition for the Homeless and the Illinois Union for the Homeless to discuss the "moral disgrace," as he called it, of homelessness and housing injustice. He began his remarks by informing the audience, and reminding the media, that King sought to serve those at "the bottom of the Empire."

The city of Chicago has transformed the lobby of the King Legacy apartment building into a small museum, showcasing the governmental-capital conspiracy that created the "ghetto." Through decades of redlining and other discriminatory lending practices, public infrastructural programs to preserve segregation, police enforcement of residential borders, and "neighborhood covenants" among white homeowners and landlords to never sell or rent to Blacks, Northern cities became white fiefdoms. Jackson first visited the building when it was a "slum," after helping to convince his boss, King, to make housing injustice the next focus of his movement and to choose Chicago—a northern city not officially under any Jim Crow regime—the staging ground. King spent time living in the slum apartments to call attention to their dangerous and filthy living conditions. He and his aides also organized marches and rallies to bring pressure to bear on the municipal government to end racial discrimination in housing and to ensure that public housing along with all privately operated apartment complexes were safe, clean, and in working order.

"We never saw hatred, not even in the Deep South, as severe as what we encountered in Chicago with the ethnic, Catholic whites," Jackson recalled about one of those Chicago marches. He explained that in Alabama, for example, the fear was always that the Ku Klux Klan or the police themselves, as in Selma, would turn violent on the protestors. In Chicago, it was as if the entire white majority was overcome by wicked mania, acting out their psychosis without shame or restraint. Ordinary civilians, from school teachers to auto mechanics, were charging the marchers, attempting to intimidate and assault them. The violence was so shocking that King canceled a second march planned for the nearby suburb of Cicero. Richard Daley, then mayor of Chicago, was hardly an ally, nor was he an opponent of political violence. Three years later, he would distinguish himself by giving a "shoot to kill" order to police during the riots following King's assassination in 1968. Daley, a Democrat, was the kind of "law and order" extremist that President Nixon and, later, President Trump would lionize and emulate in an effort to demolish the promise of multiracial democracy.

Reverend Martin Luther King convinced Daley to adopt a number of fair housing policies, but it proved merely a nominal victory. Daley did not fund or authorize the enforcement of his promises, and Chicago, like most cities, did not make any progress on housing until the federal government forced its hand with the passage of the Civil Rights Act of 1968, which "prohibited discrimination concerning the sale, rental and financing of housing based on race, religion, national origin, or sex." While more effective than Daley's empty promises, the federal law still failed to prevent racist and segregationist assaults on Black, Latino, and Native aspirations of citizenship. Redlining persisted throughout the 1990s, and even as recently as 2008, Black applicants for home mortgages, regardless of respective qualifications, were far more likely to receive disastrous subprime loans than white applicants.

In *White Space, Black Hood: Opportunity Hoarding and Segregation in the Age of Inequality*, Georgetown law professor Sheryll Cashin identifies and condemns three methods of white supremacy at work throughout the United States: boundary maintenance, opportunity hoarding in the form of commercial exclusion and educational apartheid, and stereotype-driven surveillance.

A young and precocious Jesse Jackson confronted these complex mechanisms of oppression, alienation, and injustice as the director of Operation Breadbasket, a Southern Christian Leadership Conference campaign that, in 1971, Jackson morphed into an independent organization, Operation PUSH. As acting president of PUSH, Jackson, his staff, and volunteers initiated a series of consumer boycotts, protests, and media efforts to strike a blow against the apartheid economy of Chicago. Even businesses in Black neighborhoods often refused to hire Blacks for anything beyond menial labor, trade unions routinely denied admission for Black workers, and grocery and retail stores would not stock products from Black-owned companies. PUSH's project was successful beyond most observers' expectations. Blacks secured thousands of jobs and millions of dollars in ancillary income through product placement and entrepreneurship made possible only because of PUSH's pressure on banks and other lending institutions to grant commercial loans irrespective of race. Due to PUSH's triumphs, Chicago became the 1970s and 1980s epicenter of Black banking and media. Jackson would take his economic efforts national, managing to fight the racism of major companies and negotiate deals on the behalf of Black workers and consumers with General Motors, Burger King, and other multinational corporations. He also effectively mediated disagreements between public unions and their host cities, most especially in Chicago when the firefighters union almost bifurcated by race. Jackson convinced them that creating multiple unions would only dilute their power as workers against a municipal government aiming to cut their salaries and benefits.

It was not the failures but the victories of PUSH that taught Jackson the most crucial of political truths: no amount of private successes could transform a public system working against the interests of poor and working people. Corporate capitalism, and government that acts at its behest, would continue to enrich the few, while immiserating the many.

"If you have a size nine foot, you aren't going to fit into a size six shoe," Jackson said during one of our conversations, "There is nothing wrong with your foot. There is something wrong with the structure into which you are trying to fit it. So, the structure determines your placement and movement, or inability to do either."

Democracy, Jackson came to believe, offered the means to transform the "tyranny" of "corporate structures" through governmental imposition and reformation. "We are dealing with public districts versus private territories," Jackson articulated as contrast between laws that are, at least ostensibly, open to public inspection and revision, and the impenetrable authority of capital. "You can inherit a company," Jackson told me while talking about the "unfairness" of the American system. "You cannot inherit a congressional district."

Acting as a practitioner and theoretician of democracy, Jackson formulates an unbreakable bond between the potential triumph of representational government and economic justice. Without the latter, the former will ultimately ring hollow and fail to create the culture and sociology of equality necessary for the boons of constitutional democracy to resonate with the majority of the electorate. Poverty is a threat to human life, but because it is also a threat to human rights, it undermines democracy.

"There are still millions of 'working poor,'" Jackson said at the press conference at the King apartments before punctuating the statistic with repetition of the words "moral disgrace." Referring to a 2019 study from the Chicago Coalition for the Homeless, Jackson offered another set-up for his refrain: "There are nearly 60,000 homeless people on the streets of Chicago. Moral disgrace."

In October of 2021, Jackson, and the Rainbow/PUSH Coalition, applied sufficient pressure on city, state, and federal officials to intervene on behalf of the residents of Concordia Place apartments on the South Side of Chicago. The public housing complex subjected its inhabitants to daily torture of asbestos, mold, rat infestation, unreliable appliances and faucets, and as if structural and environmental abuses were not enough, women tenants faced routine sexual harassment from roving security guards.

The public status of the housing complex is partially deceptive, because even though the apartments are taxpayer funded, the Chicago Housing Authority and HUD have outsourced management to Capital Realty—a private real estate firm guilty of similar violations against the law, and fundamental human rights, in Washington DC, and other cities. Rainbow/PUSH convinced the Secretary of Housing and Urban Development Marcia L. Fudge, and Chicago mayor Lori Lightfoot, to meet with residents, and pledge millions of dollars for repair and renovations.

"We want Concordia to become a model for public housing," Jackson declared, before also striking a blow against anyone so complacent or delusional to believe that the squalor of its units is aberrant. "There are Concordia's everywhere."

Jackson's assessment of the universality of poverty, and the pain it causes, is certainly correct, but unfortunately, there are not Jesse Jacksons everywhere. The American left suffers from a deficit of leadership—one reason why movements like Black Lives Matter, MeToo, and Occupy consistently fail to reach their full potential for political reform and social transformation. In his eighties, and fighting against the increasingly debilitating effects of Parkinson's disease, Jackson still reports to work nearly every day and, as the work with Concordia demonstrates, still marshals his intelligence, resources, and stature to serve, in the words of one of his favorite Bible passages, "the least of these brothers and sisters." The elevation of the bottom of the Empire necessitates the full force exercise of not only democracy but participatory democracy—a society and culture where people invest themselves into the manifestation of justice and the preservation of freedom.

*   *   *

A growing understanding of the essentiality of leaders who can inspire and build an infrastructure of support for participatory democracy is one reason why Jackson is receiving more accolades as he ages. As his earlier forecasts and analyses regarding the dangers that hatred presents to democracy, and the need for aggressive social liberalism and economic programs of equity, prove prescient, even former critics, like President Joe Biden, have acknowledged a debt to Jesse Jackson—the human rights leader who was never permanently at home in power or outside of power, but manages to step in and out of both zones. He leads protest movements of external agitation when necessary, and negotiates deals and compromises with corporate and governmental executives when possible. As his voluminous record of accomplishments shows, a leader of his caliber, his skillset, his commitment, and his courage is rare. When the sad day comes that he can no longer lead, march, fight, work, and speak, anyone who hopes for liberation from the age-old prejudices, the establishment of peace as a governing force in international and social relations, and the triumph of a beloved community where all children, no matter their color or class, have clothing for their bodies, food and water for their stomachs, books for their minds, and clean air and medicine for their growth, will feel the heavy weight of his absence.

Jackson has acknowledged that he has "entered a season of reflection"—a time to consider the highs and lows of his work, which is an opportunity to evaluate his legacy. During an interview we did together for the television program of one of Chicago's leading journalists, Hermene Hartman, he allowed himself a moment of pride when pressed to examine how everyone from Barack Obama to countless graduates of PUSH Excel's educational programs have cited his work as formative to their own success and happiness. "You plant trees," Jackson said, "and you never know who will enjoy the shade."

In yet another interview Jackson, and a longtime friend and ally, most beautifully captured the profundity, poetry, and power of his example. In 1982, two white men in San Francisco beat Vincent Chin, a Chinese-American, to death. They targeted Chin for their hate crime, because of xenophobic propaganda blaming Asians for the decline of the American automobile industry. Nearly alone among political leaders outside of California, Jackson visited San Francisco and collaborated with local organizers to address the surge of hatred against Asian immigrants and natural-born citizens. He never dropped contact with those organizers, one of whom, Rev. Norman Fong, the former director of the Chinatown Community Development Center, sat next to Jackson in 2022 for an interview to promote the work they were doing to combat another spike in anti-Asian bigotry. During the worst months of the Covid-19 pandemic, Donald Trump insisted on calling the virus the "China Virus" and the "Kung Flu." Conspiracy theories seized the internet, leading many Americans to develop ignorant animus toward the Chinese and resulting in increased hate crimes in city after city against anyone who appeared Asian.

"Growing up in Chinatown," Fong told the reporter while sitting next to Jackson, "there was segregation. All the teachers were white, and all the kids were Chinese. I go over to North Beach, and I get beat up by an Italian gang called, 'Damn All Chinamen.' They tied me to a fence. They picked on me all the time. I just felt like nobody." As his voice began to crack in the interview, Fong suppressed his tears with laughter and continued, "And who is the guy who started with, 'I am somebody'? So, I said 'I am somebody' everyday, and I'm still doing it—like Reverend Jackson, my hero in terms of doing justice." The journalist looked at Jackson and asked, "How does that make you feel?" His voice weak, from Parkinson's, but his eyes clear and bright, and his determination steely, Jackson answered:

> There's a kind of joy. There's also a reward for the work you've done. The rewards are not monetary awards. These awards are spiritual. . . . A will to do justice: This is my ministry. This is my life.

NOTES

All quotes from Jesse Jackson, unless otherwise indicated, derive from interviews conducted by the author.

Introduction

1   The video of the funeral service for Rosa Parks, which took place on November 2, 2005, at the Greater Grace Temple Church in Detroit, MI, is available at https://www .c-span.org/video/?189704-1/rosa-parks-funeral-service

2   "Taylor Branch and the 'Civil Rights Miracles.'" *CNN*, 1998. http://www.cnn.com/b ooks/news/9803/16/taylor.branch/index.html

3   William W. Falk and Bruch H. Rankin. "The Cost of Being Black in the Black Belt." *Social Problems*. Vol. 39, No. 3 (August 1992), pp. 299–313.

4   Taylor Branch offered his assessment of America's distortion of its own racial history in an interview with Tavis Smiley on March 30, 2010.

5   For additional information on the *Shelby v. Holder* case, see the following: P. R. Lockart. *Vox*, June 25, 2019. "How Shelby County v. Holder Upended Voting Rights in America." https://www.vox.com/policy-and-politics/2019/6/25/18701277/shelby -county-v-holder-anniversary-voting-rights-suppression-congress

6   "Free Voter IDs Are Costly, Harvard Law Report Finds." *Harvard Law Today,* June 26, 2014. https://today.law.harvard.edu/free-voter-ids-costly-harvard-law-report -finds/

7   Rebecca Leber. "In Texas, You Can Vote with a Concealed Handgun License—But Not a Student ID." *New Republic*, October 20, 2014. https://newrepublic.com/article /119900/texas-voter-id-allows-handgun-licenses-not-student-ids

8   Brentin Mock. "Study: North Carolina's Black Voters Live in a State of 'Electoral Apartheid.'" *Atlantic*, November 30, 2015. https://www.theatlantic.com/politics/arc hive/2015/11/study-north-carolinas-black-voters-live-in-a-state-of-electoral-aparthei d/433509/

9   Ari Berman. "Wisconsin's Voter-ID Law Suppressed 200,000 Votes in 2016 (Trump Won by 22,748)." *Nation*, May 9, 2017. https://www.thenation.com/article/wiscon sins-voter-id-law-suppressed-200000-votes-trump-won-by-23000/

10 Carol Anderson. "Brian Kemp's Lead in Georgia Needs an Asterisk." *Atlantic*, November 7, 2018. https://www.theatlantic.com/ideas/archive/2018/11/georgia-go vernor-kemp-abrams/575095/

11 Albert Murray. *The Hero and the Blues*. Vintage Books: New York, 1973.

Chapter 1

1   Footage of Jackson providing his immediate analysis of King's murder is included in the PBS documentary, "Roads to Memphis," which originally aired on February 26, 2019. It is directed by Stephen Ives.

2   Toni Morrison. *Playing in the Dark: Whiteness and the Literary Imagination.* Cambridge: Harvard University Press, 1992.

3   Steve Rose. "Racial Harmony in a Marxist Utopia: How the Soviet Union Capitalised on US Discrimination." *Guardian*, January 24, 2016. https://www.theguardian.com/ar tanddesign/shortcuts/2016/jan/24/racial-harmony-in-a-marxist-utopia-how-the-sovi et-union-capitalised-on-us-discrimination-in-pictures

4   Whitman's hopeful declaration of America as a "centre for equal daughters, equal sons" comes from the poem "America" (1888). His warning against America's descent into greed and nihilism is in his essay, "Democratic Vistas" from 1871. Both are available in: Justin Kaplan (ed.). Walt Whitman. *Poetry and Prose.* New York: Library of America, 1982.

5   Amy Goodman, of the radio program *Democracy Now!*, interviewed Jackson immediately following the funeral service in Charleston, South Carolina on June 26, 2015. Footage is available here: https://www.democracynow.org/2015/6/26/rev_jesse _jackson_take_down_the

6   Douglas A. Blackmon. *Slavery by Another Name: The Re-enslavement of Black Americans from the Civil War to World War II.* New York: Anchor Books, 2008.

7   The divergence in public opinion and public policy on firearm regulation and health care, respectively, is well documented. On the former— Nate Cohn and Margot Sanger-Katz. "On Guns, Public Opinion and Public Policy Often Diverge." *New York Times*, August 10, 2019. https://www.nytimes.com/2019/08/10/upshot/ gun-control-polling-policies.html. The latter—"70 Percent of Americans Support 'Medicare for All' Proposal." *Hill*, October 22, 2018. https://thehill.com/hilltv/wha t-americas-thinking/412545-70-percent-of-americans-support-medicare-for-all -health-care

8   Stefan Wojcik and Adam Hughes. "Sizing Up Twitter Users." *Pew Research Center.* https://www.pewinternet.org/2019/04/24/sizing-up-twitter-users/

9   This quote comes from the immensely important book that proved indispensable to the one you are currently reading—Marshall Frady. *Jesse: The Life and Pilgrimage of Jesse Jackson.* New York: Random House, 1996.

10   All quotes from Al Sharpton, unless stated otherwise, derive from a personal interview conducted by the author.

11   Paul L. Street. *Racial Oppression in the Global Metropolis: A Living Black Chicago History.* Lanham, MD: Rowman and Littlefield Publishers, 2007.

12   Housing discrimination is a common subject in American journalism, history, and art. With everything from newspaper reports to the classic Lorraine Hansberry play, *A Raisin in the Sun*, dealing with the injustice. An excellent recent source, however, is Richard Rothstein. *The Color of Law: A Forgotten History of How Our Government Segregated America.* New York: Liveright Publishing, 2017.

13   As an instructor at the University of St. Francis in Joliet, Illinois, I am often stunned by the lack of knowledge among the study body. For example, in the fall of 2019 semester, most of my students were unfamiliar with the Montgomery Bus Boycott, and only nine of forty-seven students were aware of Emmett Till. For a more comprehensive, and less anecdotal, look at the failure of American schools to teach

children about racial history, see Arika Herron. "Runaway-Slave Games. Sanitized Textbooks. Schools Do a Terrible Job Teaching about Slavery." *Indianapolis Star*, March 17, 2019. Https://www.usatoday.com/story/news/education/2019/03/17/his tory-racist-teacher-slavery-curriculum-textbook-indiana/3141832002/

14 Mary Lou Finley, Bernard Lafayette Jr., James R. Ralph Jr., and Smith Pam (eds.). *The Chicago Freedom Movement: Martin Luther King, Jr. and Civil Rights Activism in the North*. Lexington, KY: University Press of Kentucky, 2016.

15 Robert McLory. *Radical Disciple: Father Pfleger, St. Sabina Church, and the Fight for Social Justice*. Chicago: Lawrence Hill Books, 2010.

16 To read Lilla's compelling case, see Mark Lilla. *The Once and Future Liberal: After Identity Politics*. New York: Harper, 2017. For more on Bernie Sanders' electoral prescription, see Samantha Reyes. "Bernie Sanders 'Deeply Humiliated' Democrats Lost White Working-Class Voters." *CNN*, November 14, 2016. https://www.cnn.com/2016/11/14/politics/bernie-sanders-humiliated-democrats-loss-working-class-voters/index.html. For more detail on Christopher Parker's research and analysis visit David Masciotra. "Trump Won on 'White Fright': Why Identity Politics Wins Elections." *Salon*, July 22, 2017. https://www.salon.com/2017/07/22/trump-won-on-white-fright -why-identity-politics-win-elections/

17 Don Terry. "Town Tries to Keep Its Balance in Wake of White Flight." *New York Times*, March 11, 1996. https://www.nytimes.com/1996/03/11/us/town-tries-to-keep -its-balance-in-wake-of-white-flight.html. See also Lindsay Haines. "White Flight and Urban Decay in Suburban Chicago" (2010). Honors Projects. Paper 112. http://dig italcommons.iwu.edu/econ_honproj/112

18 Marshall Frady. *Jesse: The Life and Pilgrimage of Jesse Jackson*. New York: Random House, 1996.

19 Charles Taylor. *The Ethics of Authenticity*. Cambridge, MA: Harvard University Press, 1992.

20 Marshall Frady. *Jesse: The Life and Pilgrimage of Jesse Jackson*. New York: Random House, 1996.

21 Harry Belafonte. *My Song: A Memoir*. New York: Knopf, 2011.

Chapter 2

1 Many studies of public opinion coalesce to prove that the majority of Americans believe that they live in a genuine meritocracy, the most interesting of which shows that even in areas of the country where income inequality is at its most extreme, and even among the poor most people believe in the clichés of the "American dream"— "work hard and you will get ahead," "anyone can make it," and so on: Frederick Solt, Yue Hu, Hudson, Song Kevan, Yu Jungmin, "Erico" Dong.

  "Economic Inequality and Belief in Meritocracy in the United States." *Research and Politics*, Vol. 3, No. 4 (October 19, 2016). https://journals.sagepub.com/doi/abs /10.1177/2053168016672101

2 An essential resource on the early years of economic work from Operation Breadbasket is the following: Martin L. Deppe. *Operation Breadbasket: An Untold Story of Civil Rights, 1966 – 1971*. Athens: University of Georgia Press, 2017.

3 Marshall Frady. *Jesse: The Life and Pilgrimage of Jesse Jackson*. New York: Random House, 1996.

4 Ibid.

5   All quotes from Frank Watkins, unless otherwise indicated, derive from an interview
    conducted by the author.

6   Martin L. Deppe. *Operation Breadbasket: An Untold Story of Civil Rights, 1966 – 1971.*
    Athens: University of Georgia Press, 2017.

7   Damien Cave. "A Young Jesse Jackson Rallies for Jobs." *New York Times*, February 4,
    2016. https://www.nytimes.com/interactive/projects/cp/national/unpublished-black-
    history/jesse-jackson-protests-construction-trade-unions-chicago-1969

8   Kathryn Vasel. "6 in 10 Americans Don't Have $500 in Savings." *CNN Money*,
    January 12, 2017. https://money.cnn.com/2017/01/12/pf/americans-lack-of-savings/
    index.html

9   U.S. Equal Employment Opportunity Commission. "Diversity in High Tech." https://
    www.eeoc.gov/eeoc/statistics/reports/hightech/

10 An outstanding monograph on "gentlemen's agreements" and their sordid history in
    American race relations is Edward R. Ward. *A Gentleman's Agreement: Secured by the
    Honor of the Participants.* Chicago: Graphix Products, 2011.

11 Enrico Beltramini. "SCLC Operation Breadbasket: From Economic Civil Rights to
    Black Economic Power." *Fire!!!* Vol. 2, No. 2, Expanding the Narrative: Exploring New
    Aspects of the Civil Rights Movement Fifty Years Later (2013), pp. 5–47.

12 The story of Jesse Jackson's involvement with the music industry and Chicago radio
    stations is told in full in Aaron Cohen. *Move On Up: Chicago Soul Music and Black
    Cultural Power.* Chicago: University of Chicago Press, 2019.

13 Enrico Beltramini. "SCLC Operation Breadbasket: From Economic Civil Rights to
    Black Economic Power." *Fire!!!* Vol. 2, No. 2, Expanding the Narrative: Exploring New
    Aspects of the Civil Rights Movement Fifty Years Later (2013), pp. 5–47.

14 L. Tepperman and J. Curtis. *Principles of Sociology: Canadian Perspectives.* Canada:
    Oxford University Press, 2006.

15 Information on the Rush-Jackson story is available at the webpage for the
    documentary, *Dusable to Obama: Chicago Black Metropolis*, WTTW: https://interac
    tive.wttw.com/dusable-to-obama/death-of-a-black-panther

16 The political relationship between King and Obama is examined in the following:
    David Remnick. "The Joshua Generation." *New Yorker*, November 8, 2008. https://ww
    w.newyorker.com/magazine/2008/11/17/the-joshua-generation

17 The historian is James Ralph, the Rehnquist Professor of American History and
    Culture at Middlebury College, and author of several books and academic articles
    on the civil rights movement. The quote appears in his own Foreword to *Operation
    Breadbasket: An Untold Story of Civil Rights, 1966 – 1971.*

18 The entire story involving Jackson's leadership on social aid legislation in
    Illinois is accessible in *Operation Breadbasket: An Untold Story of Civil Rights,
    1966 – 1971.*

19 Vidal gave a philosophical and linguistic analysis of the term "radical" during a
    lecture at Harvard University, "The Great Unmentionable Monotheism and Its
    Discontents," on April 20, 1992. The entire lecture, in essay form, is available in Gore
    Vidal. *United States: Essays, 1952 – 1992.* New York: Random House, 1993.

20 A thoughtful essay on the Kerner Commission Report of 1968 is the following:
    Alice George. "The 1968 Kerner Commission Got It Right, But Nobody Listened."
    Smithsonian, March 1, 2018. https://www.smithsonianmag.com/smithsonian-institu
    tion/1968-kerner-commission-got-it-right-nobody-listened-180968318/

21 The associate was Frank Watkins, and the story appears in Marshall Frady. *Jesse: The
    Life and Pilgrimage of Jesse Jackson.*

22   An insightful account and analysis of the PUSH Excel program is the short book, Ernest R. House. *Jesse Jackson and the Politics of Charisma: The Rise and Fall of the PUSH/Excel Program*. New York: Westview Press, 1988.

23   An excellent look at "welfare reform" and popular American attitudes surrounding poverty is Jason DeParle. *American Dream: Three Women, Ten Kids, and a Nation's Drive to End Welfare*. New York: Viking, 2004.

24   Many interviews with Jesse Jackson in the aftermath of the "gaffe," including the one with CBS News, are available on YouTube. The quotes in this passage derive from "Jackson Explains Remarks." https://www.youtube.com/watch?v=KIuimjehBvo

25   The entire Jackson-Toyota story, along with Holmes' quote, is available at Paul Holmes. "Hey Toyota, It's Jesse Jackson on the Line." *Holmes Report*, July 22, 2002. https://www.holmesreport.com/latest/article/hey-toyota-it%27s-jesse-jackson-on-the-line

26   Robert W. Patterson. "'What's Good for America…'" *National Review*, July 1, 2013. https://www.nationalreview.com/2013/07/whats-good-america-robert-w-patterson/

27   Excerpts from the letter, including the passage that I quote, were later published in Jessica Guynn. "Jesse Jackson Escalates Silicon Valley Diversity Campaign." *USA Today*, August 10, 2015. https://www.usatoday.com/story/tech/2015/08/10/jesse-jackson-silicon-valley-diversity-letter-technology-companies-apple-facebook-google-dropbox-airbnb-uber/31421955/

28   Taylor Soper. "President Obama References Steve Jobs, Bill Gates at White House Demo Day." *GeekWire*, August 4, 2015. https://www.geekwire.com/2015/president-obama-references-steve-jobs-bill-gates-at-white-house-demo-day/

29   Brian Merchant. "Life and Death in Apple's Forbidden City." *Guardian*, June 18, 2017. https://www.theguardian.com/technology/2017/jun/18/foxconn-life-death-forbidden-city-longhua-suicide-apple-iphone-brian-merchant-one-device-extract

30   Details on Senator Elizabeth Warren's position on breaking up big tech companies are available at Astead W. Herndon. "Elizabeth Warren Proposes Breaking Up Tech Giants Like Amazon and Facebook." *New York Times*, March 8, 2019. https://www.nytimes.com/2019/03/08/us/politics/elizabeth-warren-amazon.html, Glenn Reynolds' view is available at Glenn Harlan Reynolds. "Donald Trump Must Bust Facebook, Amazon, Netflix, Google Monopolies Like Teddy Roosevelt." *USA Today*, November 19, 2018. https://www.usatoday.com/story/opinion/2018/11/19/donald-trump-roosevelt-monopoly-antitrust-facebook-apple-netflix-google-column/2049321002/

31   Noam Chomsky, as is often the case, is magnificent on how Adam Smith's theories are widely misunderstood by not only the general public but also the intellectual class. See Noam Chomsky. *Class Warfare: Interviews with David Barsamian*. Monroe, Maine: Pluto Press, 1996.

Chapter 3

1   Ian T. Shearn. "Whose Side Is the American Farm Bureau On?" *Nation*, July 16, 2012. https://www.thenation.com/article/whose-side-american-farm-bureau/

2   A riveting and fascinating account of the decline of the family farm comes from Victor Davis Hanson, a classicist and farmer: Victor Davis Hanson. *Fields Without Dreams: Defending the Agrarian Ideal*. New York: Free Press, 1996.

3   Berman's entire trilogy on American decline is essential reading, but the "double down" analysis is in the third installment—Morris Berman. *Why America Failed: The Roots of Imperial Decline*. Hoboken, NJ: John Wiley & Sons, 2012.

4   Joan Didion. "Insider Baseball." *New York Review of Books*, October 27, 1988. https://www.nybooks.com/articles/1988/10/27/insider-baseball/

5   St. John of the Cross. *Dark Night of the Soul.*

6   Footage from this speech is available on YouTube—"Jesse Jackson Speech, Tendley Baptist, Phila PA, January 16, 1984." https://www.youtube.com/watch?v=9Ol_BqU1 0IM. It is also described in Marshall Frady. *Jesse: The Life and Pilgrimage of Jesse Jackson*. New York: Random House, 1996.

7   Two excellent books on President Reagan's poisonous influence on American politics and policy are Will Bunch. *Tear Down This Myth: The Right Wing Distortion of Reagan*. New York: Free Press, 2010, and William Kleinknecht. *The Man Who Sold the World: Ronald Reagan and the Betrayal of Main Street America*. New York: Nation Books, 2009.

8   Zack Friedman. "Student Loan Debt Statistics in 2018: A $1.5 Trillion Crisis." *Forbes*, June 13, 2018. https://www.forbes.com/sites/zackfriedman/2018/06/13/student-loan-debt-statistics-2018/

9   The entire address to the Mayor's Conference, along with many other speeches and policy papers from the Jackson campaigns is available in Frank Clementine (ed.) and Frank Watkins. *Keep Hope Alive: Jesse Jackson's 1988 Presidential Campaign*. Boston: South End Press, 1989.

10 Joe Walker. "'Black Faces in Limousines': A Conversation with Noam Chomsky." *Joe Walker Blog*, November 14, 2008. https://chomsky.info/20081114/

11 Linda C. Farthing and Benjamin H. Kohl. *Evo's Bolivia: Continuity and Change*. Austin: University of Texas Press, 2014.

12 Sources on the Jackson effect in the 1980s include Steve Kornacki. "1984: Jesse Jackson's Run for the White House and the Rise of the Black Voter." *NBC News*, July 29, 2019. https://www.nbcnews.com/politics/elections/1984-jesse-jackson-s-run-wh ite-house-rise-black-voter-n1029596. Sam Tanenhaus. "Jesse Jackson Created the Modern Democratic Party." *Bloomberg*, August 26, 2015. https://www.bloomberg.com /opinion/articles/2015-08-26/jesse-jackson-created-the-modern-democratic-party, and Ryan Grim. *We've Got People: From Jesse Jackson to AOC, the End of Big Money and the Rise of a Movement*. Washington, DC: Strong Arm Press, 2019.

13 Donna Brazile, Yolanda Caraway, Leah Daughtry, and Minyon Moore. *For Colored Girls Who Have Considered Politics*. New York: St. Martin's Press, 2018.

14 George E. Curry. "'Run, Jesse, Run.'" *St. Louis American*, February 26, 2014. http://www.stlamerican.com/news/columnists/guest_columnists/run-jesse-run/article_143 2cd9e-9f2d-11e3-be37-001a4bcf887a.html

15 Atwater is quoted in Marshall Frady. *Jesse: The Life and Pilgrimage of Jesse Jackson*. New York: Random House, 1996.

16 George E. Curry. "'Run, Jesse, Run.'" *St. Louis American*, February 26, 2014. http://www.stlamerican.com/news/columnists/guest_columnists/run-jesse-run/article_143 2cd9e-9f2d-11e3-be37-001a4bcf887a.html

17 All quotes from Butch Wing, unless otherwise stated, derive from an interview conducted by the author.

18 All quotes from Delmarie Cobb, unless otherwise stated, derive from an interview conducted by the author.

19 Michael Kruse. "What Jesse Taught Bernie About Running for President." *Politico*, March 15, 2019. https://www.politico.com/magazine/story/2019/03/15/bernie-sa nders-2020-race-jesse-jackson-1988-presidential-campaign-225809

20 Ja'han Jones. "Jesse Jackson Is the Most Important Figure in U.S. Political History." *Huffington Post*, January 13, 2018. https://www.huffpost.com/entry/jesse-jackson-most-important-figure-in-american-political-history_n_5a591f99e4b03c4189658f7b

21   Steve Cobble. "Jesse Jackson's Rainbow Coalition Created Today's Democratic
     Politics." *Nation*, October 2, 2018. https://www.thenation.com/article/jesse-jackson-ra
     inbow-coalition-democratic-politics/
22   Jamelle Bouie. "Keep Hope Alive." *Slate*, November 27, 2016. http://www.slate.com/
     articles/news_and_politics/cover_story/2016/11/jesse_jackson_s_presidential_cam
     paigns_offer_a_road_map_for_democrats_in.html
23   "WHYY's Susan Philips Interviews President Bill Clinton," April 21, 2008. https://ww
     w.youtube.com/watch?v=gxsrGUTcEUc
24   Alex Bollinger. "How Jesse Jackson Helped Bring Gay Rights to the Democratic
     Mainstream." *LGBTQ Nation*, February 28, 2018. https://www.lgbtqnation.com/2018
     /02/jesse-jackson-helped-mainstream-gay-rights-democratic-party/
25   While my search for an explanation of how Jackson's transformation of delegate
     allocation rules was crucial to Obama's victory was not comprehensive, I found it
     telling enough that top-selling, highly reviewed books by Peter Baker, David Remnick,
     Michael Eric Dyson, Julian Zelizer, and Michael D'Antonio fail to mention it.
26   Kevin Sack. "The 1992 Campaign: Minority Voters; Jackson Waits for Plan from
     Clinton." *New York Times*, July 18, 1992. https://www.nytimes.com/1992/07/18/us/the
     -1992-campaign-minority-voters-jackson-waits-for-plan-from-clinton.html
27   Mike Pesca. "Why the GOP Has Become a Cult of Personality," June 11, 2019. https://
     slate.com/news-and-politics/2019/06/george-will-conservatism-trump-warren.html

Chapter 4

1   The full transcript, audio recording, and video of Jackson's 1988 Democratic
    Convention Speech is available at "Jesse Jackson: 1988 Democratic National
    Convention Address." *American Rhetoric*. https://americanrhetoric.com/speeches/je
    ssejackson1988dnc.htm
2   E. J. Dionne Jr. "Jackson Rouses Democrats with Plea for Hope, Saying 'Tonight I
    Salute' Dukakis." *New York Times*, July 20, 1988. https://archive.nytimes.com/www
    .nytimes.com/library/politics/camp/880620convention-dem-ra.html
3   Abraham Heschel. *The Prophets*. New York: Harper, 1962.
4   Richard Lischer. *The Preacher King. Martin Luther King Jr. and the Word that Moved
    America*. New York: Oxford University Press, 1995.
5   Abraham Heschel. *The Prophets*. Harper: New York, 1962.
6   An outstanding, and sobering, comparison of how differing social policies determine
    different lifestyle outcomes in Western Europe and the United States is Jeremy Rifkin.
    *The European Dream: How Europe's Vision of the Future Is Quietly Eclipsing the
    American Dream*. Cambridge, UK: Polity Press, 2004.
7   Walt Whitman. *Walt Whitman's Leaves of Grass: The First (1855) Edition*. New York:
    Penguin Books, 2005. Print.

Chapter 5

1   There is extensive documentation on the vicious ridicule King faced in the final years
    of his short life. A recent essay on the subject is David J. Garrow, "When Martin
    Luther King Came Out Against the Vietnam War." *New York Times*, April 3, 2017.
    https://www.nytimes.com/2017/04/04/opinion/when-martin-luther-king-came-out
    -against-vietnam.html

2 The *Jewish Standard* essay is Shmuley Boteach. "Why Martin Luther King Was the Greatest American of the 20th Century." *Jewish Standard*, January 22, 2015. https://jewishstandard.timesofisrael.com/why-martin-luther-king-was-the-greatest-american-of-the-20th-century/, "The most dangerous man" quote comes out of leaked FBI documents. Dyson's biography of King is Michael Eric Dyson. *I May Not Get There with You: The True Martin Luther King, Jr.* New York: Free Press, 2000.

3 James C. Cobb. "Even Though He Is Revered Today, MLK Was Widely Disliked by the American Public When He Was Killed." *Smithsonian*, April 4, 2018. https://www.smithsonianmag.com/history/why-martin-luther-king-had-75-percent-disapproval-rating-year-he-died-180968664/

4 The YouGov polling data is available at https://today.yougov.com/topics/entertainment/explore/public_figure/Jesse_Jackson

5 All quotes from Santita Jackson, unless otherwise stated, derive from an interview conducted by the author.

6 Alina Cohen. "This Painting of Jesse Jackson as a White Man Provoked a Sledgehammer Attack." *Artsy*, November 7, 2018. https://www.artsy.net/article/artsy-editorial-painting-jesse-jackson-white-man-provoked-sledgehammer-attack

7 Ronald Smothers. "The Impact of Jesse Jackson." *New York Times*, March 4, 1984. https://www.nytimes.com/1984/03/04/magazine/the-impact-of-jesse-jackson.html

8 Gregory J. Payne, Scott C. Ratzan, and Robert A. Baukus. "National Newspaper Analysis of the Press Coverage of Jesse Jackson's 1984 Presidential Campaign: The Confirmation of the Candidate." *Explorations in Ethnic Studies*, Vol. 12, No. 2 (July, 1989): 35–48.

9 Emily Stewart. "Donald Trump Rode $5 Billion in Free Media to the White House." *The Street*, November 20, 2016. https://www.thestreet.com/story/13896916/1/donald-trump-rode-5-billion-in-free-media-to-the-white-house.html

10 Becket Adams. "Trump's Empty Podium Gets 30 Minutes of Airtime." *Washington Examiner*, March 3, 2016. https://www.washingtonexaminer.com/trumps-empty-podium-gets-30-minutes-of-airtime

11 "Jesse Jackson Responds to Portrait of Him as White." *Los Angeles Times*, December 5, 1989. https://www.latimes.com/archives/la-xpm-1989-12-05-ca-311-story.html

12 "Understanding Implicit Bias." *The Ohio State University Kirwan Institute for the Study of Race and Ethnicity*. http://kirwaninstitute.osu.edu/research/understanding-implicit-bias/

13 Devah Prager. *Marked: Race, Crime, and Finding Work in an Era of Mass Incarceration*. Chicago: University of Chicago Press, 2008.

14 "Jesse Jackson: 1984 Democratic National Convention Address," July 18, 1984. https://www.americanrhetoric.com/speeches/jessejackson1984dnc.htm

15 A full recounting of the Jackson-Farrakhan fiasco is available in Marshall Frady. *Jesse: The Life and Pilgrimage of Jesse Jackson*. New York: Random House, 1996.

16 Wayne King. "Three Years Later, Jesse Jackson Is Haunted by Anti-Semitism of Farrakhan." *New York Times*, June 13, 1987. https://www.nytimes.com/1987/06/13/us/three-years-later-jackson-is-haunted-by-anti-semitism-of-farrakhan.html

17 Marshall Frady tells the story of Jackson's visit with a Jewish family in the hospital quite movingly in his biography.

18 Sarah Posner. "John Hagee's Controversial Gospel." *American Prospect*, March 12, 2008. https://prospect.org/article/john-hagee-s-controversial-gospel/

19 Laurie Goodstein. "Falwell: Blame Abortionists, Feminists and Gays." *Guardian*, September 19, 2001. https://www.theguardian.com/world/2001/sep/19/september11.usa9

20 Brad Polumbo. "'Liberty' University? When It Comes to Free Speech, It's Anything But." *Daily Beast*, June 30, 2018. https://www.thedailybeast.com/liberty-university-w hen-it-comes-to-free-speech-its-anything-but

21 Stephen Prothero. "Billy Graham Built a Movement. Now His Son Is Dismantling It." *Politico*, February 24, 2018. https://www.politico.com/magazine/story/2018/02/24/bill y-graham-evangelical-decline-franklin-graham-217077

22 Journalist Joshua Green recounts Bannon's successful strategy to place anti-Clinton slander in the *New York Times* in his book, Joshua Green. *Devil's Bargain: Steve Bannon, Donald Trump, and the Storming of the Presidency*. New York: Penguin Press, 2017.

23 Masochists can consult Kenneth R. Timmerman. *Shakedown: Exposing the Real Jesse Jackson*. New York: Regnery Publishing, 2002.

24 "Born on Third Base." United for a Fair Economy. 2012. http://www.faireconomy.org/ bornonthirdbase2012

25 Irina Ivanova. "If Black Families Were as Rich as White Ones, U.S. Economy Would Be $1.5 Trillion Bigger." *CBS News*, August 15, 2019. https://www.cbsnews.com/news/ racial-wealth-gap-costs-economy-1-5-trillion-dollars-report-finds/

26 Noam Chomsky. *Media Control: The Spectacular Achievements of Propaganda*. New York: Seven Stories Press, 2002.

27 *Newsweek,* May 7, 1984.

28 William Raspberry. "What Does Jackson Want?" *Washington Post*, March 20, 1988. https://www.washingtonpost.com/archive/opinions/1988/03/20/what-does-jackson -want/329b3c95-15f7-4759-badc-afabe4ac5662/

29 Karen Tumulty. "Jackson Assails Bush 'Hustler' Comment." *Los Angeles Times*, May 8, 1988. https://www.latimes.com/archives/la-xpm-1988-05-08-mn-3834-story.html

30 James Ylisela Jr. "Under the Radar." *Chicago*, June 19, 2007. https://www.chicagomag .com/Chicago-Magazine/July-2007/Under-the-Radar/index.php

31 This story also appears in Marshall Frady. *Jesse: The Life and Pilgrimage of Jesse Jackson*. New York: Random House, 1996.

32 Jennifer Calfas. "One-Third of Americans Unaware ObamaCare, ACA Are the Same." *Hill*, February 7, 2017. https://thehill.com/blogs/blog-briefing-room/news/318297 -one-third-of-americans-didnt-know-obamacare-aca-were-same-law

33 Bryce Covert. "The Myth of the Welfare Queen." *New Republic*, July 2, 2019. https:// newrepublic.com/article/154404/myth-welfare-queen

Chapter 6

1 Joan Didion. "Insider Baseball." *New York Review of Books*, October 27, 1988. https:// www.nybooks.com/articles/1988/10/27/insider-baseball/

2 Ibid.

3 Michael Crozier, Samuel P. Huntington, and Joji Watanuki. *The Crisis of Democracy: On the Governability of Democracies*. New York: New York University Press, 1975.

4 Ibid.

5 Ibid.

6 Jackson makes his comments in the documentary, *Crashing the Party: The Rise of Bill Clinton and the New Democrats*, directed by David Sigal, and released in 2016.

7 Tom Happold. "'The Democratic Wing of the Democratic Party." *Guardian*, January 20, 2004. https://www.theguardian.com/world/2004/jan/20/uselections2004.usa8

8   Both the New Orleans and Cleveland stories are told well in the documentary, *Crashing the Party*.

9   Gore Vidal. "State of the Union, 2004." *Nation*, August, 26, 2004. https://www.the nation.com/article/state-union-2004/

10 The Sister Souljah fiasco, along with Clinton's remarks, are available in Marshall Frady. *Jesse: The Life and Pilgrimage of Jesse Jackson*. New York: Random House, 1996.

11 Jean Claire Kim. "Managing the Racial Breach: Clinton, Black-White Polarization, and the Race Initiative." *Political Science Quarterly*, Vol. 117, No. 1 (Spring, 2002). https://www.jstor.org/stable/pdf/798094.pdf

12 Marshall Frady. *Jesse: The Life and Pilgrimage of Jesse Jackson*. New York: Random House, 1996.

13 Ibid.

14 In addition to the memorable quote, Hitchens provided a review of the coverage of the Rector execution in Christopher Hitchens. *No One Left to Lie To: The Triangulations of William Jefferson Clinton*. New York: Verso, 1999.

15 Jesse Jackson. *Legal Lynching: Racism, Injustice, and the Death Penalty*. New York: Da Capo Press, 1996.

16 Jackson appeared on the Charlie Rose program on June 26, 1995. https://charlierose .com/videos/5184

17 "Jesse Jackson Testimony on Crime Bill." https://www.c-span.org/video/?c4545493/u ser-clip-jesse-jackson-testimony-crime-bill

18 Jackson appeared on the Charlie Rose program on June 26, 1995. https://charlierose .com/videos/5184

19 Robin DiAngelo. *White Fragility: Why It's So Hard for White People to Talk About Racism*. Boston: Beacon Press, 2018.

20 Dan Balz. "Obama's Accidental Sister Souljah Moment." *Washington Post*, July 10, 2008. http://voices.washingtonpost.com/44/2008/07/obamas-accidental-sister-soulj. html

21 Eduardo Silva-Bonilla. *Racism Without Racists: Color Blind Racism and the Persistence of Racial Inequality in the United States*. Oxford, UK: Rowan & Littlefield, 2005.

Chapter 7

1   Alice Slater. "The US Has Military Bases in 80 Countries. All of Them Must Close." *Nation*, January 24, 2018. https://www.thenation.com/article/the-us-has-military-b ases-in-172-countries-all-of-them-must-close/

2   An excellent resource for tracking the bloat of the Pentagon budget is *National Priorities Project*: https://www.nationalpriorities.org/

3   The Ernest Hemingway reflection appears in his novel *A Farewell to Arms*.

4   Andrew J. Bacevich. "'Permanent War for Permanent Peace:' American Grand Strategy Since World War II." *Historically Speaking*, Vol. 3, No. 2, 2001, pp. 2–5. Project MUSE, doi:10.1353/hsp.2001.0075.

5   Zach Fitzner. "Is American Geographic Illiteracy a Security Threat?" *Earth*, February 5, 2019. https://www.earth.com/news/american-geographic-illiteracy-security-threat/

6   Chinta Strausberg. "Rev. Jackson Honored by Black Firemen for Saving Lives and Their Union." *Chicago Crusader*, June 20, 2018. https://chicagocrusader.com/rev-jac kson-honored-by-black-firemen-for-saving-lives-and-their-union/

7   Jacques Derrida. *Specters of Marx: The State of the Debt, the Work of Mourning & the New International*. New York: Routledge, 1994.

8   For an interesting look at the Reagan administration's policies toward terrorism, consult Michael Stohl. "Terrorism, States, and State Terrorism: The Reagan Administration in the Middle East." *Arab Studies Quarterly*. Vol. 9, No. 2, Terrorism and the Middle East: Context and Interpretations (Spring 1987), pp. 162–72

9   A good summary of the Reagan-Syria conflict is Micah Zenko. "When America Attacked Syria." *Council on Foreign Relations*, February 3, 2012. https://www.cfr.org/blog/when-america-attacked-syria

10 A short but factual and insightful analysis of Jackson's mission to Cuba, and the unreasonable hostility it provoked, is available in William M. LeGrande and Peter Kornbluh. *Back Channel to Cuba: The Hidden History of Negotiations between Washington and Havana*. Chapel Hill: University of North Carolina Press, 2015.

11 James A. Baer. *A Social History of Cuba's Protestants: God and the Nation*. London: Lexington Books, 2019.

12 Don Terry. "The Day That Reverend Jesse Jackson Took Fidel Castro to Church." *Capital Outlook*, January 4, 2017. http://capitaloutlook.com/site/the-day-that-reverend-jesse-jackson-took-fidel-castro-to-church/

13 William M. LeGrande and Peter Kornbluh. *Back Channel to Cuba: The Hidden History of Negotiations between Washington and Havana*. Chapel Hill: University of North Carolina Press, 2015.

14 Lucius Barker and Ronald W. Walters (eds.). *Jesse Jackson's 1984 Presidential Campaign: Challenge and Change in American Politics*. Urbana: University of Illinois Press, 1989.

15 Tom Raum. "Bush Says Saddam Even Worse Than Hitler." *Associated Press*, November 1, 1990. https://www.apnews.com/c456d72625fba6c742d17f1699b18a16

16 E. J. Dionne Jr. "Kicking the Vietnam Syndrome." *Washington Post*, March 4, 1991. https://consortiumnews.com/2012/12/28/kicking-the-vietnam-syndrome/

17 The definitive source on the monstrous carnage of the Vietnam War is Nick Turse. *Kill Anything That Moves: The Real American War in Vietnam*. New York: Metropolitan Books, 2013.

18 Most of the description of Jackson's mission to Iraq derive from our own conversation, but a few important details come from Frady's journalism, available in *Jesse: The Life and Pilgrimage of Jesse Jackson*.

19 The *New York Times* and Klein reactions are recounted in *Jesse: The Life and Pilgrimage of Jesse Jackson*. The Florida insult, which is actually a headline, comes from Cody Shearer. "Jackson Becoming an Unfunny Joke." *South Florida Sun Sentinel*, September 9, 1990. https://www.sun-sentinel.com/news/fl-xpm-1990-09-09-9002130268-story.html

20 Stuart Lockwood. "That's Me in the Picture: Stuart Lockwood with Saddam Hussein, 24 August 1990 Baghdad, Iraq." *Guardian*, June 5, 2015. https://www.theguardian.com/artanddesign/2015/jun/05/thats-me-picture-stuart-lockwood-saddam-hussein-iraq

21 Joe Wilson's assessment of Jackson's work is also in Frady's book.

22 Norman Solomon. *War Made Easy: How Presidents and Pundits Keep Spinning Us to Death*. Hoboken, NJ: John Wiley & Sons, 2005.

23 All quotes from Ramirez and Stone, except where stated otherwise, derive from an interview conducted by the author.

24 Ben Brumfield. "Gambia Frees 2 Americans Imprisoned for Treason; Agrees to Halt Executions." *CNN*, September 18, 2012. https://www.cnn.com/2012/09/18/world/africa/gambia-prison-release/index.html

25 Huxley is quoted in Norman Soloman's *War Made Easy.*

26 The meeting of Jackson and Alexander, along with his comments on her release, is viewable at "Jesse Jackson Meets Anthropologist He Helped Free from Algerian Detention." https://www.youtube.com/watch?v=qSsdGQOx5rA

27 The entire program preceding the anti-war march, including Jackson's speech, is available from *C-Span.* https://www.c-span.org/video/?189011-1/anti-war-rally

28 King's quote appears in his own book, *Where Do We Go from Here: Chaos or Community.* It was originally published in 1967.

29 Jesse Jackson. "Trump's 'March Massacre' Budget is Ruthless." *Chicago Sun-Times,* March 20, 2017. https://chicago.suntimes.com/2017/3/20/18321839/trump-s-march -massacre-budget-is-ruthless

30 Jackson's remarks are viewable at the United Nations website: http://webtv.un.org/ search/annual-commemoration-by-the-general-assembly-of-nelson-mandela-inter national-day/4372812029001?term=nelson%20mandela

31 I read a transcript of Jackson's remarks in PUSH offices shortly after his return from Guadeloupe.

32 Jackson's entire remarks are viewable at "Jesse Jackson – Globalization & Human Rights." https://www.youtube.com/watch?v=24UuZZMCVmQ&t=1582s

33 "Rev. Jackson Meets with Holocaust Survivors and Young Activists in Poland and Declares 'Your Struggle Is Our Struggle.'" *Rainbow/PUSH Coalition,* August 1, 2019. https://rainbowpush.org/blog/rev-jackson-meets-holocaust-survivors-and-young-act ivists-poland-and-declares-%E2%80%9Cyour-struggle

34 Emily Eakin. "Group Lists Unpatriotic Remarks on Campuses." *Chicago Tribune,* November 25, 2001. https://www.chicagotribune.com/news/ct-xpm-2001-11-25-0 111250423-story.html

35 Morris Berman. *Why America Failed: The Roots of Imperial Decline.* Hoboken, NJ: John Wiley & Sons, 2012.

36 Ibid.

37 "Origins and Future of US 'Exceptionalism.'" *National Public Radio,* May 2, 2008. https://www.npr.org/templates/story/story.php?storyId=90126925

Chapter 8

1 The tragic vision is most associated with F. A. Hayek and Thomas Sowell, respectively.

2 Martin Gilens and Benjamin I. Page. "Testing Theories of American Politics: Elites, Interest Groups, and Average Citizens." *Perspectives on Politics,* Vol. 12, No. 3 (2014), pp. 564–81. doi: 10.1017/S1537592714001595.

3 Cornel West and Christa Buschendorf (eds.). *Black Prophetic Fire.* Beacon: Boston, 2015.

4 Gary Younge. "Jesse Jackson: Power, Politics, and the Preacher Man." *Guardian,* April 17, 1999. https://www.theguardian.com/world/1999/apr/17/uselections2000.usa

5 James Warren. "What Foreigners Really See When They Come to America." *Vanity Fair,* October 9, 2017. https://www.vanityfair.com/news/2017/10/what-foreign-re porters-really-see-when-they-come-to-america

6 James Nuechterlein. "A Nation of Hustlers." *First Things,* January 2009. https://www .firstthings.com/article/2009/01/003-a-nation-of-hustlers

7 Niall Ferguson. "Is the Business of America Still Business?" *Harvard Business Review,* June 2013. https://hbr.org/2013/06/is-the-business-of-america-still-business

8   Erica Sweeney. "Kantar: US Ad Spend Reached $151B in 2018, a 4.1% Jump." *Marketing Dive*, January 24, 2019. https://www.marketingdive.com/news/kantar-us-ad-spend-reached-151b-in-2018-a-41-jump/546725/

9   Rushkoff tells the sad story of teenagers turning themselves into commodities, often with the assistance of their parents, in the PBS documentary, "Generation Like."

10   Aristotle's definition of politics appears in his classic book, *Politics*.

11   I attended the rally.

12   Barbara Reynolds. *Jesse Jackson: The Man, the Movement, the Myth*. New York: Burnham Inc., 1975.

13   Reynolds' conversation with Studs Terkel took place on May 27, 1975, and is available at https://studsterkel.wfmt.com/programs/barbara-reynolds-discusses-her-book-jesse-jackson-man-movement-myth

14   Gary Younge. "Jesse Jackson: Power, Politics, and the Preacher Man." *Guardian*, April 17, 1999. https://www.theguardian.com/world/1999/apr/17/uselections2000.usa

15   Adolph L. Reed. *The Jesse Jackson Phenomenon: The Crisis of Purpose in Afro-American Politics*. New Haven, CT: Yale University Press, 1986.

16   Marable Marable. "The Jesse Jackson Phenomenon: The Crisis of Purpose in Afro-American Politics. By Adolph L. Reed, Jr." *Journal of American History*, Vol. 74, No. 4 (March 1988), p. 1395. https://doi.org/10.2307/1894510

17   Ernest R. House. *Jesse Jackson and the Politics of Charisma: The Rise and Fall of the PUSH/Excel Program*. New York: Westview Press, 1988.

18   John Schoeffel and R. Mitchell (eds.). *Understanding Power: The Indispensable Chomsky*. New York: The New Press, 2002.

19   Michael E. Porter and Mark R. Kramer. "The Competitive Advantage of Corporate Philanthropy." *Harvard Business Review*, December 2002. https://hbr.org/2002/12/the-competitive-advantage-of-corporate-philanthropy

20   Marianne Bertrand, Matilde Bombardini, Raymond Fishman, and Francesco Trebbi. "Tax-Exempt Lobbying: Corporate Philanthropy as a Tool for Political Influence." *National Bureau of Economic Research*, March 2018. https://www.nber.org/papers/w24451

21   Zizek's thoughts are available in the video, "RSA Animate: First as Tragedy, Then as Farce." https://www.youtube.com/watch?v=hpAMbpQ8J7g

22   Adolph L. Reed. *The Jesse Jackson Phenomenon: The Crisis of Purpose in Afro-American Politics*. New Haven, CT: Yale University Press, 1986.

23   Abby Goodnough. "Jesse Jackson Takes Up Cause of Schiavo's Parents." *New York Times*, March 30, 2005. https://www.nytimes.com/2005/03/30/us/jesse-jackson-takes-up-cause-of-schiavos-parents.html

24   Norman Mailer. *The Fight*. New York: Random House, 1975.

25   Ibid.

26   Jesse L. Jackson. "Jesse Jackson: Ali Was Not Controversial. Segregation Was." *CNN*, June 4, 2016. https://www.cnn.com/2016/06/04/opinions/muhammad-ali-jesse-jackson/index.html

Chapter 9

1   The entire story of "The Crisis of Confidence" address is adeptly told in Kevin Mattson. *"What the Heck Are You Up to, Mr. President?": Jimmy Carter, America's Malaise, and the Speech That Should Have Changed the Country*. New York: Bloomsbury, 2009.

2   Joan Didion. "Eyes on the Prize." *New York Review of Books*, September 24, 1992.

3 The quote appears in Ralph Waldo Emerson's seminal essay, "Self-Reliance."

4 Albert Murray. *The Hero and the Blues*. New York: Vintage Books, 1973.

5 Berman made this comment in a conversation with the author.

6 "Rev. Jackson Acknowledges Fathering Child Out of Wedlock." *Associated Press*, January 1, 2001. https://www.nytimes.com/2001/01/18/politics/rev-jesse-jackson-ack nowledges-fathering-child-out-of-wedlock.html

7 Marshall Frady. *Jesse: The Life and Pilgrimage of Jesse Jackson*. New York: Random House, 1996.

8 Bruce DuMont interviewed Jesse Jackson on April 4, 1974. Audio is available at http:/ /www.beyondthebeltway.com/bruce_dumont_archives.htm

9 Result of the CSpan Presidential Historian Survey are available at https://www.c-span .org/presidentsurvey2017/

10 Phil Rogers and Lisa Blade. "'I'm Sorry I Let Everybody Down'": Jesse Jackson, Jr." *NBC Chicago*, February 20, 2013. https://www.nbcchicago.com/blogs/ward-room/Ja ckson-Jr-Federal-Court-Guilty-Plea-192060041.html

11 Tracy Klein. "Update: Congressman Jesse Jackson, Jr." *Mayo Clinic*, August 13, 2012. https://newsnetwork.mayoclinic.org/discussion/update-congressman-jesse-jackson-jr/

12 Naomi Nix. "Jesse Jackson Sr. to Push Voting Rights Amendment in Newark Today." *NJ*, January 8, 2015. https://www.nj.com/essex/2015/01/jesse_jackson_sr_to_push_vo ting_rights_amendment_in_newark_today.html&=1

13 The best source on the destructive influence of Republican gerrymandering is David Daley. *Ratf**ked: The True Story Behind the Secret Plan to Steal America's Democracy*. New York: Liveright Publishing, 2016.

14 Statistics on poverty in America are available from Poverty USA. https://www .povertyusa.org/facts

15 Shawn Fremstad. "The Official U.S. Poverty Rate Is Based on a Hopelessly Out-of-Date Metric." *Washington Post*, September 16, 2019. https://www.washingtonpost.com/outl ook/2019/09/16/official-us-poverty-rate-is-based-hopelessly-out-of-date-metric/

16 The Center for Poverty Research at the University of California, Davis provides data and description of the "working poor". https://poverty.ucdavis.edu/faq/who-are-working-poor-america

17 The National Center on Family Homelessness provides information on the amount of homeless children in the United States. https://www.air.org/center/national-center-fa mily-homelessness

18 Alisa Chang. "'Insane': America's 3 Largest Psychiatric Facilities Are Jails." *KCUR 89.3*, April 25, 2018. https://www.kcur.org/post/insane-americas-3-largest-psychiatric -facilities-are-jails#stream/0

19 Hoffman's words can be heard in the opening of Steve Earle's rendition of the song, "Time Has Come Today." He is also quoted in Matt Hern. *Common Ground in a Liquid City: Essays in Defense of an Urban Future*. Oakland, CA: AK Press, 2010.

20 "Noam Chomsky on Propaganda – The Big Idea – Interview with Andrew Marr." https://www.youtube.com/watch?v=GjENnyQupow

Chapter 10

1 "Jesse Jackson on Holy Saturday: Jesus Was an Occupier." https://www.youtube.com/ watch?v=oyLdYYIVdd8

2 "Christians Celebrate Easter Across Chicago." *ABC-7, Chicago*, March 27, 2016. https ://abc7chicago.com/news/christians-celebrate-easter-across-chicago-area-/1265181/

3   "Hitchens delivers one of his best hammer blows to cocky audience member." https://
    www.youtube.com/watch?v=MJ2LehsA1dk

4   Robert N. Bellah. "Civil Religion in America." *Journal of the American Academy of
    Arts and Sciences*, Vol. 96, No. 1 (1967), pp. 1–21.

5   See Frederick Mark Gedicks. *American Civil Religion: An Idea Whose Time Is Past*,
    March 2009. http://dx.doi.org/10.2139/ssrn.1440351, and Morris Berman. *Why
    America Failed: The Roots of Imperial Decline*. Hoboken, NJ: John Wiley & Sons, 2012.

6   The emergence of the religious right as a lobby for the right to unlawfully
    discriminate against black Americans is told brilliantly in Randall Balmer. *Redeemer:
    The Life of Jimmy Carter*. New York: Basic Books, 2014.

7   Hunter Moyler. "As Christianity's Popularity Declines, More Americans Identify as
    Religiously Unaffiliated, Study Finds." *Newsweek*, October 17, 2019. https://www.new
    sweek.com/christianity-decline-americans-religion-unaffiliated-pew-study-1466035

8   James Warren. "Billy Graham's Troubling Nasty Nixon Moment." *US News & World
    Report*, February 28, 2018. https://www.usnews.com/opinion/thomas-jefferson-st
    reet/articles/2018-02-28/dont-forget-billy-grahams-anti-semitic-turn-with-richard
    -nixon

9   John Paul Brammer. "Billy Graham Leaves Painful Legacy for LGBTQ People." *NBC
    News*, February 22, 2018. https://www.nbcnews.com/feature/nbc-out/billy-graham-le
    aves-painful-legacy-lgbtq-people-n850031

10 "The Extraordinary and Odd Adventure of Being a Christian." *Biola University Center
    for Christian Thought*. Stanley Hauerwas in conversation with Evan Rosa: https://cct
    .biola.edu/extraordinary-odd-adventure-christian/

11 Darryl Pinckney. "The Afro-Pessimist Temptation." *New York Review of Books*, June 7,
    2018. https://www.nybooks.com/articles/2018/06/07/ta-nehisi-coates-afro-pessimist
    -temptation/

12 Ta-Nehisi Coates. "The First White President." *Atlantic*, October 2017. https://www
    .theatlantic.com/magazine/archive/2017/10/the-first-white-president-ta-nehisi-coates
    /537909/

13 Salim Muwakkil. "Ta-Nehisi Coates and the Absurdity of Hope." *In These Times*,
    October 5, 2017. https://inthesetimes.com/article/20572/ta-nehisi-coates-and-the-a
    bsurdity-of-hope

14 Imani Perry. *Breathe: A Letter to My Sons*. Boston: Beacon Press, 2019.

15 Although my search was not comprehensive of their respective catalogues, I did
    investigate Coates' much celebrated *Between the World and Me: Notes on the First
    150 Years in America,* and Perry's *Breathe* for the vocabulary of political reality and
    reform.

16 *Small Planet Institute*. https://www.spifastfacts.org/single-post/2015/06/04/It-is-th
    eory-which-decides-what-we-can-observe—Einstein

17 Albert Camus. *Neither Victims Nor Executioners: An Ethic Superior to Murder*.
    Eugene, OR: WIPF and Stock Publishers, 1946.

INDEX